The Question of Astrology

The
Question of Astrology

*A PERSONAL
INVESTIGATION*

DEREK PARKER

EYRE & SPOTTISWOODE
LONDON

First published 1970
© Text 1970 Derek Parker
© Appendix I 1970 Anthony Stevens
© Figs 1, 2, 3, and Appendix II 1970 Julia Parker
Printed in Great Britain for
Eyre & Spottiswoode (Publishers) Ltd
11 New Fetter Lane, EC4
by Cox & Wyman Ltd, London, Reading & Fakenham
SBN 413 259609 2

To
my mother
and the memory of
my father

Contents

Diagrams in the text

Acknowledgements

Many astrologers have given me their help in this survey. They include John Addey, M.A., D.F.Astrol.S. (President of the Astrological Association of England); Roy Allin, D.F.Astrol.S.; Denis Bartlett; the late Charles Carter, D.F.Astrol.S. (late Principal Emeritus, Faculty of Astrological Studies); Anne Cilliers, D.F.Astrol.S. (South Africa); Ronald Davison (President, Astrological Lodge of London); Reinhold Ebertin (Germany); Dennis Elwell; Irene M. Foy, D.F.Astrol.S. (South Africa); Harriet Friedlander, D.F.Astrol.S. (USA); L. Furze-Morrish, D.F.Astrol.S. (Australia); the late Margaret E. Hone, D.F.Astrol.S. (late Principal Emeritus, Faculty of Astrological Studies); Dorothy B. Hughes (USA); Marc Edmund Jones (USA); Jeff Mayo, D.F.Astrol.S. (Principal and Tutor, Faculty of Astrological Studies); Pauline Messina (USA); Jaroslav Mixa (Czechoslovakia); Al H. Morrison (USA); José Murgui-Munoz, D.F.Astrol.S. (Spain); B. V. Raman (Editor, *Astrological Magazine* of India); Dane Rudhyar (USA); Sanders Salcedo (Spain); Youko Shiojima (Japan); Katina Theodossiou; Dr Rosanna Zerilli (Italy).

The following non-astrologers have been helpful with information and advice: R. S. Belasco (W. Foulsham & Co. Ltd); William Golightly (Taipei, China); Fr John McDonald; Alan Mann (Honeywell Controls Ltd); W. D. Nagle (L. N. Fowler & Co. Ltd); R. J. Ogden (London Weather Centre); Professor Alec Samuels.

I am grateful for the assistance of the following astrological and non-astrological organisations: the American Federation of Astrologers; the Astrological Association (Great Britain); the

Astrological Association of Puerto Rico; the Astrological Guild (USA); the Astrological Lodge (Theosophical Society, London); Bombay Astrological Society; the Church of Light (Los Angeles, USA); Eva Petulengro Publications; Friends of Astrology, Inc. (Chicago, USA); Horoscope Publications (USA); the International Society for Astrological Research (USA); Maurice Woodruff Promotions Ltd; Mass-Observation Ltd and Professor Tom Harrisson, with acknowledgements to the archives of the University of Sussex; Michigan Federation of Astrologers (USA); Ordinastral (Paris); Professional Astrologers, Inc. (Los Angeles, USA); Research Associates, Los Angeles (USA); Royal Greenwich Observatory. Three libraries – the British Museum Library, the London Library, and the Library of the Meteorological Office – have been of great help.

I am particularly indebted to three astrologers – Charles Harvey, D.F.Astrol.S., Ingrid Lind, D.F.Astrol.S., and John Naylor – who have given me permission to quote at length from astrological analyses of my own Birth Chart which they provided.

Mr Addey, Dr Anthony Stevens and Clifford L. Brettelle, D.F.Astrol.S., were kind enough to read the manuscript, and to offer various suggestions, although the responsibility for the views expressed remains mine. I am grateful to Dr Stevens for his Appendix, and to Susan Rowe, who typed my manuscript.

Permission to use quotations from copyright works, as detailed in the footnotes, has been given by the following in respect of the authors named:

Charles Carter, *An introduction to political astrology*: L. N. Fowler Ltd.

W. E. Davis, *Weather*: the author and the Royal Meteorological Society.

Margaret E. Hone, *The modern textbook of astrology*, and astrological chart forms designed by her: L. N. Fowler Ltd.

C. G. Jung, various works: Routledge & Kegan Paul Ltd.

Alan Leo, *Astrology for all; The progressed horoscope*: L. N. Fowler Ltd.

Jeff Mayo, *Teach yourself astrology*: English Universities Press Ltd.

Henry Miller, Introduction to *Henry Miller, his world of Urania*:
the author, Sydney Omarr, and the Ninth House Publishing
Co.

Opinion Research Centre and the *Sunday Times*.

The Times.

Alan Whicker and the editor, the *Listener*.

Louis de Wohl, *The stars of war and peace*: Hutchinson Publishing Group Ltd.

In a few cases, I have made use of material from sources ac-
knowledged in the footnotes, but have been unable to contact the
copyright-holders. No discourtesy is implied in these cases.

Finally, I must acknowledge the help of my wife, Julia
L. Parker, D.F.Astrol.S. Her technical knowledge has been of the
greatest assistance, as has her constant criticism. My continual
scepticism must have been extremely irritating to a committed
astrologer, and she has borne it with the greatest patience. I am
also grateful to her for allowing me to reprint, as Appendix II, a
complete example of one of her analyses. I must thank, too, its
anonymous subject for permission to reproduce this work. It has
never been truer of any book that without my wife this one would
neither have been started, nor finished.

DEREK PARKER

1970

Preface

This book presents neither a blind defence of astrology nor a blind attack on it. It is – as its title suggests – a personal enquiry into how an ancient science is surviving after three hundred years of denigration; how it is being used to advise, to warn, to reveal; how it is being used in medicine and weather forecasting and business. I can provide no conclusive proof that astrology 'works', although I offer some evidence which may confirm the subject's inherent interest, and suggest the need for a proper and scientific examination of the theory that certain facts about terrestrial life can be discovered by studying the movement of the planets. I believe that anyone who becomes convinced of this is probably convinced less by abstract argument than by personal experience; and a good deal of the evidence I offer is personal. It is not 'scientific', and I do not pretend to have made a scientific experiment under test conditions.

Although I have corresponded with astrologers and astrological institutions all over the world, of varying shades of opinion and various degrees of accomplishment, my researches are inevitably sketchy. As astrologers know, there is an immense amount of astrological activity at the present time, and a book of ordinary length – especially a non-technical book – could not hope to cover the ground fully. I hope (not too confidently) that astrologers who have been kind enough to help me will not find the book impossibly lightweight. I have been impressed by their serious-minded devotion to their theory, and I am aware that in many particulars I may seem to have skated over important aspects of their work. My excuse must be that I am a layman writing for laymen, and attempting to avoid complete opaqueness.

I have sketched the methods used by astrologers to reach their results and draw their conclusions. I am very conscious that to anyone with even a rudimentary knowledge of astrology, this can only appear as an immense over-simplification. However, I have intended simply to give to the lay reader some indication of the complexities of the work involved; and there are a very great number of textbooks in print which will enable him to go further, should he wish to do so.

The Question of Astrology

I

Introduction – The Fascination of Astrology

'To prejudge other men's notions before we have looked into them,' wrote John Locke, 'is not to show their darkness but to put out our own eyes.' It is a sensible warning; but to attempt to write seriously about the subject of astrology is to risk the reaction Dr Mervyn Stockwood met when he attempted to write about his psychical experiences – 'embarrassment, annoyance, and pity'.

And what of the credulous? What interest can they find in the subject? I have always tended to believe that *occult* experience occurs within the minds of those who relate it; and to listen to ghost stories with the same interest as I listen to dream narratives – as fascinating unconscious evidence of the character of the narrator. But the astrologer's notions are not even an extension of his own mind: they originate in the movements of the planets, in the opposition of Mars and Jupiter or the conjunction of the Sun and Moon – less likely to have anything to do with the habits of man than the traditional Red Indian spirit guides, who seem often to have a very definite effect on those who see them.

And if individual astrologers at least write for individual clients, the world of newspaper astrologers seems quite lunatic. Who could believe that the population of a country can be divided into twelve sections, and even the vaguest predictions offered for a day or a week on that basis?

It is clear that there would be interesting facets to an historical study of astrology; there are several astrologers who evidently played an important part in history – Dr Dee for example, Queen Elizabeth's astrologer. But that astrology *per se* could be taken seriously, and that 'serious astrology' existed in the twentieth century, did not occur to me until comparatively recently. The few press allusions I saw were all of the 'silly season' variety; and the books on the subject either written by committed astrologers wholly convinced of their position and its probity, or by splenetic opponents such as the astronomer Robert Eisler, whose *The royal art of astrology* is as unappealing and unentertaining as an astrological apologia!

So I was mildly surprised when one day in a reference library I came across a book in the series published by the English Universities Press. This particular volume was called *Teach yourself astrology*, and it was written by Jeff Mayo, who printed after his name the letters D.F.Astrol.S., and styled himself 'Tutor, Faculty of Astrological Studies'. The letters, I discovered, signify that Mr Mayo holds the diploma of the Faculty. His book, incidentally, had by 1969 been reprinted several times, and during that year its sales increased by no less than 60 per cent!

That evening I happened to mention Mr Mayo's book to my wife. Next day she bought it. A short time afterwards she enrolled as a student of the Faculty; and two years and two lengthy examinations later, was awarded its diploma and began practising as an astrological consultant.

The fact that she persevered with the studies impressed me, because she has never seemed to me to be the sort of person who would continue to study anything which was not producing results. The first time an astrological theory failed, I would have expected her to drop the work. But she did not, and I began gradually to see why.

A number of interesting books were left about the house: notably, the two textbooks by which the Faculty's course is taught. Other recommended books – by Alan Leo, a well-known Edwardian astrologer, and by modern theorists like Dane Rudhyar and Marc Edmund Jones – also appeared. Apart from the fact that they went far more fully into the characteristics of the zodiacal signs than I had thought possible, I was impressed at first mainly by amusing coincidences. For instance, in a photo-replica of an early translation of the fifteenth-century *Kalendar and compost of shepherds*, I found a description of myself, under my Sun-sign, Gemini:

> Who so is born under Mercury shall . . . not love to go to a warfare; he shall love well to preach and to speak fair rhetoric language, and writing . . . to read ever in strange bookes. He shall have a high forehead, a long visage, black eyes and a thin beard.

The thin beard has now vanished, but the rest of the description fits fairly well.

Again, in William Lilly's *Christian astrology* (1647) I found that the Geminian was:

> An excellent disputant or logician, arguing with learning and discretion, and using much eloquence in his speech, a searcher into all kinds of Mysteries and Learning, sharp and witty, learning almost anything without a Teacher; ambitious of being exquisite in every Science, disirous naturally of travell and seeing forain parts; a man of an unwearied fancie, curious in the search of any occult knowledge;

and that on the debit side, he was:

> A troublesome wit, a kind of Phreneticke man, his tongue and Pen against every man, wholly bent to foole his estate and time in prating and trying nice conclusions to no purpose; a great lyar, boaster, prattler, busybody, false, a tale-carrier, given to wicked arts, as Necromancy and such like ungodly knowledges . . . constant to no place or opinion, cheating and theeving every where; a newes-monger, pretending all manner of knowledge, but guilty of no true or solid learning; a trifler, a meere frantic fellow; if he prove a Divine, then a meer verbal fellow, frothy, of no judgement, easily perverted, constant in nothing but idle words and bragging.

If I would like to recognise myself in the first of these passages ('manners when well placed', as Lilly put it), I have no doubt that some of my friends might recognise me in the second, and there are certain phrases in which I recognise myself all too readily. It might of course all be rubbish; but *astrological* rubbish did seem to be supported by well-tried and ancient rules. It was, in fact, to some degree empirical.

I continued, however (like most people with only the faintest notion of astrological theory), to be mainly entertained by the parlour tricks. For instance, relatively early in her studies my wife was able reliably to tell a person's Sun-sign by his appearance and behaviour; or if not his Sun-sign, then his Ascending sign (which is of equal or often greater importance in his horoscope). It was interesting that in so many cases a man born with the sign Taurus predominant in his Birth Chart should in fact look rather bull-like, with a broad rather low brow, often curly hair, almost invariably a thick neck and heavy shoulders; that an Arian should (to put it plainly) occasionally look rather sheep-like, with the Arian sign or glyph ♈ appearing on his face in his heavy eyebrows and straight, almost Jewish nose. That Mercurial people should have quick, light movements; Saturnine people rather gangling, loose, clumsy and slow movements.

Other old astrological traditions often turned out to be true. People suffered from the illnesses traditionally associated with the signs prominent in their charts; others particularly liked cities or countries traditionally associated in the same way with the map of the sky at the moment of their birth. I wanted to know how the trick was done.

Then, gradually, my wife began to build up a list of clients – at first experimentally among our friends and relatives, and later professionally. It became more and more clear that it was possible for her to tell them something about themselves by examining data discovered, after certain calculations, from the moment and place of their birth. What my wife told her clients could not, I knew, have been discovered by any other means open to her.

She was, of course, convinced of the relevance of an astrological theory earlier than I was; but she was working full-time on the study, while I was an interested spectator. However, it was impossible not to be impressed by her clients' repeated assertions that she had been accurate in dating events in their past, and helpful in giving advice about present problems (of which she had, usually, only a vestigial notion). They were often having their first experience of astrology and they were initially unenthusiastic and sceptical; but I never met one who was not finally at the least intrigued. A father, for instance, who produced a career guidance report prepared for his son by a reputable national careers advisory service found that it tallied almost word for word with a report prepared for him by my wife from the boy's birth data.

Again, late in 1969, a father sent my wife the birth data of his three-year-old son, with no comments whatsoever. My wife drew up the child's Birth Chart, and felt that there were signs that he might have suffered some brain damage at birth, possibly with the result that he might be extremely aggressive. She telephoned the home and asked the mother if the birth had been a difficult one The mother said that she 'did not know' – she had been unconscious throughout it; but that her son was very aggressive, and that she had sometimes said to her husband that perhaps he should be taken to a psychiatrist. A psychiatrist later confirmed that brain damage could have given the child psychopathic tendencies, and recommended that he be taken to a child guidance clinic as soon as possible.

Reading the reports written by my wife for her clients, I soon realised the scope of the consultant astrologer's work. She was, for instance, called upon to tell the parents of a two-year-old child something about her still emerging character: perhaps to warn them—

She is naturally an enormously friendly little girl, [and] during these early years [her independence] could express itself through her desire to go off on her own in the park to enjoy herself in her own particular way. This is in many ways splendid; but care is necessary, and more than an average careful eye is advisable in this respect, since she could tend to stray just a little further than is comfortable or safe. . . .

She has extremely refined and very sensitive feelings, and therefore could become worried or upset if anyone has been unkind, or has hurt her in any way. The direct result of worry would probably be a stomach upset, and her digestion could easily suffer – probably this will be the first indication that she is upset about anything.

There was also a comparison of the personalities of twins, born only ten minutes apart:

The indications are that C— tends to have more will-power and determination than P—, and perhaps more ability to express a dynamic and somewhat dramatic urge. P— may well let him take the lead, and while he is by no means lacking in fighting spirit, there may not be quite such a strong need in him to express himself in this way. There may be something of a 'holding-back' on P—'s part. With C— the answer is 'Yes'; but with P— it is quite likely 'Um . . .', followed by 'Yes' when he has heard C—'s answer.

In both these cases the parents confirmed the findings. When we met the seven-year-old twins for the first time, after the report had been sent to their mother, their characteristics emerged in startling confirmation.

A married couple wanted their charts compared, to reveal or confirm certain tendencies, similarities or differences:

It may be that Mrs X's emotions tend to flow in rather a different way from Mr X's; I think I can compare hers to Vesuvius – dormant for a long time, and then erupting when feelings are intensely moved. Mr X's perhaps more resemble the Mississippi – a steady, deep flow which is always there; greater in quantity and somewhat deeper. . . .

Perhaps another very positive indication which shows when looking at your two charts is the ability of Mrs X to contribute much to the success of your marriage. She has the necessary flair to make it run on well-oiled wheels by recognising and identifying with Mr X's objectives in life. I believe that this indication is of primary importance to both of you, and that you will over the years feel this link steadily growing. Although having a natural love of comfort, beautiful surroundings, and so on, there is a powerful element of work in Mrs X's chart, and this energy-force is very strongly and positively tied up with the moral support a wife can contribute to the well-being of a marriage.

A man contemplating a change of career wanted confirmation of his desire to give his life a new direction (or, maybe, dissuasion from it):

I think that (especially at present) you need to have business interests which are stimulating and a challenge to yourself as a person. But at the same time, you need rather more mobility and perhaps more freedom than you have had in the past. It is perhaps possible to assess your coming moods and feelings as needing greater freedom of expression and expansion, along with an interesting and lively challenge, with new ambitions to aspire to. This may not seem easy; but I think you will only be really happy for the next few years if you accept that you really need something of this sort. The time is ripe for you to expand in several ways . . . the most important of course being in your career and business interests.

When one client complained that she 'did not recognise herself' in my wife's report (the only time, incidentally, that this has so far happened), it subsequently turned out that she had not only been unable to give a correct birth time, but had given a place of birth some five hundred miles from her actual birthplace, unaware that this would make any difference!

According to my wife's clients she was much more often right than wrong about their personalities and the characteristics of their lives. Could coincidence be at work? Was it coincidence that the client whose character she got completely wrong was the client to give her false birth date? – that of the twin boys, C should indeed have been the dominating one?

No. Anyone who looks at astrology with an open mind will eventually have to abandon the theory that coincidence can account for the accuracy of the astrologer's character analyses or forecasts. Chance is unthinkable on this scale.

We have all had the experience of a spectacular coincidence now and again in life: of reading a word on a page while at the same moment someone speaks that word on the radio, for instance. It may even be possible under some circumstances (such as, for instance, when one switches on the radio and immediately hears a tune one has been humming for some minutes) to suspect that some extra-sensory power is at work. But in the field of astrology the range is too wide. The 'coincidences' are of too many degrees, too many kinds – as the various examples I shall give throughout this book will, I think, demonstrate.

My wife and I visited, not long before his death, the distinguished astrologer Charles Carter, author of many astrological textbooks and books of theory, who had spent almost the whole of a long life in a careful study of astrological theory.

In August 1955 Mr Carter had written to John Addey, now the President of the Astrological Association:

> I confess I'd like to live to hear about man's first trip to the Moon, but this seems rather improbable. In 1968 my progressed Moon is in conjunction with progressed Sun and progressed Mars, near radix Moon and opposed to radix Jupiter which seems to indicate a heavy strain; also at this time . . . the whole family joins in with typical 'bereavement' directions! We shall see; but as a good astrologer I feel I ought to place on record my own forecast on this point! Uranus is also at this time on my progressed M.C. and the commonest sign of death seems to be a malefic on an angle, though of course this often happens without much effect on health.

The technical terms need not perhaps be explained here; they are all good astrological usage. And the fact is that Mr Carter died on October 4, 1968.

Not long before his death he was visited by an old friend, the astrologer and weather forecaster Denis Bartlett. The two men looked at Mr Carter's progressed Birth Chart. 'What d'you think, Denis?' asked Mr Carter. 'The same as you,' replied his friend. 'Ah!' said Mr Carter; 'not long for this world.'

The psychiatrist could argue that Mr Carter, over the years, on the basis of his own astrological experience, had become so convinced that his death would occur late in 1968 that whether or not the astrological theory is valid, he persuaded himself into the grave at that time. It is possible, but I find it difficult to believe.

The more I read and heard about astrology the more fascinating I found it. I heard of the experiments of Dr Eugen Jonáš in Prague, who claims to be able to predict accurately the sex of babies according to the time of their conception, and can produce statistics to prove it. I heard of recent meteorological data which tended to confirm astrologers' centuries-old claims about the planets' effect upon terrestrial weather.

I read Jean Overton Fuller's biography of Shelley,[1] and realised that as an astrologer she was able to put forward acceptable and interesting theories about his behaviour and character and had carefully examined his Birth Chart. I learned that men's horoscopes survived them, and that – for instance – the unveiling of Byron's memorial in Westminster Abbey might be expected to show up in a progressed chart of his nativity.

Then there were several startlingly accurate predictions. In May 1963 Leslie McIntyre, the American astrologer, had sent a letter to the editor of *American Astrology*. He had noticed certain indications in the progressed horoscope of the United States: 'In the past, such configurations have coincided with personal danger to our head of state,' he wrote, 'all the more so in this case in view of the grievous attack by Saturn on the President's natal Mars, Mercury and Jupiter.'

Could this astrological attack be in any way connected with the physical attack of November 22 – six months later – by which President Kennedy was murdered?

As I read on, and as I met astrologers – some working as consultants, some as members of the Theosophical Society, some who were professional psychiatrists or doctors – it became clear that a greater range of intelligence was working in this field than I had thought possible. It was also perhaps a greater range of practitioners than ever before, from the serious astrologer who had faith in the empirical basis of his subject, to the occultist who drew up a Birth Chart and, more clairvoyant than astrologer, switched on some music, turned the light low, and sank into a semi-trance from the depths of which the oracle might or might not utter.

It was clear too that interest in astrology was far more widespread than I had imagined. There are more astrologers at the

[1] *Shelley: a biography* (Jonathan Cape, 1968).

present time than at any other in the history of the world – although it may not indeed be true that the increased number of astrologers is in direct proportion to the increased world population.

A number of them may be charlatans and hacks; a lot of them study astrology as part of a search for some kind of 'eternal truth' (whatever they may feel this to be). But whatever brings people to astrology, one fact is indisputable: of those who study the subject with an open mind, not uncritically but not with undue prejudice either, those who are able afterwards to dismiss it completely are in a tiny minority. Even the most sceptical enquirer must admit that there is sufficient evidence to suggest that some basic tenets of astrology may be founded in fact.

Despite a recent revival in popular interest, it is still difficult to find anyone who is unprejudiced about astrology. (For this the newspaper astrologers are almost totally to blame; and I shall have more to say about them later.) Anyone who is in even a minor official position seems almost always terrified to show a serious interest in any slightly 'off-beat' activity. I was talking one time to probably the best known professional astronomer in Great Britain. Having dismissed astrology as 'absolute bunkum,' he added: 'But of course I used to say that about dowsing – until I discovered I could do it.' I asked him (we were preparing for a radio interview) whether I could mention this. 'God, no!' he said, 'my colleagues would think I had gone mad!'

People who are worried that their names may appear in connection with a serious astrological experiment are partly responsible for the lack of statistical proof of the astrological theory (or, if they would rather have it this way, of proof that that theory does not work). For instance in the 1930s a member of the Department of Psychology at Edinburgh University conducted intelligence tests upon 'a representative group of Scottish children' on behalf of the Scottish Council for Research in Education. All the children born in Scotland on the first days of February, May, August and November 1926 were traced and given a comprehensive intelligence test at about the age of ten. There were some 870 births on those four days; about nine births an hour.

In Scotland the time at which a child is born is recorded on his birth certificate; and in the 1960s the detailed intelligence test results were still in existence. The Astrological Association decided that it would be interesting to use this data to attempt to discover any correlation between intelligence test performance and identical or near-identical moment of birth.

A national newspaper agreed to contribute to the financing of the work to the extent of providing an independent observer to collect and tabulate the available data. The Scottish Registrar's Office agreed to help with the provision of the birth times. A psychologist of Edinburgh University (and not an astrologer) gave the Scottish Council for Research in Education firm assurances of the respectability of the Astrological Association and of its president, John Addey. But the Council, hearing that the data was to be used in an attempt to provide statistical evidence for astrological examination, refused absolutely to release it. It would, of course, be freely available to any undergraduate who went to the Council with a note from his tutor!

This attitude is, unfortunately, all too typical. It is strange that organisations are unwilling to release information when care has been taken to assure them that it will be used in a properly scholarly manner, under proper supervision. At the worst, after all, astrological students can only be wasting their own time. The publication of results which favoured astrology might indeed be mildly embarrassing in that it might provoke more serious thought about the subject.

Astrologers themselves have admittedly often done their best over the past hundred years to cloud the issue. Dogmatism has resulted from the irritation serious astrologers feel at the apparent determination of scientists to dismiss their ancient theory as rubbish. Tedious theory has been elaborated, interminable occult glosses have been published; much astrological writing is illiterate, quarrelsome, and tendentious. And as Nietzsche pointed out, 'we often refuse to accept an idea merely because the tone of voice in which it has been expressed is unsympathetic to us'.

By the time my wife had been studying the subject for two years and practising for two more, I found myself sufficiently intrigued to wish that there was a book which examined, in as detached a way as possible, what was going on in the world of astrology in our own time. There were, no doubt, the quacks and the frauds; but there were also, obviously, serious men and women who believed that astrology worked and could be useful to society. I could find no such book. The books available either set out to assert what the author already knew (that astrology did/did not work), or – like Louis MacNeice's excellent coffee-table book – concentrated too much on the past, ignoring or ducking the question whether astrology was in fact worth serious consideration.

I decided to try to write such a book myself. There seemed to be evidence, generally available, and capable of being checked on a personal as well as a statistical level, which to a certain extent supported the astrological theory. I would not set out to present this evidence in detail. It was available elsewhere if I could interest people sufficiently to look it out. I would simply try to show in a general sense why I had come to think that the astrological theory was worth more serious respect than is usually shown it.

Perhaps in the end it is impossible to *prove* whether or not astrology 'works': statistics are only statistics – and too often astrologers refuse to compile them because they do not believe them to be necessary. All one can do – all I claim to do, apart from looking at the activity of astrologers around the world today – is to present some fascinating astrological evidence, and leave the reader to form his own general conclusion.

II

The Qualities of the Moment

Relatively few people know how complex the astrological theory is. It is far simpler to accept, as most people still do, that when one talks about astrology, one is talking about the kind of astrology on display in the columns of the popular press. A layman who picks up even the most straightforward of astrological textbooks will soon founder in a welter of technical terms, while the more advanced theoretical astrological works written in this century – Dane Rudhyar's *The astrology of personality,* for instance – will quickly leave behind any reader not prepared to face arguments at least as abstract as those in many textbooks of psychology.

The objection is often made that astrologers hide a lack of concrete argument behind a mist of jargon. It is not a new objection. The astrologer has always set out his arguments in technical language; and it would be surprising if he did not. It would be as difficult for him as it is for an astronomer to write without technical terms. An argument can be carried only so far without such terms. Yet the shout of 'jargon' still goes up today, as it did in Dryden's day:

'What think you, Sir, of the taking of Hyleg? or of the best way of rectification for a Nativity? have you been conversant in the Centriloquium of Trismegisthus? what think you of Mars in the tenth when 'tis his own House, or of Jupiter configurated with malevolent Planets?'[1]

[1] John Dryden, *An evening's love, or, The mock astrologer* (1671).

If Dryden knew what his character meant (and, in fact, he did) his audience did not; the astrologers had been scored off again.

However, there is no reason to suspect that the serious astrologer attempts to blind his clients with science. The best astrologers always include in their report to a lay client a basic explanation of what they are doing when they interpret a Birth Chart. If pressed, they will in the end have to use technical terms, much as a radio engineer, pressed to explain the intricacies of a television set, will eventually use terms unlikely to be understood by the layman. And there are plenty of astrological textbooks – as there are radio textbooks – to which the layman can go for a definition of those terms, if he cares to take the trouble.

In a report written for a fellow-astrologer, technical terms will be freely used. An astrologer may explain a client's tendency to overwork and cause strain on his nervous system by writing that

> astrologically, this can be seen through his rising Moon being in opposition to Mars in intellectual Sagittarius in the Sixth House. The Sixth House is the Virgo House, and Mars is squared by Mercury in Virgo. These strenuous aspects have a direct bearing on his health.

'The serious astrologer' is a term which need not disturb even those who disbelieve in astrology as a 'science'. It is not necessary to believe every article of the Athanasian Creed to accept that there are others who hold each article to be literally true. Similarly, I find it easy to dismiss the arguments of those who assert that astrology is a nonsense because there is no apparent *reason* why the course of a man's life should be affected by the pattern made by the planets against a background of stars artificially grouped into a constellation. It is as *reasonable* to believe in astrology (certainly in that part of the science which deals with character analysis, and perhaps in the possibilities of prediction) as it is to believe in Buddhism or Christianity. The religious man can produce no rational reason why he believes in the existence of God; he regards that existence as manifest in reported 'miracles', and by the 'evidence' of his own faith.

As with all religions, the question is not how or why astrology works, but *whether* it works. There are not inconsiderable twentieth-century minds which believe that it does.

Jung was the most important lay apologist for astrology in this century, and remains so. He seems to have become interested in the subject while studying the Chinese *I ching*, published in a translation by Richard Wilhelm as *The secret of the golden flower*. In an address in memory of Wilhelm, subsequently printed as a foreword to the book, Jung explained and examined the principle of causality in connection with some unexplained coincidences which he had come across while working on the psychology of the unconscious.[1] The appearance of simultaneous identical thoughts or instincts seemed to him to be connected in some way with the moment of their conception. He called this moment 'synchronistic', and in his address said

> Astrology would be a large scale example of synchronism, if it had at its disposal thoroughly tested findings ... In so far as there are any really correct astrological deductions, they are not due to the effects of the constellations, but to our hypothetical time-characters. In other words, whatever is born or done this moment, has the qualities of this moment of time.

Not surprisingly, these last fifteen words have been quoted in evidence (and generally out of context) by almost every astrologer who has written a book or a paper, or given a lecture, since they were first spoken.

Jung took his theory further in a long essay (with which I will deal later). In it he set up 'an astrological experiment', explaining the sometimes extraordinary coincidences which occurred during his research by postulating 'a secret mutual connivance' between the psychic state of the investigator and the material itself. A theory no easier to accept, it may be, than the astrological theory.

However, at the end of his life, Jung stood by the conclusion that

> there are some facts adequately tested and fortified by a wealth of statistics which make the astrological problem seem worthy of

[1] C. G. Jung, foreword to *The secret of the golden flower* (Routledge & Kegan Paul, 1931).

philosophical investigation. It is assured of recognition from psychology, without further restrictions, because astrology represents the summation of all the psychological knowledge of antiquity.[1]

So an interest in astrology might be said to be respectable. And by 'the serious astrologer' I mean the man or woman who has studied the subject in depth, can accurately set up a Birth Chart (that is, a map of the heavens seen at the moment, and from the precise place of birth of an individual) and having studied the classic works on the subject from antiquity to the present time, can interpret it in the same way as a psychiatrist would interpret the evidence provided by his patient's dreams and imaginings. The astrologer can interpret the patterns of the Birth Chart with strict relevance to the subject's human condition and environment.

The latter clause is a vital one: it is there that St Augustine's objection to astrology (on which the churches still – as far as one can discover – base their objections to the science) fails. This hinges on what modern astrologers consider a misconception. In his youth, St Augustine had been inclined to astrology. The Proconsul Vindicianus warned him that the whole structure of the science was based on coincidence; but Augustine was unconvinced, and persisted in accepting astrology as a possible means whereby God revealed the future to man. In due course, however, an acquaintance, Firminus, produced what Augustine took to be a final and conclusive argument.

When Firminus' mother was with child by himself [sic], a certain slave-girl, who served a friend of his father, was with child also. Which fact was not known to her master, who used even with the most exact diligence to observe the birth of his puppies.

Now it so fell out that, when these men – the one for his wife and the other for his slave – had counted the day, the hour, and the minute of their being brought to bed, they were both delivered at the same instant; insomuch that they were both constrained to allow the very same horoscope to both the children,

[1] C. G. Jung, *Synchronicity: an acausal connecting principle* (Routledge & Kegan Paul, 1955).

one for his son and the other for his slave ... And yet Firminus, being honourably born in his parents' home, had his course with ease in the sunnier paths of the world, while the slave – as he that told the history knew well enough himself – continued to serve his master, without ever being eased from the yoke of that mean position wherein he was born.[1]

Augustine, taking the point, promptly announced that astrologers, presuming to forecast events, 'take themselves to be high and bright like the stars', and 'desired to set upon and to confute with scorn the dotards who follow this trade'. Both Roman Catholic and Church of England clergy produce St Augustine's argument still, with enormous *élan*, but agreeing that provided no firm forecast of actual events is promised, there can be no real *theological* argument against astrology. (And no serious modern astrologer will ever guarantee to forecast events.)

Incidentally, if St Augustine is perhaps the main Christian antagonist to astrology, one can produce from the long list of saints (not surprisingly, perhaps, considering its length) some who would support the theory – chief among them, St Thomas Aquinas, who felt convinced that 'it may be proved to demonstration that the celestial bodies are guided by some intelligence, either directly by God, or by the mediation of angels'. He pointed out, too, that the stars could not absolutely rule the actions of men: that while 'the celestial bodies are the cause of all that happens in this sublunary world' and 'act indirectly on human actions', 'not all the effects produced by them are unavoidable'.

Theologians who debate the astrological theory on the assumption that it denies free will misunderstand the attitude of contemporary astrologers, and indeed of most ancient astrologers also. Ingrid Lind, an astrologer with a keen religious bent, has pointed this out:

The natal Chart is the starting-point; it portrays where things will go easily and where there will be struggles or tests; but it is up to the individual as a living, breathing human being with the divine spark of life within him to meet such tests with courage

[1] *The Confessions of St Augustine*, tr. Sir Tobie Mathew (Collins, Fontana, 1957).

and intelligence. He is not an automaton to react at the lowest
material level to a given stimulus. In fact the whole advantage
of man as a conscious being is that he has freewill. Not freewill
to choose his beginnings and the natal pattern of his potential
strengths; but from the moment that he takes over his particular
starting-pattern he has freewill as to his own reactions, tinged
as these will inevitably be by the natus.[1]

Miss Lind also deals with the problem of the dissimilarity of the
lives of 'astrological twins'. Apart from the fact that Augustine did
not mention the distance between the two mothers, and that it
may be possible to doubt the accuracy of the timing (only four
minutes is sufficient to make a considerable difference in a Birth
Chart), he failed to recognise that children born under different
sets of circumstances must, of course, have different lives – which
is not to say that the general trends in those lives may not be
similar.

At the same moment of time three or four babies may utter their
first cry in the same town [Miss Lind wrote], animals too will be
born, business projects started or ships launched . . . All of these
would have the same Chart which must be studied in relation to
the subject or object. Further, I maintain that widely different
uses may be made of identical Charts. This is demonstrated
often enough in the case of twins. . . . The simplest explanation
is that two different spirits, perhaps at very different stages of
evolution, are animating the same Chart.[2]

This of course introduces elements of reincarnation and the
occult with which many astrologers would not agree; but Miss
Lind goes on to point out that the client 'must learn the strengths
and weaknesses of each planetary principle as it works through
him, and where he needs to tone down an excess and where to
remedy a weakness'. That is, a client will interpret his chart to suit
his own circumstances (through the medium of the astrologer);
another with the same chart may apply it to his quite different

[1] *Astrological Journal*, vol. IV, No. 4 (Autumn 1963); see also Ingrid
Lind, *Astrology and common sense* (Hodder & Stoughton, 1962).
[2] *ibid.*

circumstances. 'Men as plants increase, Cheered and checked even by the selfsame sky.[1]

The 'serious astrologer' must regard astrology as a science – using the term in the dictionary sense of 'an organised body of the knowledge that has been accumulated on a subject'. The term 'pseudo-science' is often used by antagonists; but the astrological body of knowledge is only 'pseudo' so long as one does not believe it to be true, and this is certainly not the case with astrologers. Indeed, it is an empirical science; if it were not, its theory would very probably not have survived. That as a theory it is imperfectly understood in its means of action is beside the point. However wildly out-of-the-way an astrologer's analysis or forecast may seem to be, if he is conscientious he will be able to produce his reason for making it: a certain pattern of planets, or certain planetary movements, interpreted by a set of rules which may have originated over three thousand years ago, but which has certainly been reconsidered and re-thought many times since then, and in any event will be applied specifically to one particular case. 'Proof' may not be available that planet A in conjunction with planet B provokes condition X; but the serious astrologer predicting condition X will always be able to produce a text supporting that prediction on the basis of the positions of planets A and B.

This is not to say that the astrologer must be devoid of imagination, or even of instinct. Many astrologers contend that there is a most important occult aspect to the science; and most will say that they have a 'feeling' about Birth Charts which will reliably inform them if a mistake has been made in calculation.

However, the vaguely occult air hanging over most astrological advertisements in the popular astrological press is perhaps unfortunate. The catalogue of astrological books published by Messrs L. N. Fowler of London (a firm founded in 1880 by an American whose main interest was in phrenology) contains 150 works, many of them serious astrological textbooks. It also contains a blurb advertising C. C. Zain's *Astrological signatures*, suggesting that

With the knowing before you, and the means of proving it, that

[1] Shakespeare, *Sonnets*, XV.

there is a conscious survival of personality after the dissolution
of the physical body you will next desire to know the meaning
of life. Here is set forth, in proper detail, where your soul had its
origin, through what process it reached the earth, why human
incarceration was necessary, and the purposes of joy and
sorrow.

All for 28s 6d, or $3.95.

Mr Zain's work and, indeed, Dane Rudhyar's is unlikely to
become popular with the lending libraries, and perhaps it is as
well. But Jung saw at the very end of his life that astrology was on
the edge of not only a popular, but a scientific and academic
revival.

The cultural philistines believed until recently that astrology
had been disposed of long since, and was something that could
safely be laughed at [he wrote]. But today, rising out of the
social deeps, it knocks at the doors of the universities, from
which it was banished some three hundred years ago.[1]

The popular revival has certainly taken place. The increased
number of clients queuing for astrologers' time, the thousands of
astrological postcards and posters, pennants, birthday cards and
amulets, shopping-bags and calendars; the newspaper columns,
the gramophone records, the magazines, all testify to this. And the
popular interest seems more than simply decorative; it is in a sense
almost 'magic'. Astrology is built into our language – in the names
of the days of the week, for instance; in adjectives such as 'saturnine', 'jovial'; and also because almost everyone who knows the
sign with which their birthday is particularly associated knows
also the qualities generally associated with that sign, their Sun-
sign, and have come perhaps to some extent to identify with those
qualities.

And there is another reason why astrology is increasing its hold
on the popular interest. Man still, for the most part, seems to need
a belief in some supernatural force – if only one which he can
blame for natural disasters, or for the fifty-odd wars of the past
fifty-odd years. God has ceased to exist except for a minority

[1] C. G. Jung, *The spirntual problem of modern man: civilisation in transit*
(Routledge & Kegan Paul, 1964).

(indeed more people probably now believe that 'there may be something in astrology' than in the existence of God; although of course the two beliefs are not mutually exclusive).

In America in particular, but also in some European countries, there are signs of university interest; in 1959 an American student, Marcia Moore, submitted a socio-psychological survey entitled 'Astrology Today' as a thesis for her degree. She graduated from Harvard phi beta kappa, *magna cum laude*.

Sales of astrological textbooks mount year by year. The number of students who sit the examinations of the British Faculty of Astrological Studies also increases annually. Businessmen hire astrologers to advise on the sale of stocks and shares; astrologers have programmed computers to work on experimental correlations of charts; and most astrologers have a waiting list of from one to six months for private clients.

The number of full-time professional astrologers working today in Britain is comparatively small; the Astrological Association has a membership of about three hundred at home (many others abroad); but from time to time the Secretary has an application from someone who 'has been an astrologer for years, but has never heard of the Association'. The Faculty of Astrological Studies has over sixty diploma-holders in Great Britain, although many of these are not in practice.

But estimation is difficult all over the world: Spain, for instance, has not been considered a stronghold of astrology, yet suddenly at the end of 1969 an astrological conference was announced to run in Spain for a week, during 1970, and organised by a group of astrologers of whom no one outside that country had apparently ever heard!

Whether or not the increasing interest in astrology is capable of statistical proof, however, popular interest is still, in the broadest sense, confined to newspaper columns or to 'playtime' astrology in the end-of-the-pier sense, or the revelation of the approach of the tall, dark, handsome suitor, or the sudden visitation of wealth. But this, a 'touch of the old bead curtains', is not what astrology is about. Astrologers have varied attitudes to prediction; but the serious astrologer will insist that the most he can do is to predict tendencies in the subject's life. This causes, inevitably, some disappointment, especially if the astrologer is not honest enough to explain before he undertakes a horoscope, precisely what he can and cannot do. Many astrologers do so. Ingrid Lind, for instance, despatches in response to enquiries, a printed order form which includes 'Advice to Enquirers':

> Please do not expect any form of exact fortune-telling. The progressed Chart shows the trends in your basic pattern that are stimulated in a particular year. The years when important events are likely to occur show up clearly (although not the precise nature of the event) and also years when the tide, so to speak, is with you or against you.

It is impossible to escape the feeling that the serious astrologer often mistrusts his capacity for more or less precise prediction, even of 'trends'. It is fair to say that in my own limited experience these trends have often been fairly accurately forecast. But Charles Carter, for instance, was extremely suspicious of prediction; and one would be wary of any astrologer who claimed to be able to forecast on any other basis than that set out by Miss Lind.

Louis de Wohl probably put the matter most plainly:

> It [astrology] has nothing to do with fortune-telling. It does not say what is going to happen, but what *tendencies* appear. An astrologer can never say, 'At six o'clock in the afternoon of the seventeenth of September you will have an accident and will be taken to hospital where two hours later you will die'. Such a prediction is either clairvoyance or a swindle – and in 999 cases out of a thousand, the latter. What the astrologer *can* say is: 'On the seventeenth of September between five and seven you have a bad Mars aspect, which owing to the unfavourable position of Mars in your natal horoscope, brings with it the danger of an accident.'[1]

Character analysis – the detailed examination of a Birth Chart as it reveals the character of the subject – is quite another matter, and it is perhaps the most interesting aspect of modern astrology. There is virtually no limit to be placed on the claims made

[1] Louis de Wohl, *Secret service of the sky* (Cresset Press, 1939).

by astrologers in this direction: and the results are often surprising.

Modern astrologers, therefore, have learnt caution; they will nor normally claim to be able to forecast events with the certainty of some of their ancestors, although it is true that no adequate attempt has yet been made to evaluate how the astrologers of Europe between the twelfth and seventeenth centuries affected the history of their times. Dr A. L. Rowse, in the forthcoming final volume of his Tudor trilogy, will present new material about Dr Dee, Elizabeth's astrologer, who for a considerable period of time was extremely close to the court, and without any doubt must have influenced political decisions. But I know of no serious or detailed study of the subject.

This is remarkable, for during those five hundred years astrology affected almost every aspect of life; kings and popes had their private astrologers, authors invoked the planets to support the actions of their characters, artists relied on the Zodiac for decorative purposes and for allegories, and no family of consequence would fail to have a horoscope drawn up for its children. Dr Dee in England was matched by Cosmo Ruggieri at the court of Louis XI, Guido Bonatus earlier yet at the court of Frederick II, and Joannes Camateros at that of the Byzantine Emperor Manuel I.

Martin Luther, in a preface to an astrologer's manifesto, pointed out that the planets could 'warn and threaten the godless lands and countries'; Luc Gauric set up the horoscope of a young man, Giovanni de Medici, and predicted that he would become Pope. After his prediction had come true, he published his *Kalendar and compost of shepherds*, a charming astrological text which was one of the first printed books to have a wide circulation in Europe.

In literature, the astrological influence seems limitless (and here, again, no real study has been made). Scarcely an important writer can be found between 1100 and 1600, who does not allude extensively to astrological lore. The pages of Dante, Chaucer, Shakespeare, are full of such allusions. A concordance will reveal almost a hundred direct astrological allusions in Shakespeare, for instance; and they are shrewd enough to make it clear that his was a reasonably accurate knowledge of the subject. It has been suggested that he was an opponent of astrology; but, as John Addey has pointed out, the anti-astrological allusions are invariably placed in the mouths of his villains (as in the speech of Edmund, in *King Lear*), while the accurate allusions, or the favourable ones, are given to virtuous men.[1]

It would be easy enough to give a catalogue of distinguished astrologers in history, their influence in their time, and their effect on their contemporaries; but this is not the place for it. It is impossible, however, to read at all deeply in the history of those five hundred years, without becoming aware of astrology as an important force. These earlier astrologers were distinguished astronomers (there were no printed ephemerides listing the positions of the planets; they had to work these out accurately for themselves); and while the great body of textbooks available to twentieth-century astrologers did not exist, they had large quantities of manuscript sources, as well as a body of information passed down orally from astrologer to apprentice. And the work of setting up a Birth Chart and interpreting it was basically the same as it is today. It is, as will be seen, by no means a simple operation.

[1] See *Chaucer and the country of the stars*, by Chauncey Wood (Princeton, 1970), for an exhaustive study of Chaucer's extensive astrological imagery.

III

Beginnings and Complexities

The one astrological fact which almost everyone knows about himself is his Sun-sign – the zodiacal sign in which the Sun stood at the moment of his birth; whether he is a 'Leo' or a 'Virgo' or a 'Pisces'. (It is this that enables newspapers to print columns in which the entire population is split into the twelve zodiacal categories, and the week laid out for their inspection.)

The consequent air of ease and approximation which seems to be given to astrological prediction has done great damage, and caused considerable confusion. Very few readers have any idea of the amount of work which goes into the proper reading of a Birth Chart or into its preparation. But for the serious astrologer, the complexities of preparing an analysis are considerable. The relative positions of all the planets at birth, the angles made between them and their general relationship to each other; the Houses in which they stand – not only in the Birth Chart itself, but in the 'progressed' chart which tells the astrologer of the future trends . . . all these factors make proper interpretation a lengthy business.

It is difficult to explain the process in lay terms; any reader interested would do well to go directly to a textbook. I shall attempt here only to indicate the extent of the work to be done; and first I should perhaps provide a little background information – in so far as this is available.

The origin of the Zodiac itself is lost in the uttermost distances of man's history. In the earliest recorded years of Babylonia and

Egypt, man was already worshipping the Sun and Moon and some of the planets. Some cities had their planet-gods: Ur of the Chaldees relied for protection on Sin, the Moon-god; Nineveh on Ishtar, the goddess of Venus; and at Abydos the ruling god was associated with Jupiter, and the constellation of Orion. Already by that time a band of sky spreading out for a few degrees on either side of the apparent path of the Sun (the ecliptic) was recognised to contain a number of groups of stars identified with certain figures of men or of beasts. These were drawn in such a way as to contain within them the groups of stars to which they referred; although it often seems now that the imagination which created them allowed itself more licence than might reasonably have been permitted.

These zodiacal figures were referred to as early as 3000 B.C., although the earliest manuscript depicting them is from Babylonia, c. 600 B.C.; we are unlikely to discover how they became universal, or how they gained their astrological significance, and speculation is unrewarding. It is at least possible that their astrological meaning was attached to them by general observation; Gemini became associated with quickness of movement, duality, artistic sensibility, simply because it was noticed that Geminian subjects possessed these qualities. The many hundreds of years during which astrology developed would certainly allow plenty of time for observation!

Here, at all events were the Lion, the Scorpion, the Heavenly Twins, moving in continuous procession about the sky; though in reality their positions are without reference to the band of the Zodiac, *from earth* they appear to confine themselves to it; and it is this fact which, one supposes, made astrology in the first place possible, with the realisation that one could define the moment of one's birth by referring it to the apparent position of the Sun within the ecliptic: if one was born between December 22 and January 19, the Sun was 'in' Capricorn; if between September 23 and October 22, 'in' Libra.

It is no longer true that between those dates the Sun is 'in' either of those signs; the slow shift of the stars, the 'precession of the equinoxes', as it is called, has resulted in a general upsetting of the original plan. Critics of astrology have made much of this; but in

fact astrologers use zodiacal terms only for convenience – they
work not with the constellations, but with the sectors of the ecliptic
itself: with twelve sectors of 30° each, irrespective of the position
of fixed stars within those sections. It is convenient to refer to them
in the ancient zodiacal terms.

Moving against the background of the Zodiac (or, if you wish,
against the background of these sections) are the planets – which
must, with their apparently inexplicable changes of speed and
direction, have seemed to the ancients almost to have a life of their
own. It is fairly easy to guess how the planets were endowed with
their traditional 'personalities': Venus, the clearest and brightest,
had already by Babylonian times been associated with propa-
gation; Mars, dully red and angry, with its sudden changes of
direction; Jupiter with its steady implacable movement and regal
bearing; Saturn, distant, faint and old – each has its individual
characterisation. One can sense how the signs of the Zodiac, and
the planets, were associated with their traditional qualities. Traditionally, these qualities connect the zodiacal signs with the four
elements: there are three fiery signs, three watery, three earthy
and three airy. These attributions have significance today, though
they are less firmly interpreted. Astrologers up to the beginning of
this century were more definite about their meaning. John Varley,
a nineteenth-century astrologer, wrote in *A treatise on zodiacal
physiognomy*:

> The firey trigon [the triangle made by the signs Aries, Leo and
> Sagittarius] contains the spirited, generous, magnaminous and
> princely natures. The earthy trigons, Taurus, Virgo and Capri-
> corn, contains the careful, sordid and penurious qualities; the
> aerial trigon, Gemini, Libra and Aquarius, contains the
> humane, harmonious and courteous principles; and the water
> trigon, Cancer, Scorpio and Pisces, the cold, prolific, cautious
> and severe qualities.

Modern astrologers would qualify this; but the statement still
has significance. One will still find in modern astrological textbooks, summaries of the characteristics of 'the Aries man' which
are not too widely different from the summaries given a century or
several centuries ago. For instance, Raphael (Robert Cross Smith,

the first of a number of astrologers to take that pseudonym at the turn of the eighteenth-nineteenth century) wrote of Aries that it is 'a vernal, dry, fiery, masculine, cardinal, equinoctial, diurnal, moveable, commanding, eastern, choleric, violent and quad-repedian sign'.

Margaret Hone, an astrologer of our own time, writes of the 'predominantly Arian person':

> He is very much of a firebrand or battering-ram. He will force his way through life with courage, daring, energy and initiative and enterprise. . . . Overstress or misuse of these traits will mean selfishness, crudeness, egotism, pugnacity, bad temper, foolhardiness, churlish behaviour.[1]

If the Arian subject happens to have been born at sunrise, he may well find his Arian characteristics heavily underlined: for then as well as a Sun in Aries, he will have an Arian Ascendant – that is, the zodiacal sign Aries will have been in process of rising above the eastern horizon at the moment of his birth. Generally speaking, no sign of the Zodiac is so uniformly admirable that anyone may count himself fortunate to have been born at sunrise. Yet the double-Arian need not despair: the position of the Moon can be of equal importance, and an array of planets in some other sign can very greatly modify the result even of a Sun and Ascendant in the same sign. Nevertheless, someone born approximately at sunrise may well find that the newspaper predictions for his Sun-sign are marginally more accurate than a neighbour whose Ascendant and Sun-sign are different.

Once one has realised that other factors besides the time of the year affect one's horoscope, then a professional astrologer of greater or lesser ability becomes necessary; for until a Birth Chart is set up – a chart which will show the positions of the planets within the zodiacal signs or sections of the ecliptic – the other factors involved cannot be known.

The starting points for the setting-up of the Birth Chart are the moment and place of birth, which must be as accurate as possible. Most people know the place of their birth. The birth *time* is a

[1] Margaret E. Hone, *The modern textbook of astrology* (L. N. Fowler, 1951).

different matter, although in some countries (including Scotland and some states in the US) this is recorded on the birth certificate. Most astrologers call the birth-time the time of the first cry, when the baby becames an individual. Of course there have been, and there still are, arguments about why this particular moment should have significance; some astrologers have worked from the moment of conception (in practice this is virtually impossible to time and modern astrologers have almost completely abandoned it). One has, I think, to accept the fact that the moment of the first cry seems on the whole to be the significant *moment* in the Jungian sense. Argument on the point is fruitless: astrologers reply, 'It works.'

If the precise time of birth is not known, some astrologers may 'rectify' the Birth Chart in the light of what it shows. This is generally risky, although it too may occasionally work. Normally, a Birth Chart is set up for noon or perhaps for sunrise on the day of birth. If the astrologer knows the subject very well, and perhaps knows of several important events which might be expected to show in his progressed chart, he may infer that the Ascendant is *probably* a specific sign, and will then calculate a chart for the time at which that sign was ascending. If then the appearance of the chart seems to support certain events in the subject's past life, the time of birth may be narrowed down still further. But even so, events may show in so many different ways in a chart, and there are so many qualifications to be made, that the most experienced astrologer may, quite simply, guess wrong. So, in her textbook,[1] Margaret Hone warns that it is unwise to attempt to rectify a chart when birth is only known to have occurred on a certain day. She does allow rectification when the birth-time is known to within two hours or so; and birth-times are fairly often rectified when it appears to the astrologer that the error is one of minutes.

This kind of rectification – an astrologer may very well inform one that one's birth-time was 4.36 p.m. rather than 4.30 p.m. – is not a conjuring trick; it is based on observation, and the astrologer, if pressed, can produce good reason for suspecting such a correction to be necessary. There are certain tricks which can be

[1] *ibid.*

performed with reasonable ease by a practised astrologer, and which are extremely effective in disarming any sceptical critic. Mr Cecil King[1] has told how, before the war, he took the *Daily Mirror* astrologer to lunch. She pointed out a waiter, and said he was a typical Leo, born, she would guess, around August 11. Mr King called the waiter over and asked him the date of his birthday. It was August 11.

This was certainly a lucky guess, but based, no doubt, upon specific observations of the waiter's appearance, movements, general characteristics. It is only possible when the subject *is* strongly characteristic of a dominant sign in his chart, Sun-sign or Ascendant. In that case, it was obviously the Sun-sign. But if a subject can say that his Sun-sign is Leo, yet he obviously has some of the characteristics of, say, Gemini, in his appearance and behaviour, then the astrologer (knowing his date of birth) can say that he was born perhaps at 2 a.m., when Gemini would have been ascending over the eastern horizon. Of course when other planets strongly modify the chart the trick fails; and in any event, astrologers generally hate performing it. To invite an eminent astrologer to do so would be rather like inviting Sir Bernard Lovell to demonstrate the means of calculating the distance of the Moon from the Earth.

Provided, then, with the moment and the date of birth, and the place, the astrologer begins his calculations. He needs, for these, the longitude and latitude of the place of birth, and an emphemeris for the year of birth – an astronomical almanac detailing the positions of the planets on each day of the year concerned. These are published annually – for the use of astronomers and navigators as well as astrologers – and have the kind of grandiloquent title-pages associated with the astronomical works of the sixteenth century. Perhaps the most famous, published since the early nineteenth century by Foulsham's, is entitled:

RAPHAEL'S

ASTRONOMICAL EPHEMERIS

of the

PLANET'S PLACES

for 19—

with tables of houses for London, Liverpool, and New York

[1] Lecture at the Royal Institution, 1969.

*containing the Longitudes of all the Planets daily and their
Latitudes and Declinations for every other day, with the
Lunar and Mutual Aspects for every day, etc., etc. A COM-
PLETE ASPECTARIAN. Ephemeris Time Observed
throughout ... Caution: Refuse inaccurate imitation
issues.*

Using the ephemeris (some astrologers prefer the *Nautical
Almanac*) the local sidereal time at birth must be calculated. This
will enable the Ascendant and M.C. (*Medium Coeli*, mid-heaven:
the degree at which the ecliptic reaches its highest point at the
meridian of any single place) to be found, and the planets to be
placed in their respective Houses.

Sidereal time relates to the *actual* time the earth takes to revolve
on its axis: not twenty-four hours precisely, but twenty-three
hours, fifty-six minutes and 4.9 seconds. Astronomers assume that
the first point of Aries (which in fact is no longer 'in' Aries, but still
provides a useful fixed point from which to measure) is fixed; it
appears to cross the meridian of any place at a more or less precise
interval of time. This interval of time is known as a sidereal day,
and is divided into hours, minutes and seconds in the same way as
our conventional day. So 00.00 hours sidereal time is the moment
at which the first point of Aries crosses the meridian of any given
place.

Having the local sidereal time of birth for the place where the
subject was born, the astrologer goes on to plot the position of the
planets at that time on a chart which represents the heavens [see
Fig 1]. Various charts are in use (some astrologers have devised
their own); but I show the one designed by Margaret Hone, and
completed from my own birth data. The astrologer draws the
divisions of the Houses in the inner space, which is used also to
show the angles between the various planets; and the divided
inner ring is marked with the zodiacal signs as they apply to the
chart under consideration. The aspects made by the planets are
shown also in the squared spaces marked on the chart, on which
the necessary calculations are also given.

The process of calculation need not be detailed here. Proportional logarithms, consideration of the Moon's nodes, the

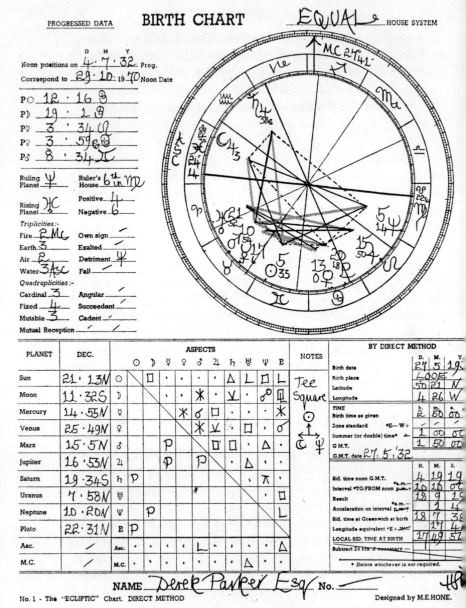

BIRTH CHART — EQUAL HOUSE SYSTEM

PROGRESSED DATA

Noon positions on 4 . 7 . 32 Prog.

Correspond to 29 . 10 . 19 70 Noon Date

	D	M	Y

PO 12 . 16 ♉
P☽ 19 . 1 ♉
P☿ 3 . 34 ♌
P♀ 3 . 59 ♌
P♂ 8 . 34 ♊

Ruling Planet ♆
Ruler's House 6th in ♍

Rising Planet ♓ ♄
Positive 4
Negative 6

Triplicities:-
Fire ♂♇♃ Own sign ✓
Earth 3 Exalted ✓
Air 2 Detriment ♆
Water 3 ASC Fall ✓

Quadruplicities:-
Cardinal 3 Angular ✓
Fixed 4 Succeedent ✓
Mutable 3 Cadent ✓
Mutual Reception ✓ ✓

PLANET	DEC.	ASPECTS										NOTES
		☉	☽	☿	♀	♂	♃	♄	♅	♆	♇	
Sun	21 . 13 N	☉	□	.	.	.	.	△	∟	□	∟	Tee Square
Moon	11 . 32 S		☽	.	.	✳	.	⩒	.	⚼	⚸	
Mercury	14 . 55 N			☿	✳	☌	□	.	.	.	✳	
Venus	25 . 49 N				♀	✳	⩒	.	□	.	☌	
Mars	15 . 5 N			P		♂	□	□	.	△	.	
Jupiter	16 . 53 N			P		P	♃	.	△	.	.	
Saturn	19 . 34 S	♄	P					♄	⊼	.	.	
Uranus	7 . 58 N	♅							♅	.	□	
Neptune	10 . 20 N	♆	P							♆	∟	
Pluto	22 . 31 N	♇	P								♇	
Asc.	/	Asc.	.	.	.	.	∟	⌐	.	.	.	△
M.C.	/	M.C.	.	.	.	.	.	.	.	△	.	.

BY DIRECT METHOD

	D.	M.	Y.
Birth date	27	5	19
Birth place	LOOE		
Latitude	50	21	N
Longitude	4	26	W

TIME	h.	m.	s.
Birth time as given	2	50	00
Zone standard •E— W+			
Summer (or double) time*	1	00	00
G.M.T.	1	50	00
G.M.T. date 27 : 5 '32			

	H.	M.	S.
Sid. time noon G.M.T.	4	19	19
Interval *TO/FROM noon •a.m. p.m.	10	10	00
Result	18	9	19
Acceleration on interval p.m.*a.m.		1	4
Sid. time at Greenwich at birth	18	7	38
Longitude equivalent •E + W—		17	4
LOCAL SID. TIME AT BIRTH	17	49	57
Subtract 24 hrs. if necessary —			

* Delete whichever is not required.

NAME Derek Parker Esq No. ____

No. 1 - The "ECLIPTIC" Chart. DIRECT METHOD

Designed by M.E.HONE.

Fig. 1. Birth Chart of the author

declination of the planets, and other niceties are involved; but the mathematical work is a matter of drudgery rather than difficulty. And when it has been applied to a Birth Chart, the astrologer has before him a map of the heavens at the moment of the subject's birth, as this might have been seen from the place of that birth. This is the raw material. The real work must now begin.

I have used already certain astrological terms which need definition. First of all, the Houses: the twelve equal triangles into which the inner space of the chart is divided. These are not, as I have pointed out, identical with the twelve signs of the Zodiac. In order to grasp the nature of the Houses, one must imagine the earth to be the centre of the solar system, with the Sun revolving around it (a major assumption, certainly). As the sun at daybreak rises on the eastern horizon, a line passing from it through the centre of the earth would, extended to the perimeter of the circle formed with the earth at its centre, hit the *cusp* of the first House. The ecliptic (i.e. the circumference of the circle of the Birth Chart) is then divided into twelve equal Houses of 30° each. The *cusp* of the first house falls invariably on the Ascendant degree: so naturally the cusps of the remaining houses fall on the same degree of each subsequent sign.

I have been referring to the Equal House system: this is the one taught by the Faculty of Astrological Studies, and is considered there to be the most satisfactory. But there are various systems of House division – Placidus, Campanus, Regiomontanus – and the arguments which have been going on for several hundred years about their relative merits show no signs of being resolved; it is unlikely, indeed, that they will be. Perhaps the Placidean system is on the whole still the most popular – despite the fact that, as Margaret Hone points out in her textbook,[1] it distorts the charts of subjects born in the higher latitudes, and indeed a strict devotee of Placidus would have to uphold the contention that at certain times in the year no births could take place in the northernmost latitudes.

The history of the Houses themselves is ancient and symbolic –

[1] *The modern textbook of astrology,* op. cit.

QA–D

full, as is the general history of astrology, of elegant and graceful assertions which are deeply rooted in many generations of considered thought (reminding one, certainly, of Jung's comment about 'the summation of the psychological knowledge of antiquity'). Even if astrology as a whole should be a worthless trickery, it can scarcely be denied that it provides, in a study of its rules and traditions, a fund of the most fascinating evidence about the nature of man.

Each House of the astrological chart has its own significance: planets placed within it will refer to the matters traditionally associated with it. The First House, for instance, has to do with the personal characteristics of the subject; the Second refers to possessions and emotions; the Third to communications, and close relatives; the Fourth to the home; the Fifth to the subject's instinct for living and creating . . . and so on. Thus Mars (representing strength and energy) placed in Gemini in the Third House might be interpreted as pointing to the use of forceful energy in a lively, perhaps loquacious manner (Geminian characteristics), and concerning itself with matters of communication, or perhaps with brothers or sisters or other close relatives.

But I have taken this example straight from a textbook, using 'key-words' supplied for the Houses, the planets, the signs. An astrologer would properly be aghast at the naïvety of such a judgement; he would modify, expand and refine it by reference to the positions of the other planets and their aspects.

An astrological aspect – an astronomical one, for that matter – is the angle made by the line drawn from one planet to the centre of the earth, and the line from another to the same point. These angles are measured simply on the Birth Chart by counting the degrees which separate the two planets along the ecliptic. The lines connecting the points within the chart are simply drawn for the astrologer's convenience, and for quick reading – the colour and form of the line suiting his own convenience (the Faculty recommends using red lines for the 'helpful' aspects, and black for the 'disruptive' ones).

The angles between the planets are described by traditional terms which refer to the number of degrees involved: a square aspect is, naturally, one of 90°; a trine, of 120°. Two planets 'in opposition' are separated by 180°; if they are sextile, the angle is one of 60°. Other terms include the semi-square (45°), and sesquiquadrate (135°), quincunx (150°), and semi-sextile (30°). Two planets in conjunction fall on the identical degree. As with the zodiacal signs (familiar from the various decorative uses to which they have been put), each of the angle definitions has its shorthand significator – its 'glyph'.

The aspects have their own significance: the planets concerned act on each other within their own astrological natures, but they are affected also by the astrological nature of the aspect they make with each other. These are deeply traditional, although they are constantly under review within the individual astrologer's experience of them. In the earliest time, the Houses referred only to the positions of the planets and signs they 'ruled'; the more sophisticated implications developed gradually – as did the meanings of the aspects. Both had reached some degree of complication by the time the *Syntaxis* and the *Tetrabiblos* appeared.

These two books can be used as examples of the many publications that have affected the development of astrology, more or less radically, over the past one thousand years or so. Astrology of course had been in the air for many centuries before 400 B.C. Personal predictions (made, naturally enough, to rulers, and referring not so much to their personal lives as to the conduct of public affairs) were made in Babylonia, it seems; and the destruction of Ur was forecast by astrologers of that time, who based their forecasts on a lunar eclipse (as did the astrologers, centuries later, who forecast the San Francisco earthquake). Some fragments of documents known as the *Anu-Enlil* series, derived from the reign of Sargon of Akkad (*c.* 2350–2300 B.C.) detailed predictions obtained by observation of the Moon, the Sun, 'the five planets', constellations, stars and comets, and from storms, winds, rains, thunderbolts and lightning. Morris Jastrow, an American scholar, believes these documents to have formed part of an important astrological handbook 'published' as early as 1500 B.C.

But by far the most important early textbooks for astrologers were the *Syntaxis* and the *Tetrabiblos*. The former was the work of the Alexandrian mathematician, astronomer and geographer

Claudius Ptolemy – a work based on the teachings of Hipparchus, and propounding a quite extraordinarily detailed examination of the condition and behaviour of the observable universe.

Ptolemy was observing during the reign of Hadrian (A.D. 127–141), at Alexandria, where pillars were erected on which were carved his astronomical theories and discoveries. The *Syntaxis* describes a spherical world in the centre of the universe, circled by the heavenly bodies; and goes on to discuss their dimensions, to catalogue 1,022 separate stars, and to discuss Mercury, Jupiter, Venus and Saturn in some detail.

The *Tetrabiblos*, a purely astrological work, was for some time ascribed to Ptolemy, although internal evidence now suggests, rather, that it is an anthology of Babylonian and Egyptian astrological traditions, perhaps with a Greek flavour. Whatever its origins, however, the book is unquestionably the most important of the early astrological documents; it broadened the whole concept of the science. As man's knowledge of the movements of the planets had increased, so had the numbers of variations observable in their behaviour; so that the scope of interpretations now possible was almost endless. The *Tetrabiblos* demonstrated this with conviction, almost with relish; and it remains required reading for every astrologer.

Book One classifies the planets and signs, attributing general properties to them: Mars causes dryness and heat, is male, nocturnal, a portent of evil, the ruler of the signs Scorpio and Aries. Taurus is female, nocturnal, and one of the Houses of Venus (an example of the early use of the term *Houses*). In Book Two, the *Tetrabiblos* deals with races, countries and cities, dividing them according to their climates. It points out that the position of the Sun and Moon is important at the founding of a city, as far as its subsequent history is concerned (incidentally, the authors had very different ideas from Ptolemy's on geography!). Eclipses of the Sun and Moon affect a city in whose sign the eclipse takes place; and the nature of the event foretold varies according to that sign, and by the nature of the ruling planets. Jupiter, for instance, was considered excellent for the happiness of domestic animals, weather, navigation and harvest!

The Third and Fourth Books deal with individual predictions

and horoscopes, based on the moment of conception (if known) or the moment of birth. Although the *Tetrabiblos* uses the word *House* in its old sense, in Book Four considerable care is given to the interpretation of the positions of the Sun, Moon and planets within the various Houses. Longevity, for instance, was determined by the First House, the Eleventh (the 'House of the Good Demon'), the Tenth (containing the M.C.), the Ninth (the 'House of God'), and the Seventh (containing the Descendant, the sign sinking below the western horizon at the moment of birth). All these Houses would be considered with reference to the planets placed within them. But one is warned also to consider the Ascendant, the Part of Fortune (a point as far from the Ascendant as the Moon is from the Sun), the planetary rulers of the Sun-sign, and the preceding conjunction. Special rules declared which of these points was most important in any one case.

Charles Carter, the twentieth-century British astrologer, lists in one of his textbooks[1] the Fourth, Eighth or Twelfth Houses as the most important ones to consider (with special reference to Jupiter contained within one of them) where longevity is concerned. He goes on to comment on the importance of having Saturn well placed in the Fourth House; on the good configuration of Venus and Libra; and to detail the facts revealed by his own careful examination of the charts of a number of octogenarians.

But obviously the contemporary astrologer cannot rely on any single source. He must draw on a combination of the many theories of astrologers who have built up a wealth of comment on the various attributes which might be found in any one chart. Like a solicitor consulting the law books published between the sixteenth century and the present day, he must take shifts of judicial astrological opinion into consideration, while at the same time retaining an open mind, and using his own experience and common sense to interpret a chart.

Perhaps this is some indication of the difficulties of conscientious interpretation – and it may already be clear that the more an astrologer knows about his client, the better his work will be for that client. While the results of 'blind astrology' are

[1] Charles Carter, *The encyclopaedia of psychological astrology* (Theosophical Publishing House, 1924).

sometimes spectacular, it is silly to expect an astrologer to be able to tell from a look at the Birth Chart whether a subject is a rich man, poor man, beggar-man or thief. The Birth Chart provides, as I have said, the raw material for a psychological study, as well as showing the tendencies towards certain physical weaknesses or strengths.

It is the *progressed* chart which provides evidence of these 'trends'. There have been, during the centuries, several methods of 'progressing' a chart – that is, of producing a map of the sky not for the moment of birth, but for some time in the future when the client's life will be influenced by new planetary configurations. Generally speaking, the method used for progressing a horoscope today is the 'day for a year' method, and it had better be admitted again that (as indeed is the case with astrology in general) there is no proper explanation of why this should work. Each day after the client's birth is taken to represent, symbolically, a year in his life: the movements of the planets during, say, the seventh day after his birth are taken to represent the manner in which his life will fall out during his seventh year.

The method is immeasurably old (Jeff Mayo points out[1] that it is mentioned in *Ezekiel*: 'I have appointed thee each day for a year'), and it correlates with the orbital movements of the planets. The Primary System, which is less often used, correlates with the revolution of the Earth itself; but it has considerable disadvantages – great nicety of calculation, for instance, being necessary, since an error of four minutes in the birth-time will throw progressions out by twelve months.

Generally speaking, then, the astrologer who is asked to discover the tendencies affecting a client's life for his thirtieth year would recalculate the Birth Chart for the same time and place as before, but using the ephemeris to give the new positions of the planets for the thirtieth day after birth. This new chart is then read in the same way as a Birth Chart.

As far as *daily* predictions of good or evil tendencies are concerned, however, a very simple method is used, based on transits. A transit is taken to mean the movement of a planet over another

[1] Jeff Mayo, *Teach yourself astrology* (English Universities Press, 1964).

planet, or over some given point in the horoscope. This requires no
calculation: simply the use of the ephemeris for the year concerned. Incidentally, it is possible in this way to read the daily
horoscope of someone long dead: an ephemeris for 1820 would, for
instance, reveal the tendencies affecting Keats during the last year
of his life. Some fascinating experiments have been conducted
along those lines; and evidently there is continuing interest, since
the printers of ephemerides are able to keep 'back numbers' in
print as far at least as 1860.

The importance of transits seems to vary with the astrologer's
own attitudes and theories. Jeff Mayo, for instance, writes:

> Transiting aspects appear to correlate with . . . the develop-
> ment of circumstances in the life, which are invariably outside
> the individual's power to prevent happening. They do some-
> times correlate purely with psychological development, though
> more frequently this is due to exterior happenings, which
> demand particular reactions from the individual or force prob-
> lems upon him which test his character or ability to cope with
> them.[1]

Alan Leo, in his classic, *The progressed horoscope*,[2] has weighed
the differing effects of various transits, and gives a 'key' to them:
i.e. 'Mars passing through the Fifth House inclines prodigality,
violent demonstration of feeling and the awakening of the passions'.
Or 'Mercury in transit over Jupiter is fortunate for business and
all literary occupations; it brings friends, social success, honour
and pleasure'.

The transits and progressed aspects have to be read, of course, in
relation to the character of the Birth Chart: they affect the client's
life accordingly, strengthened or weakened by their relationship to
the original positions. As Jeff Mayo puts it,[3]

> When interpreting the progressed or transiting aspects
> always base your reasoning on the principles of the planets,
> signs and Houses involved, but *especially* the planets. You must
> also assess the probable effects, and the likely reaction of the

[1] *ibid.*
[2] Alan Leo, *The progressed horoscope* (L. N. Fowler, 1906).
[3] *Teach yourself astrology,* op. cit.

individual concerned, according to the natal Chart *as a whole*, and the status and circumstances of the individual.

But it seems to be rarely possible to tell precisely what the effects of a transit will be; there are so many incalculables, not all of them embodied in the progressed chart.

All positions and aspects [writes Alan Leo[1]] denote the nature of events likely to happen, *sooner or later*, the actual time usually depending upon opportunity, impulse, and also, to some extent, the directions operating in the nativities of others closely affecting the native's life – the latter an important consideration that is generally overlooked.

There are other branches of astrology, two of which perhaps should be mentioned here: mundane astrology, and electional astrology. It is claimed that by mundane astrology it is possible to predict tendencies for cities, states, political parties, etc., in the same manner as for individuals. A decision has to be made of course, as to the moment for which to draw up the necessary Chart: and here is where the difficulty arises. For Great Britain, for instance, no less than three moments are suggested: midday on December 25, 1066 (the moment of the crowning of William the Conqueror); midnight on May 1, 1707 (the moment of the union of England and Scotland); and midnight on January 1, 1801 (the moment of Union of Great Britain and Ireland). Charles Carter 'found the 1801 map more reliable'; but other astrologers would argue about that. And in any case a choice seems fairly arbitrary – how often with a city can one judge the moment marking its foundation: with a company, the moment of its formation? And would not the various charts of individuals in the city, state, company, affect its programme to the extent where any central chart might prove almost unreadable?

A body of people astrologically inclined, forming a company, might well make sure of auspicious stars by *electing* a moment at which to sign the necessary documents; this was certainly done, for instance, at the moment when the International Society for Astrological Research was incorporated in Ohio. An astrologer may be asked (taking into account the horoscopes of those con-

[1] *The progressed horoscope,* op. cit.

cerned, the type of business involved, the place at which the meeting is to be held, and other factors) to calculate the most favourable moment at which to start a particular venture, sign the papers for a take-over, or whatever.

Of all astrological lore, I find mundane astrology the most difficult to accept: the impossibility of knowing the precise timing of a relevant moment, or of the other factors involved, makes it extremely difficult to accept a chart drawn up for any particular moment (certainly, historically); and it is even more difficult to fathom how by any theory the astrological and historical facts can be reconciled. In my experience, which is small, mundane astrology seems as often to be wrong as right. But it must be said that many astrologers do support it with tenacity. In an excellent introduction to the subject, Charles Carter wrote: 'Sooner or later, I believe "mundane" astrology will have to be replaced at the top of the astrological tree, and the more the State controls the individual, the truer this will be.'[1]

Certainly, *physical* happenings – earthquakes, typhoons, the weather in general – have been predicted, in the past, with accuracy; and certain brilliant predictions of mundane astrology are recorded such as the sinking of the *Titanic* and the *R-101* disaster; but I find it difficult to escape the feeling that these may have had more to do with the occult than the astrological. And certainly astrology still reels from the effect of the numerous predictions of lasting world peace so confidently made by almost every major astrologer during 1938 and 1939. The kindest thing that can be said about mundane astrology (as Carter admitted) is that a great deal more work is needed before any dogmatic statement can be made about its efficacy.

[1] Charles Carter, *An introduction to political astrology* (L. N. Fowler, 1951).

IV

Astrology in Action

Ultimately, the only evidence likely to convince anyone that there is truth in the astrological theory, is personal evidence – for instance, an analysis of his own Birth Chart in which an astrologer refers to facts about his own character or behaviour of which the astrologer can have had no previous knowledge.

This in itself may not constitute *proof*, but I have found three analyses prepared for me by three different astrologers in various ways extremely persuasive.

I obtained readings[1] of my Birth Chart from Charles Harvey, a young astrologer of relatively slight experience; from John Naylor, whose practice must be among the busiest in England; and from Ingrid Lind, who is more experienced than Mr Harvey, but less so that Mr Naylor. Mr Harvey met me briefly on two occasions before he worked on my chart. Mr Naylor had never met me, and I wrote to him from an address in Cornwall under a nom-de-plume. Miss Lind and I had never met, although she knew one or two very basic facts about me – that I earned my living in literary and radio journalism, and that I was married. In each case, I provided only my birth-time and date (May 27, 1932, at 1.50 a.m. GMT) and the place of my birth (Looe, in Cornwall).

Mr Harvey's analysis concentrated very much on my character and personality, as he saw them revealed on the Birth Chart. It was

---

[1] I discuss the presentation of the analyses in Chapter IX.

divided into six sections: the first giving 'an overall picture of your make-up' and describing 'the main outlines and central characteristics of your individuality'. The second section provides an 'analysis of your immediate response to life and the type of habit patterns which you are likely to have developed, especially in early childhood, and that are likely to continue to dominate your emotional life'. The third examines 'the way in which you attempt to put yourself or "pull" yourself together as a co-ordinated individual'; the fourth deals with my personality 'in the Jungian sense of the term *persona*'; the fifth analyses my 'reflective attitude to life', and the sixth is a summary.

> In an analysis [Mr Harvey writes in a prefatory note], it is often necessary to over-accentuate contradictions and tendencies in the individual in order to bring out underlying tensions which in day-to-day life will not be immediately apparent. Thus the frequent use of the words 'conflict' and 'contradiction' are not meant to imply that you are permanently in a state of neurotic anxiety and indecision. But rather to throw into sharper relief the interactions of your life pattern so that it may be more readily understood.

This paragraph could be read as an excuse to cover generalisations. I consider it, however, fair; the kind of warning a psychiatrist might be likely to give when talking to a patient on the same level.

Mr Harvey's analysis has been read by a psychiatrist, Dr Anthony Stevens,[1] who has not analysed me, but has known me well for fifteen years. Dr Stevens approved a proportion of Mr Harvey's analysis as being true of my character, as far as the former is able to judge. Among the statements he approves are several which I personally doubted. I respect his opinion, although obviously psychological analysis would be necessary to confirm it. Perhaps five per cent of the analysis seems both to myself and Dr Stevens untrue; a few remarks, it is felt, could apply to anyone of my own general cast of personality, and Mr Harvey could in any case have derived them from the very limited personal knowledge he had of me at the time.

[1] See Appendix I.

Mr Harvey's analysis begins with a general statement which might well apply to anyone who works in any creative or artistic field, from a newspaper reporter to a major novelist; but it nevertheless includes a passage (my italics, below) which I recognise as being true of myself in a particular sense:

Your life pattern is dominated by the need to give concrete form and shape to your everyday personal experience: thoughts, feelings, impressions, sensations and fantasies. And to communicate these in a significant and meaningful way to the outside world – to society. At a conscious reflective level you will wish to strive to do this in broad ambitious terms, in direct creative activity, experiencing yourself as a creative and cultural focus and centre. *In practice, however, you find that you tend to centre yourself more in terms of passive communication – acting as an agent, a translator of experience, a go-between.*

Mr Harvey goes on to mention that 'a desire to push forward with energy, assertion, persuasion and aggression is offset by an almost sentimental, soft-hearted, romantic and impressionable longing for emotional containment'. This statement may be true, but I recognise immediately the truth of the following passage of the analysis:

You desire ... a sensitive response from others – a two-way exchange – for your own emotional fulfilment. These forceful emotional experiences can either be translated into rational form through the arts, or allowed to dissolve into irrational dreams and fantasy. Uncontrolled dreaming of this nature ... leaves you open to unscrupulous exploitation by others. This in turn produces inner discontent, self-doubt and a sense of personal inadequacy.

While I do not wish to claim that I have been unscrupulously exploited by anyone, I recognise that any antagonistic act towards me results perhaps in defiance on my part, but certainly also in 'self-doubt and a sense of personal inadequacy'.

The next passage seems both to Dr Stevens and myself to be true and relevant, to an extent which makes it doubtful whether it could be applied with equal strength to anyone else:

At the level where you seek to organise and co-ordinate your conflicting drives and motives into some kind of coherent whole, you attempt to find order both inwardly and outwardly by a continual dialogue with your environment. Taking your day-to-day experiences, feelings, sensations, thoughts, you will experience the need to formulate them and then to pass them on, to communicate them with all the persuasion in your power so that others may share your experience. . . .

To communicate your thoughts, feelings and sensations totally and meaningfully is, at this level, your greatest satisfaction. For through such communication and the logical and rational processes that go with it you experience a sense of purposeful self-hood, being and identity. For in some senses this is your *purpose* – to act as a line of communication.

This passage seems to reflect the truth. The urge to communicate is one which is not, as far as I am aware, shared by all writers in this special sense. While some writers are protective of their writings to the extent that they actually, like Kafka, attempt to suppress them totally, it is also true that a very great number of writers are uninterested in acting as a medium for the opinions and experiences of others. Many writers are oblivious to, or even disdainful of, their audience. But communication in the sense in which Mr Harvey speaks of it, has always been of the greatest interest to me.

Mr Harvey goes on to write three paragraphs which I at first dismissed as untrue. Dr Stevens, on the other hand, considers these could go far to explain certain traits in my personality that he has observed.

Because [the instinctive and integrated] levels of behaviour represent (to you as a child at any rate) almost incompatible attitudes – the irrational, sensitive, vague, chaotic, emotionally receptive female *v*. the rational, controlled, purposeful male – your relationship with your parents was probably extremely ambivalent. And, regardless of the actual relationship between them, to you their relationship would almost certainly have seemed uncertain, incompatible and somehow insecure. So that you, for your own part, would have found it extremely difficult to learn to resolve the masculine-feminine rôles in life and thus to learn a coherent pattern for relationships.

While no doubt you will long since have come to terms with
the resultant tensions created by these conflicting attitudes, this
mental-emotional conflict can still produce a subtle under-
mining effect in your psyche so creating inner discontent, dissat-
isfaction and tension – most especially where close relationships
are involved. And in this area of experience there is always liable
to be an underlying uncertainty and insecurity that will tend to
reassert itself under pressure. Likewise this uncertain division
between masculine and feminine elements could create strong
emotional stress regarding your own rôle in relationships unless
both sides are accepted and accommodated as equally part of
yourself.

In day-to-day terms, the conflict between your instinctive
and integrated levels is that between self-abnegation and service
to the community at a totally impersonal level and self-expression and achievement at a personal level within the immediate environment. It is a conflict between personal
subservience to a large whole, involving what seems like total
sacrifice of personal freedom and the paramount need for total
freedom of movement and freedom within your occupation.

There can be no comment, again, about this statement except
at a personal level; and the balance between the masculine and
feminine elements of any personality is a fragile one. But the fact is
that Mr Harvey deduced from my Birth Chart a state of psychological imbalance which Dr Stevens recognises as probably accurate.

There are other passages in the analysis which strike home with
what seems to me to be reasonable accuracy:

Essentially passive as a personality, whatever the circumstances
you can 'play it by ear', and can blend into the environment,
catching its mood, identifying with its needs and generally
acting as a universal solvent and peacemaker, adapting and
readapting, adjusting and readjusting to the needs of the
moment.

While I would question the term *peacemaker*, the rest of this
statement is recognisably true; and indeed I have often had cause
to deplore it. As Mr Harvey goes on to say, 'at a reflective level

your whole direction is towards cutting through [a] sometimes passive mask and releasing the energy that is hampered by this outward self-denial.'

The summary contains one or two statements which could be guessed at without astrology. A 'demand for personal freedom', 'a strong need to succeed', even 'desire to establish personal influence over your environment mitigates against any long-term relaxation' – all these, while true, could apply to a great number of people. The final paragraph reads:

> Tensions must be worked out and your dynamic energy must be applied. If they are not, these tensions can sap your strength and your constructive formative energy and then turn into depressive fears of social inadequacy and fruitless worry over objectives not realised! Nonetheless, such depressions should never last long, for consciously your creative enthusiasm and versatility will win through.

Dr Stevens, as sceptical about astrology as any critic could wish, comments: 'I hesitate to say this, but I would almost call that last paragraph brilliant. I think it is remarkably percipient. I don't know how Mr Harvey does it.' (With the predictable acidity of the persistent sceptic, he adds: 'But I'm sure it has nothing to do with the stars!')

One of the common complaints heard about astrological analyses is that they contain generalisations which might apply to any reader. This must of course be true: it would be difficult to write at any length about one person without including phrases which could be applied to others. When Mr Harvey speaks of my 'need to preserve and defend my *self* from submersion in a formless sea of experience', he is saying something that could be generally applied. It is interesting that the points about which I would consider him wrong, are specific – he speaks of 'the immediate direction of your energy towards service for others, and the utilisation of your imaginative and artistic impulses for the benefit of the community', and goes on:

> This immediate drive towards self-abnegating service goes to reinforce an essential conflict in your make-up between personal freedom and self-expression, and this equally strong drive

towards impersonal self-sacrifice for the good of the community.

However much I would like this to be true, I cannot lay claim to it. Nor is it true that my 'reflective thoughts will focus on communal and group rather than on individual enterprises'. I would say that precisely the opposite was true. But it is at least the kind of statement that would be either distinctly true or untrue of any person. It is hardly a generalisation.

Mr Harvey's analysis contains fewer generalisations than those of the other two astrologers. This is partly due to the manner in which it is written, and its whole tenor, which is more 'serious' than either Mr Naylor's or Miss Lind's. It is, it must be admitted, not the kind of analysis which would be welcomed by the average man or woman applying to an astrologer for information. For various reasons, Mr Naylor's report would probably not only please the average customer, but be more what the average customer would expect. Like Mr Harvey's, it falls into six sections: psychological characteristics; career, finance and business affairs; family affairs, friendship, marriage; health; future probabilities generally; month-by-month possibilities.

Mr Naylor, alone of these three astrologers, had never met me *and* could have had no idea of my nature or occupation. Some of the assertions he makes are broad enough to apply to a large degree to a large number of people; others are more strikingly individual.

> Yours is a basically flexible, adaptable, versatile and restless temperament [he says]; travel, change, variety of experience will hold a strong appeal for you. You will like to keep on the move both mentally and physically. A very quick and assimilative mentality is indicated. You will be something of an 'ideas man'. Imaginative, you will find it easy to envisage many diverse possibilities and probabilities. . . . You will possess a keen wit, a strong sense of humour, probably have a flair for mimicry, possess the potential of developing into a good linguist. Your powers of expression in speech and writing should be good.

The qualities in this paragraph are to some extent qualities which most people might persuade themselves they possessed. My powers of mimicry equal in poverty my flair for linguistics; but the last sentence seems reasonably accurate.

> You will be idealistic, something of a theorist, inclined to see life and people through rose-coloured spectacles and to lay yourself open to disillusion. There will be a very sensitive side to your personality, but this may manifest in that you are very intuitive, very responsive to and fond of music, that you are rather drawn towards things artistic.

The only mistaken remark in this paragraph is that about intuition. I believe myself to be unintuitive, certainly where other people are concerned.

Mr Naylor almost invariably mentions the planetary indications from which he draws his conclusions. For instance, he continues:

> The prominence of the two planets Neptune and Uranus in your horoscope will give you a somewhat 'off-beat' approach to life and people. You will be unorthodox, posses a vein of unconventionality. At the same time, you will possess a vein of originality, of creative abilities which are well worth developing.

This seems fairly acurate, although I am not sure that my 'originality' is creative in nature.

'Yours will be a "dual" personality', Mr Naylor remarks, evidently leaning heavily on the Gemini Sun-sign – an interpretation fairly obvious even from a layman's point of view. However, he takes it further:

> On the one hand, you have a very quick, clear active brain. On the other hand, you will be a very impressionably and emotionally responsive person. On a number of critical occasions in life you will find that heart and head disagree – and the probability is that your heart will rule your head. Because of your quick sympathies, you will involve yourself in situations which your brain tells you are quite impossible.

The first two sentences might apply to anyone; the last, however, seems peculiarly my own. It may even be thought that my involvement, such as it is, in astrology is indicative of it.

QA–E

The next paragraph might be drawn from a school report:

With your particular type of personality there is a very obvious need deliberately to cultivate your powers of concentration. You must develop objectivity of thought and action, the capacity to eliminate irrelevances from your life. You must tackle one thing at a time and learn to finish off everything you start. By all means make use of your adaptability and flexibility to achieve your aims, but be very careful indeed not to vary your basic objectives or targets in life too frequently!

If this paragraph is singularly apposite, so is the following one: 'You obviously possess powers of expression in speech and writing which are well worth developing. These will be combined with a very useful dramatic instinct. You will be a natural mimic and actor.' Since I have spent my entire adult life writing and broadcasting, have been involved in amateur theatricals, and at one time seriously considered an acting career, Mr Naylor's statement (with simply a Birth Chart to judge from) must surely be considered accurate. Many people would claim it was a guess. Is this fair? Is it even probable?

In the second section of his report, Mr Naylor underlines my 'mercurial' temperament – my inclination towards frequent changes, a varied way of life. He emphasises the 'creative, imaginative vein' which he considers worth developing. Mr Harvey was more accurate in seeing this as *interpretative* (and although he knew that my work was mainly in this area, he did not know that my attempts at creative writing had been relative failures).

It is in this second section that one or two misfires by Mr Naylor seem directly attributable to his use of the Placidus rather than the Equal House system of House Division. By Placidus, Mr Naylor placed the Sun in my Second rather than Third House; and Jupiter in the Sixth rather than the Fifth. This led him to suggest that I am 'well suited to any type of activity concerned with the movement of people, money, ideas, goods. You would tend to flourish in any type of business activity connected with transport or communication, the sea or shipping'; and that I might well be suited to 'any type of career actively concerned with medicine or nursing'. When I mentioned this to Mr Naylor, he remarked that he used Placidus because it generally seemed to work; there is no answer to this except that, in my case, it did not.

Turning to family affairs, Mr Naylor comments on 'quite a good start in life'; this is certainly not untrue. 'You may,' he goes on, 'have some sort of family tradition which is connected either with the sea and shipping or with some branch of art or creative artistic work.' This is general enough to be true of a great number of people: few families in Cornwall have not at some time or another been connected with the sea. He remarks on my 'gregarious temperament', and love of 'good food, good company, good conversation'; true. He goes on to warn that

> the placing of the planet Saturn in the Eleventh House of your horoscope is not too fortunate a factor in regard to friends and friendships. It warns against being too demanding of, or reliant upon, your friends. There is an obvious danger that you will be let down at critical periods in your life by friends you trust.

This has not so far been true; but I have not, as far as I am aware, been 'too demanding of, or reliant upon' my friends!

The suggestion that 'individuals born during late January, late February and late September' will be most likely to prove congenial and helpful associates in business or work may be true or untrue; just as it may be equally true or untrue that those born during late August or late November are uncongenial. But Mr Naylor's next paragraph is extraordinary:

> Here is a curious point which might perhaps interest you. Assuming you came into close contact with an individual of either sex who was born within a few days of January 25 or July 27 in any year, that individual would be likely to affect your life and affairs considerably for good or ill. There would be a kind of link of destiny between you, as it were.

My wife's birthday is July 27. We had been married for over ten years before I sent Mr Naylor my birth date, and he was not aware that I was married.

'With your particular type of horoscope you will be a natural flirt,' Mr Naylor goes on. It is difficult to comment on this; but when he adds that I 'have probably been involved in a comparatively large number of light-hearted flirtations', I fear I must part company with him.

He goes on to make assertions which I consider positively dangerous:

> There is a very obvious possibility that you will marry more than once. There is an equally obvious probability that sooner or later you will be deeply involved in a close relationship with a lady whom you are unable to marry because of previous ties on one side or the other. The probability is that you are already married and that family factors or family influences were an important factor in your choice of marriage partner. [The opposite was in fact the case.] You are heading towards a period of life 1970–2 when ... there is an obvious probability of one or more new ties of affection developing. There is equal probability of the break-up of relationships which have been important in your life in previous years. There will be at least one parting or estrangement which leaves a big gap in your life. You are heading into a period when there is very obvious danger of your becoming involved in a relationship which conflicts with your marriage. There is obvious possibility of a major domestic upheaval 1970–2.

I have grave doubts of the propriety of an astrologer telling this sort of thing to a client he does not know. Surely a suggestible reader might take it too seriously? The astrologer might well reply that he *does* know the client concerned, because he has studied the Birth Chart. And when I raised the point, Mr Naylor replied that while he never predicts a client's death (although he can almost always see it clearly), he will always mention a possible marital crisis, so that the client concerned may have the opportunity of considering what action to take. This is all very well, but to predict marital difficulties and 'a relationship conflicting with marriage' to a client who is 'a natural flirt' seems to be asking for trouble.

Miss Ingrid Lind's report is more 'chatty' than Mr Naylor's, and the extent to which one finds it amusing or satisfactory depends on one's reaction to Miss Lind's personality, which comes through her work very strongly.

Chatty though she is, her involvement with her subject is such that, try as she may, she cannot help using technical terms that her reader may not understand. Having pointed out that my Sun-sign is Gemini and my 'Rising-sign' (Ascendant) Pisces ('I find we grow more like our Sun-sign as we grow older, while the Rising-sign is the vehicle on which we ride through life'), she goes on:

You are only able to have this combination of Gemini and Pisces because you were born just at the right moment – most Pisceans with the Sun in the Third House in Gemini would have Aries rising – very pioneering, forceful and brilliant – but you have managed to combine the strong Third House Gemini urge for brains/communication/writing/speaking with the quite different Piscean qualities.

Miss Lind combines Mr Naylor's remarks about my possible acting ability with Mr Harvey's remarks about 'communication':

Pisces is one of the 'stagey', actor signs, and it dilutes the purely intellectual, academic Gemini strength – or perhaps dilute is not the right word – cloaks or veils or disguises the serious, brainy purposefulness and presents facts in a form more readily assimilable by the public ... so you see you have chosen the right outlets in work connected with the public and entertainment and knowledge-communication.

With a delightful reliance on the literal aspect of my ascending sign, Miss Lind points out that 'many people with this combination take to drink – in short they misuse the liquid side of Pisces'. But I am apparently safeguarded somewhat from this course of events by my 'most elevated planet', Saturn, 'the driest ... of all the planetary forces'.

Like Mr Harvey (and, similarly, mistakenly, perhaps), Miss Lind emphasises that I should have a particular interest in 'hospitals, drugs, the public, drunks ... road accidents, institutions, schools, reformatories' (Mr Harvey suggested 'a compelling desire to reform and regenerate ... hospitals, mental homes, prisons'). I do not find this in the least to be so.

It is at this stage in Miss Lind's report that the first occult emphasis is laid. 'Bad aspects,' she writes, 'of course are there uniquely because we have put them there in some (generally a series) past life or lives . . . Frankly, I think in a past life you had a lot of fun. The pattern shows excess in pleasure, sex and entertainment.' My only regret, if this was indeed so, is that I have no clear memory of it.

Miss Lind applies her occult instincts to an examination of my general character:

The *balance* of your Chart is very good and even, and this will reflect in your ability to get on with most types of people. Fixity of purpose is there to a degree that will not let you rest until you have accomplished what you set out to do. There is energy-plus and a sort of ruthlessness that will help in the rat-race. I like it very much that you are not over-balancedly the 'mental', ratio-cinating Gemini – it seems to me that you can use the curiosity and quickness and brilliance of this sign in a far wider range than many of your fellow Geminians. This shows in the fact that you can contemplate investigating a subject like astrology. Your ceiling is high. I wonder if you are at all psychic or me-diumistic? [I am not.] I would suggest that you use the 'higher self' technique in your work, as you clearly have the ability to do this. I mean by this that you should relax rather than think until blue smoke comes out of your ears. Relax and see what your higher self feeds into your mind. This is how inspiration comes.

Any tendency to dismiss this suggestion out of hand is perhaps premature, for I have certainly for some years tended to 'relax into' problems which seem over-complicated, or subjects which need a broad view. While Miss Lind terms this 'using the "higher self",' others might simply call it mental laziness.

I think your more sensational successes will come if you allow your originality and – dare I mention the word? – spirituality free rein [Miss Lind goes on]. Finances certainly seem to benefit through this less down-to-earth side of you – and they are also tied up with your writing/speaking talents. You have a charm-ing speaking voice. Maybe you sing like a lark, too?

My speaking voice has certainly brought me financial reward; I have also sung, but my friends are unconvinced of my voice's excellence.

Miss Lind seems to strike another bull's-eye with the assertion that I am 'in fact rather an odd mixture of convention and unconvention without these two clashing'. I am aware of a clash in fact in my own mind; but this may not be obvious to others. Mr Harvey mentions in his analysis that I 'seek to identify with social objectives, with the current needs of the time', while at the same time I see myself 'in a central creative rôle and aspire both to personal social power and leadership and a high degree of self-knowledge and mystical awareness'. Taken together these two statements are illuminating. I am not proud of admitting to an aspiration to 'social power', which in another sense I despise; rather an odd clash of instincts.

Miss Lind dives again into the occult when she says that I

have power and punch and common sense, and people will take truths from you that they might reject from others. You have quite a responsibility. Don't misuse it. I am increasingly sure that this is what you did in a former life – misused your communicative powers and misled to the point of creating confusion or even madness. The pattern is there.

She sees in my character a certain interest in the occult.

In some ways [she says], you take naturally to 'inner plane' values and may do good work and well-rewarded work of a practical or productive nature that forwards a much more intangible or other-worldly wisdom. ... Your service to Humanity should be the communication of the unknown. You may think now that your present work is just this, but it will develop unimaginably.

I am not aware of having any occult properties; an interest in the occult, certainly – but also a mistrust of it. However the difficulty of proving or disproving an astrological (or, I suppose, psychological) report once more arises. Miss Lind may be right. I would have dismissed Mr Harvey's remarks about my childhood relationship with my parents out of hand; yet a psychiatrist independently feels they may be true. One cannot afford to be over-dogmatic in any matter concerning the human mind, and most particularly one's own.

Miss Lind's summing-up equates my 'reliable and steadfast' efforts at achieving my aims with 'a deep and possibly sub- conscious sense of duty'. In my view my sense of duty is weak; and it may indeed (though I am not sanguine) be the result, as Miss Lind goes on to say, of my wishing to 'pay off considerable wrongs done to friends in some past life in the furtherance of [my] own aims'.

Through a mistake either on my part or Miss Lind's, her report was at first based on a birth-time which was twelve hours out: she drew up the chart for 1.50 p.m. GMT, rather than 1.50 a.m. This made some minor differences in the chart – minor at any rate to the layman – making my Ascendant Virgo rather than Pisces; Gemini on the Mid-Heaven rather than Sagittarius; the Moon on degree 10 of Pisces rather than degree 4; the Sun half a degree further into Gemini than it should have been, and the other planets similarly slightly displaced. At first I did not notice this, and my reaction was that for the first time I had found an astrol- oger who had got my character almost completely wrong. It was suggested that sex and money were linked in my chart ('Perhaps you ought to run a sexy cabaret . . . or write sexy scripts'). Miss Lind felt I was emotionally violent, and should make a particular effort to 'introduce into my work some therapeutic element'. She suggested that this violent element might be a product of a former life: 'I would go as far as to hazard a guess that you have misused it in a past life to the detriment of your own (or other people's) health.' There was even an indication of cruelty to children, and I was advised to work for the promotion of children's health and safety, to counteract it.

Finally, Miss Lind pointed out that the bad aspects in my chart were 'mostly past their peak before birth. . . . Probably you used them in full activity in some past life. What you now have to face is more like a hang-over of the worst phase'.

If I had been an ordinary client and failed to notice the faulty figures entered on the Birth Chart, I would no doubt have been confirmed in the conventional view of astrology as unhelpful rub- bish. In fact, this mistake gives the astrologer some ammunition, for it deals with the argument that astrological analyses are so generally written that any single one could apply to several different clients. The faulty analysis in this case could not, I think, apply to me – except in so far as the indications were *generally* the same (the Geminian duality, for instance).

If it is difficult to look fairly at any analysis of one's own character, and to decide whether or not it can be said to be revelatory; it is even more difficult to look fairly at astrological predictions, and to judge how far they are accurate. The difficulty arises often because the predictions are extremely general. But can one expect them to be specific? Mr Naylor saw 'developments which work out rather to your financial advantage' in March and September of 1968. If one is a freelance writer, one hopes that developments working out to one's financial advantage will be fairly common; and I was not notably blessed with them at the times Mr Naylor suggested. But I had no right, surely, to expect him to predict a large cheque from a specific source. If the stars reveal anything, they reveal trends. How particularly those trends can be predicted, is an equivocal question. I have not been particularly fortunate with Mr Naylor's or Miss Lind's predictions. Mr Naylor said 'You are particularly likely to get on well with neighbours during 1968 and may find yourself acquiring a new neighbour to whom you are very attracted in the autumn of 1968'; alas, untrue. 'There is a heightened probability of your making plans and arrangements for overseas travel in 1968'; well, possibly. I did at the end of 1968 holiday abroad for the first time for some years. 'There is a pleasant possibility of events within the family circle and involving a relative of your own generation which gives you pleasure'; not as far as I am aware. '1968 is a most favourable year for concentrating on activities connected in any way with writing or speaking'; well, again, perhaps – Mr Naylor did not, of course, know that journalism and broadcasting was my business.

But it would be tedious to go on quoting at length. The predictions must be dismissed, unfortunately, on what evidence there is in the section entitled 'Future Probabilities Generally'. The same must be said, unfortunately, for the more detailed month-to-month predictions, as far as I have been able to check them. These are admittedly so general that some of them are bound to work out. Mr Naylor suggests 'a strenuous and trying period' at one time, 'a widening of horizons and the chance offered to gain new experience' at another; or 'You may find yourself feeling that something is about to happen – whether it does or not'!

Miss Lind's predictions are equally vague, with a touch of the occult added. They sometimes run parallel to Mr Naylor's. Both of them see 1971 as being peculiarly important (and peculiarly unattractive). This is apparently due to transits of Jupiter and Saturn affecting my Sun. 'A most crucial and curious year,' says Miss Lind, 'don't be surprised if you go through a strange and gruelling inner experience. A sort of "death of the ego", when you feel everything is taken away so that you can reassess yourself and start afresh.'

Mr Naylor is more specific. I can look forward to 'a death of the ego' with interest. 'Unfavourable implications in regard to your worldly interest, your business and financial fortunes' are less interesting. 'The development of discontent, of difficulties and problems in this sphere ... adverse working conditions, heavy expenses, a falling-off in income, difficulties in your relationships with important business associations' bids fair to be positively boring. It might all be very worrying, if it were not that one does not implicitly trust astrological prediction.

I do not think that this is being unduly unfair. As Mr Naylor himself points out, 'much depends on your circumstances and the way you influence events by your own will-power and effort.' If, in due course, 1971 turns out to be spectacularly successful where my 'worldly interests' are concerned, and if the magnificent blonde is rejected in favour of my wife, Mr Naylor can safely say that this was due to my own vigour in combating unfavourable planetary influences. This, like so many astrological arguments, would be unanswerable.

This question of prediction is obviously a difficult one. Perhaps not until an astrologer can work with, say, five clients for five years, noting carefully how each aspect, each transit, affects them, and *still* fail to predict reasonably accurately for them, will one dismiss prediction completely. It is obviously true that some indications are only capable of very vague interpretation unless the astrologer knows the client very well, and sometimes not even then. My wife has had some spectacular successes in predicting for me. Other predictions have sunk without trace.

And of course the 'blind' prediction undertaken by Mr Naylor has problems of its own. The indication which in the chart of an international financier might mean huge gains on the stock exchange would obviously not mean the same thing if applied to a charwoman in Bethnal Green, a sea captain in the South Seas, or a Minister of religion in Scotland.

Eventually, new techniques may emerge which make prediction easier, though I have doubts. What is clear is that a number of serious astrologers are developing their own views about prediction. A British astrologer, Dennis Elwell, who has given much thought to the astrological theory in general, writes in a letter:

On this question of prediction one must distinguish two stages. There is the scientific appraisal of the point reached by a person in his psychological evolution, which can be stated in the most precise terms, and there are informed guesses based on that appraisal. What we call 'objective events' are not linked *directly* to the stellar pattern, but are at one remove. The stars are directly linked with the implication of events for us, the construction we put on them, the way in which they stimulate our development, round out part of our character. An astrologer may use this information to speculate about objective happenings if he wishes, but he ought to be clear in his own mind that this is an additional step, undertaken on his own responsibility, and one in which he can all too easily exceed the limits of his science.

Astrology has itself to blame for its dismal reputation in prediction, for the more accurate 'first-stage' has never been properly developed. . . . Suppose one sees that a person is coming under a strong Mars configuration. We know from that that he will have some sort of fight on his hands, an opportunity to develop the self-assertive, incisive side of his nature. And we know that, if it is a major configuration, what he will acquire for himself at this point in life will remain his for the rest of his days: he will have built something into himself.

Surely it is of some interest to know that our destiny is organised in this purposeful way? What can we say to the person who retorts: 'I don't care about that. What I want to know is whether I shall win the fight or lose it.' Will he believe us when we tell him that winning and losing do not seem of such import- ance to the heavens as they do to us? After all, to win or lose in this instance may not matter in a few years' time; but what sort of person one has become goes on mattering.

Done properly, 'first stage' predictions ought not to be vague, however. They may seem vague if one's client expects to be told details of events which he imagines to be already laid up in heaven. You have to make it plain that you are not attempting to describe events, but the *meaning* of those events. And you can do it exactly enough for him to add a dimension of under- standing to his experience of life, to show him there is more to it than he even suspected. Surely that is of some value?

Having said all that, I must admit that there are cases when a definite event jumps out of the Charts at you – when you know it's a racing certainty that a man is going to have an accident, or a woman lose her husband. This swift transition from stage one to stage two comes about because of the entirely *passive* relation to the stars of the ordinary person. The fact that events are being brought about by largely unconscious processes means that some of the options are already closed. We are such sleep- walkers! But this does not mean that 'the forces to be unleashed' – if I may dramatically so express it – could not be diverted into some positive outlet. Or defused by some kind of inner alchemy. We do not know yet what could be achieved by *consciously* working with the stellar patterns.

Mr Elwell's attitude, although many astrologers would dissent from it, is strongly appealing. While astrological predictions of tendencies in my own life have been, on the whole, disappointing, there have been areas in which they have run parallel to my life. It seems strongly probable that astrologers in general, cautious though many of them are, may well be wrong in their attitude to prediction. Mr Elwell's attitude, on the contrary, would obviously commend itself to the psychiatrist; and the use of astrology along the lines he suggests could be of the greatest value to a man in search of himself, and in seach of his own value and meaning in a putative order of events in time and space.

V

The Language of Symbols

I consulted the three astrologers for the purpose of this book, and out of general interest. But who, more broadly, *uses* astrology, and why? When the general tendency is, publicly at any rate, to denigrate astrologers as 'fortune tellers', what kind of person keeps the average professional astrologer busy week after week, returning to him year after year for new sets of 'progressions'? I had to wait for six months for John Naylor to send me his analysis; and the usual waiting period seems to be between one and six months.

Many clients approach an astrologer in the first place because of some personal problem; but many seem to go to him for no other reason than curiosity – and often, at first, sceptically. They want to know something about their future prospects; but they also feel, however vaguely, that astrology may provide a means of imposing some order or putative order on the anarchy of life. It may be true that anyone who claims by clairvoyance, astrology, psychiatry, physics or any other method, to be able to explain us to ourselves, can make a living by doing so – the richness of that living being in direct proportion to the plausibility of his tongue. Perhaps we are more receptive to what we are told if we happen to be emotionally inadequate or in some way deficient in personality (and this is where some psychiatrists claim that astrology can be of use); but on the whole we seem to be drawn to astrology by the same sort of force that draws us to religion. A need for reassurance can certainly be served by Christianity or Buddhism, by psychiatry or community service, by golf or table-tapping or business or ambition or any single-minded purpose. But the occult forces which have been netted by the founders of every religion seem to be at the back of a very strong attraction towards 'the stars'; and the attraction is as old as the 'personalities' of the planets and their attendant gods (if, indeed, the planets are not attendant upon the gods, for which came first is a matter of conjecture).

The forces which compel us towards the supernatural are rarely openly repressed, and this repression is usually extremely unpopular. The anger which was directed against the humanists, for instance, when they first began to be heard in the public media, reflected the unease of the majority in the face of human beings apparently content to cut themselves loose from traditional outward manifestations of the collective unconscious. Now, the generation loosely known as 'hippies' (or, by some astrologers, as 'the first Aquarius generation') is beginning to turn back to the heavens for 'readings' of events on earth, perhaps for astrological reasons, perhaps because of social inadequacies in their environment. They have not all turned single-mindedly to astrology, but most of them show an interest in it.

The concept of the collective unconscious explains in part why astrologers are so addicted to Jung, claiming, as so many of them do, that he believed in astrology and made much use of it. He was in fact less of an enthusiast than astrologers might have hoped or may wish people to believe. Wilful misquotation and highly selective quotation have set him up as the twentieth-century Ptolemy – ironically, since he would have been as quick as Ptolemy to deny a total commitment to astrology. He was, nevertheless, extremely interested in the subject, and used it to some extent in his work. He also wrote interestingly about it. Moreover, the instinct which draws people towards astrology can perhaps best be explained in Jungian terms.

Jung believed that the brain of man was shaped and influenced by his remote history; that

> although our inheritance consists in physiological paths, still it was mental processes in our ancestors that created the paths. If these traces come to consciousness again in the individual, they

can do so only in the form of mental processes; and if these processes can become conscious only through experience and thus appear as individual acquisitions, they are none the less pre-existing traces, which are merely 'filled-out' by the individual experience. Every 'impressive' experience is such an impression, in an ancient but previously unconscious stream-bed.[1]

That stream-bed is indeed so ancient that we can scarcely hope to have evaded it. A leader-writer in *The Times* put the matter strongly in 1936:

The humbugs in astrology – the giant humbugs like Casanova, or the hedgerow humbugs that need little searching for in these days – are too easy prey to be worth mocking, while behind and beyond them lies the immemorial dignity of a system that took its being from man's inextinguishable need to form a harmony between the universe and himself, to make, first through magic and then through religion, a settled order on which he might count in the macrocosm and the microcosm alike. . . . Think as we may about horoscopes, astrology has grown so deeply into our language and our thought that we can never be free of it.[2]

The signs of the Zodiac with which we grow up are archetypal; that is to say, they exist in us before we are conscious of them intellectually. As Jung points out, we experience archetypes as emotions as well as symbols and images, and we are particularly conscious of them in highly emotional situations such as the presence of birth or death, of great danger or great happiness or some evidently other-worldly experience. (It is, significantly, at such times that people often first approach an astrologer.)

The most ancient of our instinctive superstitious actions and beliefs spring from the collective unconscious and its archetypal store. The archetypal *astrological* symbols are fundamentally connected with the myths of gods and goddesses, as well as with the behaviour of the planets (the two are interconnected, the gods often sharing the characteristics of the planets – swift-footed Mercury and his fast-moving panet; warlike Mars and his fiery planet,

[1] C. G. Jung, *Contributions to analytical psychology* (Routledge & Kegan Paul, 1960).   [2] *The Times*, April 15, 1936.

and so on). And here ancient myth takes its place in bolstering up our natural instinct for astrology. As Jung put it:

> The collective unconscious – so far as we can say anything about it at all – appears to consist of mythological motifs or primordial images, for which reason the myths of all nations are its real exponents. In fact, the whole of mythology could be taken as a sort of projection of the collective unconscious. We can see this most clearly if we look at the heavenly constellations, whose originally chaotic forms were organised through the projection of images. This explains the influence of the stars as asserted by astrologers. These influences are nothing but unconscious introspective perceptions of the activity of the collective unconscious.[1]

Jung felt strongly that myths both illustrated and illuminated. They not only pictured natural events and attempted to explain them rationally, they also explained how man felt about the bases of the myths. The growth of the Zodiac and its illustrative figures not only enshrines man's instincts about the planets and attempts to explain their movements, but also imposes on them the characteristics with which man at first endowed them. It is at this point that one wonders to what extent the planets and man's feelings about them are interdependent: how far is the correlation between Mars and war natural, and how far imposed? It is a field of psychological study that might repay investigation; but the difficulties are obvious. One cannot call ten thousand generations of witnesses.

It may be questioned whether the influence of the collective unconscious can really draw a modern man towards astrology. It is not, I suppose, a theory capable of very convincing demonstration. Yet it does seem to be one explanation for a real, fundamental *general* interest. The fact that perhaps a majority of astrological clients know nothing of the myths, and very little about the true or ancient meaning of the Zodiac, does not greatly detract from the theory; it certainly may be argued that the collective unconscious can work in this manner – as the most ancient symbolic images and ideas can appear in the dreams of a modern

[1] C. G. Jung, *The structure and dynamics of the psyche* (Routledge & Kegan Paul, 1960).

man who is totally ignorant of them. It is also interesting that the
astrological chart is a perfect mandala, or magic circle; naturally,
for the heavens appear circular from the view on earth, and all the
most ancient representations show it thus. Jung found that the
appearance of a mandala symbol in the dreams of his patients was
for the most part a sign of a feeling of peace and harmony. He felt
that the circle (sometimes, in fact, a square – and astrological
charts were sometimes drawn in a square form) acted as a magical
protection – there are many parallels in magic – which prevented
the disintegration of the dreamer, who was often enclosed in it.
The mandala in our own time, he wrote, was 'an involuntary
confession of a peculiar mental condition. There is no deity in the
mandala [as was often so in ancient times] nor is there any sub-
mission or reconciliation to a deity. The place of the deity seems to
be taken by the wholeness of man.'[1]

He points out, also, that 'the horoscope itself is a mandala (a
clock) with a dark centre, and a leftward *circumambulatio* with
"houses" and planetary phases. The mandalas of ecclesiastical art,
particularly those on the floor before the high altar or beneath the
transept, make frequent use of the zodiacal beasts or the yearly
seasons.'[2]

As in every religion, so in astrology, symbolism is of the greatest
importance, though a good number of astrologers would not give
this fact the recognition which, for instance, Henry Miller gives
it:

The vast difference between astrology and other sciences, if I
may put it thus, is that astrology deals not with facts but with
profundities. The solid ground on which the scientist pretends
to rest gives way, in astrology, to imponderables. To look at
man's universe with the eyes of an astrologer demands more
than the exercise of logic or reason. It requires the vision and
the imagination of the poet, for whom language has ever to be
created anew. The language of the astrologer is entirely one of
symbols – and their meaning is inexhaustible.[3]

[1] C. G. Jung, *Psychology and alchemy* (Routledge & Kegan Paul,
1958).   [2] *ibid.*
[3] Henry Miller, introduction to Sydney Omarr, *Henry Miller, his world
of Urania* (USA, Ninth House Publishing Co., 1954).

An astrologer would of course contend that the symbols contained within the mandala of the horoscope do indeed portray 'the wholeness of man', and that the order – artificial or not – imposed by the Birth Chart has often prevented the disintegration of personality in a client.

The archetypal nature of astrological symbolism deepens one's interest in it, but does not, I think, indicate that it has meaning only within some dark instinctive cavern of the mind. Within astrological lore one can recognise certain patterns of movement which seem to reflect some seemingly purposive, evolutionary tendency of the unconscious. The symbols of astrology crop up with astonishing universality throughout the whole field of man's history, and have relevance often to national and international myth and legend.

To take only one of many possible examples: the Arthurian legend. In the 1930s, Mrs K. E. Maltwood was examining the whole basis of the Arthurian story, and became convinced that the episodes of the legend were intimately connected with the area around Glastonbury, Somerton and Castle Cary. (Cadbury Hill, where recent archaeological digs have uncovered extensive remains of the period *circa* Arthur, is right in the middle of this area.) Studying the available texts, she came to the conclusion that the knights had followed each other, in their quest for the Holy Grail, in a circle, their adventures being concerned with the same beasts and giants; and one day, looking at a map of the area, she realised that the River Cary traces a path which, if one reinforced it, seemed to outline the form of a vast lion lying on the southern slopes of a low range of hills.

She outlined her extensive researches in two books, summarising them more recently in a third.[1] She finally identified, not only from maps but from aerial photographs, ten of the zodiacal signs outlined by ancient tracks, natural and artificial waterways, contours of the ground, and earthworks. The signs are in their natural order, and Mrs Maltwood suggests that the centre of the bulls-eye may have indicated the position of the equinoctial line at

[1] K. E. Maltwood, *The temple of the stars; the enchantments of Britain* (John M. Watkins, c. 1935); *A guide to Glastonbury's temple of the stars* (James Clarke, 1964).

the time of making the Zodiac: which would place that time at the end of the second millennium B.C. Of course, England is so net-worked with ancient tracks, field-boundaries, streams, rivers, roads, contour-lines, that it might be said to be possible to produce a more or less accurate representation of the Zodiac from any sizeable slice of country; and it must be said that the outlines of the figures postulated by Mrs Maltwood seem to leave something to the imagination. However, she is extremely persuasive in her hypothesis; and some of the 'coincidences' are interesting. For instance, on the tail of the lion (which lies, outlined by the river, the tongue represented in the red clay of the Somerset countryside) is a Romano-British burial ground, which Mrs Maltwood associates with the graveyard referred to in *The high history of the Holy Grail*; and in the graveyard, when it was excavated, were found representations of lions' claws!

The figure representing Capricorn lies just below Glastonbury Tor (which, local legend has it, is haunted by a goat-figure!). The Pisces figures lie near Glastonbury itself, one of them over Weary-all Hill, which local tradition connects with the burial of a vast and no doubt legendary salmon. The Phoenix-figure which was an ancient symbol of Aquarius lies over Cinnamon Lane; cinnamon was one of the spices from which the Phoenix is said to have built his nest. And so on. Mrs Maltwood's three books contain a detailed list of the many links postulated between the figures she has discerned in the countryside and the Zodiac.

This is only one example of the astrological symbolism either 'built' into the land, or left (more obviously man-made and discernible to everyone than Mrs Maltwood's outlines) as evidence if not of the truth of the astrological theory, then at least of strange coincidences which astrologers can produce to back up the importance of that theory.

The matter of the Great Year is another manifestation of astrology in the continuing history of our planet. The Great Year is marked by a complete revolution of the twelve signs of the Zodiac within a period of about 25,000 years; a Great Month therefore consists of something like 2,156 years. Since the age of Leo (about 10,000 B.C.) the Zodiac has turned half around.

This seems, like so much astrological lore, a fundamentally

meaningless and arbitrary theory; yet the astrological Ages have some of the characteristics of the signs with which astrologers would associate them. It was during the Gemini age, according to this vast calendar, that the earliest picture-writing was developed, and increased delicacy of workmanship points to a more deft use of the hands; there are examples of Geminian duality. Then, during the Taurus age (about 4000–2000 B.C.) the bull became a common figure, found in stone monuments and representations in all parts of the then civilised world. The following Aries age produced many representations of the Ram in art; and the Piscean age brought Christianity, with its fish-symbols. Now, the 'Age of Aquarius' must be beginning; an age predominantly scientific, with the blending of science and art in the cinema, television and radiophonic music.

Jung has much to say of all this. He points out[1] that a Jewish commentary on Daniel, written in the fourteenth century B.C., expected the coming of the Messiah in the age of the Sign of the Fishes. A conjunction of Saturn and Jupiter is said to have taken place *in Pisces* three years before the birth of Moses, and at least three astrologers (Don Isaac Abarnel, 1437–1508, Rabbi Abraham ben Hiyya, who died in about 1136, and Solomon ben Gabirol, 1020–70) are said to have expected the coming of their Messiah to be signalled by a conjunction of those two planets in that sign. As Jung points out, 'Saturn is the star of Israel . . . Jupiter means the "king" (of justice). Among the territories ruled by the Fishes, the house of Jupiter, are Mesopotamia, Bactria, the Red Sea, and Palestine.' In 7 B.C., there were three conjunctions of Saturn and Jupiter in Pisces – one of them very close, so that in southern latitudes the result was the apparent appearance of one massive and very brightly shining star: without any doubt that traditionally observed by the Magi.

As to the influence of Pisces: Jung, again—

According to Doelger, the Christian fish symbol first appeared in Alexandria around A.D. 200; similarly, the baptismal bath was described quite early as a *piscina* (fish-pond). This presupposes that the believers were fishes, as is in fact suggested by

[1] C. G. Jung, *Aion: researches into the phenomenology of the self* (Routledge & Kegan Paul, 1960).

THE LANGUAGE OF SYMBOLS

the Gospels (for instance, *Matthew* 4:19). There, Christ wants to make Peter and Andrew 'fishers of men', and the miraculous draught of fishes (*Luke* 5:10) is used by Christ himself as a paradigm for Peter's missionary service. . . . Above all, it is the connections with the Age of the Fishes which are attested by the fish symbolism, either contemporaneously with the gospels themselves ('fishers of men', fishermen as the first disciples, miracle of loaves and fishes) or immediately afterwards in the post-apostolic era. . . .

At first sight, all this points to no more than that the fish symbols are mythologems which have always existed, and had assimilated the figure of the Redeemer; in other words, it was a symptom of Christ's assimilation into the world of ideas prevailing at that time. But to the extent that Christ was regarded as the new aeon, it would be clear to anyone acquainted with astrology that he was born as the first fish of the Pisces era, and was doomed to die as the last ram (lamb) of the declining Aries era.

It may be said, too, that the influence of Christianity, steadily declining, is now showing signs of death precisely during the century when the Great Month of Pisces is giving way to that of Aquarius. Another coincidence? The great months give way to each other reluctantly – there are no clear-cut edges. And yet the pattern does seem to be there, whether it is imposed by the vast forces of the collective unconscious, the archetypal pattern forcing its way through on a time-scale so remote as to be almost inconceivable in terms of an ordinary lifetime, or whether it is imposed by some strange outside influence.

Biology has vast time-scales, and the physicist Wolfgang Pauli has pointed out that the latest discoveries in mutation of species seem to indicate that we should look for interrelations between the biological process and the unconscious psyche. If the selection process by which animal and plant life develop had been left to pure chance, we and the life around us would have taken far longer to evolve than the history of the planet would allow.

'Chance' is a word which must be treated with care – and it is here that Jung's theory of synchronicity can be applied – but the fact that coincidence seems to emerge when it is most needed, and that extrasensory perception may in part account for coincidence, could explain how a life-force urgently in need of some means to overcome apparently immutable laws of nature, could indeed do so. A positive evocation of 'coincidence' (as one must still call the phenomenon) seems in fact the only solution to some of the problems attached to various theories of 'evolution'.

The kind of instinctive knowledge which has guided the living things of the earth towards more positive life, and towards a full exploration of that life, may have its roots in such archetypal imagery as is contained in the Zodiac. Relatively recently, scientists and philosophers have relied on more or less mythical imagery. Descartes used the 'fact' that 'God is immutable in His decisions and actions' to confirm the law of causality. Kepler saw the 'fact' of the Trinity as providing confirmation that there could be only three dimensions of space. And so on. Similarly, it may be that man 'invented' the Zodiac in order to confirm certain patterns of existence. This does not mean that the astrological theory is any more or less an invention of man than any other quasi-religious system, or any philosophical system for that matter. It simply questions the end from which that system may or may not work.

If astrology now seeks links with science – links broken after all relatively recently in its history – some astrologers still seek to preserve its past links with magic (also of course an important area of the unconscious); and so it is not surprising that astrology is dear to those who are interested in the occult. The lingering fragments of magic refer to the centuries during which astrologers were often if not magicians then at least under the influence of magic, even if they were at the same time distinguished astronomers. They were generally supposed to be able to communicate with spirits. 'Astrologer, mathematician, and conjurer were accounted the same things,' wrote John Aubrey in the seventeenth century; and the servant of the Elizabethan mathematician and astrologer, Thomas Allen, often met the spirits 'coming up his stairs like bees'. This, one gathers, was by no means as unusual as it might seem.

It is not indeed surprising that there should have been a strong interest in astrology during the past fifty years among the theosophists. Madame Blavatsky, the extraordinary and eccentric cofounder of the sect, wrote at some length on the subject, although she had worked out her own system (as in everything else she touched). This, as far as one can judge, was a synthesis of Eastern astrology and Blavatskyism. She was not particularly interested in those aspects of Western astrology which were in any way practical; she denied that the planets could influence the characteristics of the mind. She replaced that factor, however, with another:

> When it is said that: Saturn governs the devotional faculties, Mercury, the intellectual, Jupiter, the sympathetic; the Sun, the governing faculties; Mars, the selfish; Venus, the tenacious; and the Moon, the instincts; we say that the explanation is incomplete and even misleading. For, in the first place, the physical planets can only rule the physical body and the purely physical functions. All the mental, emotional, psychic and spiritual faculties are influenced by the Occult properties of the scale of causes which emanate from the Hierarchies of the Spiritual Rules of the planets, and not by the planets themselves.[1]

Western astrology, the founder of theosophy concludes, is 'often incomplete and not infrequently distorted to conceal the real truth': it is 'high time to begin a reform in Astrology which comes to us entirely from the Chaldean and Assyrian esoteric mob!' However, she had no doubt that

> Our *duty* is written in the stars. This is not superstition, least of all is it fatalism – it is not amply proved that even horoscopes and judiciary astrology[2] are not quite based on fiction, and that stars and constellations, consequently, have an occult and mysterious influence on, and connection with, individuals.

[1] H. P. Blavatsky, *The secret doctrine*, V (Theosophical Publishing House, 1938). Ingrid Lind, who takes a great interest in the occult, has asked whether it is 'fantastic to conceive of God, or at any rate of the Solar Logos, as embodying His universe, with the Sun as His heart, and the Planets, including Earth, as vital organs of His being?' Madame Blavatsky might have sympathised.

[2] 'Judicial astrology' is an archaic term for mundane astrology, which concerns itself with things and events rather than people (i.e. affairs of state, political matters, the timing of natural phenomena, etc.).

And she conceded that Western astrology had

> done excellent work, for it has helped to carry the knowledge of
> the existence of a Secret Wisdom throughout the dangers of the
> Medieval Ages and their dark history of bigotry up to the pre-
> sent day, when all danger has disappeared.[1]

Theosophists were in at the very beginning of the major resurgence of astrology at the end of the nineteenth century; and it
seems as though Alan Leo was almost alone in beginning this
resurgence.

Leo's real name was W. F. Allen: until comparatively recently
it was a common custom for astrologers to use their ascending signs
as *noms-de-plume*. After various ups and downs, Leo became in
his mid-twenties the manager of a firm of sewing-machine manufacturers, and in his spare time studied astrology and became a
friend of W. R. Old, a young man with an intense interest in the
occult. Old was a member of Madame Blavatsky's 'inner group',
and later became known to astrologers as 'Sepharial'. He took
Leo off to Notting Hill Gate, where Madame Blavatsky was living
in the late 1880s, and – like W. B. Yeats – they both became
members of the Theosophical Society.

Leo and another friend, F. W. Lacey, started the *Astrologer's
Magazine*, encouraging readers to subscribe by giving away astrological analyses to those who actually sent their subscriptions in
cash. The subscriptions came in all right; but the work was immense. After Leo's marriage to the wealthy Bessie Phillips (an
enthusiastic theosophist who was the widow of a phrenologist, and
who married Leo on condition that the marriage should never be
consummated) he became a full-time professional astrologer. He
soon found himself so busy that he had to engage assistants.

He was the first professional astrologer of modern times. And
behind him, all the time, was the Theosophical Society, to which
he was devoted. Its members were among his most regular clients,
recommending him to their friends; and the Astrological Lodge of
the Society subsequently played its part in extending knowledge of
the techniques of astrology not only to theosophists but to 'out-

---

[1] *The secret doctrine*, op. cit.

siders' whose interest was confined to the science itself, rather than to the theosophical faith.[1]

An interesting tangent was described by Rudolf Steiner, the Austrian mystic and follower of Madame Blavatsky, who broke away from her successor, Annie Besant, and formed the Anthroposophical Society, which used astrology as an aid to the progress of the human soul through the Seven Spheres – an essentially Steinerian journey. His followers, like Madame Blavatsky's, seemed to have a natural interest in astrology – and in this context Mass-Observation, in its examination of astrology in 1941, noted that

> a considerable number of people who go to church regularly have some belief in astrology. There are also indications of a positive correlation between church-going and astrology, in the sense that there is a higher probability of astrological belief among the minority who go to church than among those who do not. This is in line with other past information suggesting that many churchgoers have a *temperamental* interest in various forms of belief, without making any logical self-communication of the possible inconsistence of different beliefs held simultaneously.[2]

Astrology's connection with theosophy (and to some extent with the Rosicrucians and other similar bodies) cannot have been said to raise its reputation; but it did contribute to an increased general interest, especially when on the margin of the occult movements there moved such men as Professor Philippe Lebas, a scientist of the Institute of France, whose article on astrology in the *Dictionnaire encyclopédique de France* at the end of the last century must presumably have had considerable influence.[3]

> Is it not true, at all events [writes Professor Lebas], that there is a physical reaction upon one another among the planets? Is it not again true that the planets have an influence upon the

---

[1] There is a full and fascinating account of the nineteenth-century English astrologers in Ellic Howe, *Urania's children* (William Kimber, 1967).

[2] Mass-Observation, *Report on astrology* (1941–2).

[3] Interestingly enough, Lebas raised a point which his fellow-countryman Michel Gauquelin has raised at length more recently, and which might have been thought to be more modern. See Michel Gauquelin, *The Cosmic clocks* (Chicago, Henry Regnery Co., 1967).

atmosphere, and consequently at any rate a mediate action on
vegetables and animals? Has not modern science demonstrated
now these two points beyond any doubt? [He takes the argument further:] Is it any less true that human liberty of action is
not absolute: that all is bound, that all weighs, planets as the
rest, on each individual will; that Providence acts on us and
directs men through those relations that it has established between them and the visible objects and the whole universe? ...
Astrology, in its essence, is nothing but that: we are bound to
recognise that an instinct superior to the age they lived in
guided the efforts of the ancient Magi. As to the materialism
and annihilation of human moral freedom with which Bailly
charges their theory – that old reprobate has no sense whatsoever. All the great astrologers admitted without one single
exception that man could react against the influence of the
stars.

Bailly, 'that old reprobate', was the eighteenth-century scientist
who described astrology as 'the very foolish mother of a wise
daughter' – the daughter of course being astronomy.

The occult influence within astrology has been responsible for a
number of eccentricities, some of which are taken more seriously
than others by astrologers themselves. The Sabian symbols, for
instance, were vouchsafed to a clairvoyant in 1925; one symbol
was 'dictated' for each degree of the ecliptic, and they were presented after some years of work in a book by the American astrologer and Presbyterian minister Marc Edmund Jones, who had
founded the Sabian Society in 1922.

Mr Jones has described[1] how he and the medium, a Miss Elsie
Wheeler, went to work. It was decided that the task of abstracting
the symbols from the great beyond, or the collective unconscious,
or wherever they originated, should take place in the midst of 'a
dense aggregation of people active in the business of being'. So Mr
Jones and Miss Wheeler parked their car in Balboa Park in San
Diego, behind some bushes, and got to work with 360 blank cards,
divided into three piles.

[1] M. E. Jones, *The Sabian symbols* (New York, Sabian Publishing
Society, 1953).

As Miss Wheeler dictated the symbol relevant to each card, Mr Jones made a note of it, and after two hours, a break for lunch, and a second session the task was complete. It was an arduous day's work. Mr Jones was, fortunately, able to call on a Brother 'on the invisible side of life' to support him, the most difficult aspect of which was to sustain 'the ancient mind-matrix which made the whole procedure possible'. Miss Wheeler's task was, maybe, easier: some of the symbols she saw 'were directly out of her own experience ... some were beyond her range of comprehension, and were impressed upon her consciousness'.

Mr Jones gives instructions as to the use of the symbols in interpreting a horoscope, and then lists them together with his own psychological interpretations. For instance, the symbol for degree six of Capricorn is

A dark archway and ten logs at the bottom [which] is a symbol of the illimitable resources of self in preserving its own integrity through the varying fortunes of everyday living, and of the satisfaction anyone may know through a conscious direction of his own destiny.

The symbols are extremely varied: from 'The Union Jack' and 'A tiny nude miss reaching in the water for a fish', to 'A large hat with streamers flying, facing east' and 'An old man attempting vainly to reveal the Mysteries'. The world of Edward Lear seems inescapably close!

The Sabian symbols provide, fairly obviously, excellent material for anyone who wishes to make fun of astrology; they seem, in themselves, absurd. But so, if one approaches them unsympathetically with a sceptical mind, do many of the dream-interpretations of the psycho-analysts. The real obstacle in the way of accepting anything as detailed as Mr Jones's theory is that while the symbols may indeed have had very considerable significance for Miss Wheeler, they need not have any significance for anyone else. Anyone capable of dredging from her mind 360 significant fragments of the collective unconscious must have our admiration. This is not to say that it could not be done; but Mr Jones's is not the only set of symbols connected with the degrees. Margaret Hone has pointed out that 'there are no less than eight books in which a degree may be looked up and a different meaning found in each. This does not encourage trust in any of them'.

The occult-orientated astrologers often make use of degree-symbols. Astrologers using straightforward traditional astrology do not, although Charles Carter in his *Encyclopaedia of psychological astrology* lists a number of 'local influences': areas of the signs which seem, after examination of a very great number of charts, to indicate certain predispositions.[1]

Personally, I find it very difficult to accept those 'rules' of astrology which have been psychically obtained; if only because it is extremely difficult to assure oneself of their genuineness. Perhaps it was for that reason that R. H. Naylor, in a set of mimeographed lessons circulated between the wars, warned at the very outset:

> I should recommend you to lay aside – as far as your early studies are concerned – any tendency you may have to treat the subject as 'Occult'. Astrology in the past has been associated with much superstition and doubtful arts and practices. To be sure, the advanced study of the subject must necessarily lead you and me into that elusive twilight that lies between the known and unknown; the seen and the unseen. In the early stages of your study it is better to keep on the plane of matter-of-fact reason.

Some, perhaps most, occult astrologers with whom I have talked are transparently and obviously honest. Whether what they say is true or not, is then in a sense beside the point; they evidently utterly believe it. More, they *know* it to be true. It is to that extent impossible to argue with them, especially when the things of which they speak are outside one's own experience. One recalls Dylan Thomas's reply to a critic who enquired how he knew a good poem from a bad one: 'I only like the good ones.' Ingrid Lind, for instance, uses a dowser's pendulum to indicate the correct birth-time of a client, subsequently rectifying it by means of events in

---

[1] Degree five of Aries/Libra, for instance, seems to indicate cruelty or even a homicidal tendency: degree twenty-five of Sagittarius, literature and also anarchism; degree twenty-two of Leo/Aquarius, appendicitis. But Mr Carter, as I have said, produced this list empirically; he did not swoon into an armchair and dictate them arbitrarily to an amanuensis.

the client's life, or by more conventional means. All one can do is sit back and – particularly if the method seems to produce adequate results – wonder. If I find it difficult to subdue my own unbelief, I can respect Miss Lind's attitude. And it is clear that her clients accept it. She has found for instance that they hardly ever raise (as I did) the question of her natural assumption that they have all lived other existences in other ages. They seem on the whole to share her own attitudes: which confirms the general belief among astrologers that their clients seem to be drawn to them in some strange way rather than to any other astrologer, so that a sympathy readily exists between them.

Even those astrologers who make no use at all of the occult tend to reserve a special sympathy for it. Most clients similarly, even if they by no means wish their astrologer to act the part of a seer, much less a medium, are ready at least to reserve judgement. The reason for this sympathy is, it seems to me, again perfectly explained by Jung.

> The first knowledge of psychic law and order was found in the stars [he writes], and was later extended by projections into unknown matter. These two realms of experience branched off into sciences: astrology became astronomy, and alchemy chemistry. On the other hand, the peculiar connection between character and the astronomical determination of time has only very recently begun to turn into something approaching an empirical science. The really important psychic facts can neither be measured, weighed, nor seen in a test tube or under a microscope. They are therefore supposedly indeterminable, in other words they must be left to people who have an inner sense for them, just as colours must be shown to the seeing and not to the blind.[1]

Most people who are naturally interested in astrology, either as astrologer or client, seem to possess this 'inner sense'; and it is worth noting that a fair proportion of astrologers, even if they are repelled by the thought of using any kind of occult or mediumistic powers in the interpretation of a Birth Chart, possess to some degree some sort of psychic power. (It may be, of course, that we

[1] C. G. Jung, *Alchemical studies* (Routledge & Kegan Paul, 1960).

all do; but that the kind of temperament sensitive to the astrological theory is also sensitive to whatever psychic power may be latent in us.)

But to return to the theme of 'chance', which its opponents see as the main bulwark of the astrological theory. It was in the course of explaining the whole area of those extraordinary and sometimes almost frightening coincidences which must at some time have staggered most people that Jung developed his theory of synchronicity, published in 1952, in the opening chapters of which he quoted the astonishing case of the plum pudding (which he had from Flammarion, the astronomer).

> A certain M. Deschamps, when a boy in Orléans, was once given a piece of plum-pudding by a M. de Fortgibu. Ten years later he discovered another plum-pudding in a Paris restaurant, and asked if he could have a piece. It turned out, however, that the plum-pudding was already ordered – by M. de Fortgibu. Many years afterwards M. Deschamps was invited to partake of a plum-pudding as a special rarity. While he was eating it, he remarked that the only thing lacking was M. de Fortgibu. At that moment the door opened, and an old, old man in the last stages of disorientation walked in: M. de Fortgibu, who had got hold of the wrong address and burst in on the party by mistake.[1]

This kind of coincidence has happened to most of us, in one degree or another; and in his essay, Jung set out if not to explain this, at least to comment on it and to propose directions in which a solution might perhaps be found. Coincidences of this order, he pointed out, fall outside the causal philosophic principle by which we explain natural law. He hedges his argument, first, in a manner many astrological apologists might do well to note. A unique *biological* specimen can be observed directly, and its existence is not on the whole in doubt. But in dealing with ephemeral events which are recorded only in the human mind and memory, then 'a single witness no longer suffices, nor would several witnesses be enough to make a unique event appear absolutely credible. One

[1] C. G. Jung, *Synchronicity: an acausal connecting principle* (Routledge & Kegan Paul, 1955).

has only to think of the notorious unreliability of eye-witness accounts.

So he proceeds with extreme caution. There are occasions, he
points out (citing several of these) when one says to oneself – as
anyone must say who has had any experience of astrological analysis – 'That cannot be mere chance.' The kind of coincidence
which occurs appears to have no relation to the normal course of
cause and effect; and Jung coined the word 'synchronicity' 'to
designate a hypothetical factor equal in rank to causality as a
principle of explanation'. He suggests several events (the appearance of symbols of death, dreams which seem to forecast
death accurately) as examples of 'synchronicity', and goes on to
suggest that if one is looking for some kind of basis for statistical
evaluation of coincidences of this sort, one can do no better than
turn to astrology, in which the 'coincidence' of certain star-pat-
terns with certain personality-patterns is a basic argument.

In order to attempt to produce some kind of statistical argument, Jung decided to concentrate on the very strong indications
of satisfactory marital relationship: the relationship between the
Sun and Moon in the charts of man and wife.

He and his assistants collected, initially, the birth data of 180
married couples, and began to investigate the relationships (conjunctions and oppositions) of Sun and Moon in the charts. He had
decided, dangerous though this was, to ignore the traditionally
important relationship of Mars and Venus, because although they
indicate a love relationship, this need not necessarily have had
anything to do with marriage.

After the initial number of charts had been examined, a
number of extra couples were found; and in the end, 483 couples
(966 separate charts) were considered – not only in their natural
pairings, but also by chance pairing: i.e. the charts of married
couples A/B and C/D were considered; but so were the charts of
A/D and C/B. So there were 32,220 unmarried 'couples'.

The results of the experiment are set out in detail in Jung's
essay; but he sums up briefly in this way:

The first batch of 180 marriage horoscopes shows a distinct
maximum of 18 for Moon conjunction Sun, and the second

batch of 220 a maximum of 24 for Moon conjunction Moon. These two aspects have long been mentioned in the old litera- ture as marriage characteristics, and therefore represent the oldest tradition. The third batch of 83 yields ... a maximum of eight for Moon conjunction Ascendant. These batches have probabilities of about 1 : 1,000, 1 : 10,000 and 1 : 50 respect- ively.

Jung then illustrates the results in a dramatic way:

You take three matchboxes, put 1,000 black ants in the first, 10,000 in the second and 50 in the third, together with one white ant in each, shut the boxes, and bore a hole in each of them, small enough to allow only one ant to crawl through at a time. The first ant to come out of each of the three boxes is always the white one.

'The chances of this actually happening are extremely im- probable. Even in the first two cases, the probability works out at 1 : 1,000 × 10,000 which means that such a coincidence is to be expected only in one case out of 10,000,000. It is improb- able that it would ever happen in anyone's experience. Yet in my statistical investigation it happened that precisely the three conjunctions stressed by astrological tradition came together in the most improbable way.

It is only fair to point out that Jung qualifies this, admitting that from the scientific point of view the result of the investigation is in some respects not encouraging for astrology, because the results obtained are not statistically acceptable in terms of scientific experimentation. It would not be true, I think, that a substantially large number of people had been brought to a belief in astrology by this essay. Yet it does reflect the process which has taken place in the minds of a great number of people to whom the coincidences evident even in newspaper astrology, and certainly in properly conducted astrological experiments, have been impress- ive.

It also reflects the increasing scepticism with which a great many people now regard the old notions of time and space as finite and shapely; in the time-space field anything now seems possible.

As Jung himself put it elsewhere,[1]

> Anyone who does justice to the [parapsychological] facts cannot
> but admit that their apparent time-spacelessness is their most
> essential quality. In the last analysis, our naïve perception and
> immediate certainty are, strictly speaking, no more than evi-
> dence of a psychological *a priori* form of perception which
> simply rules out any other form. The fact that we are totally
> unable to imagine a form of existence without space and time
> by no means proves that such an existence is in itself imposs-
> ible.

Or, indeed, that that existence does not impinge upon our own
closely enough to 'seep through' into it. A leader-writer in *The
Times* once put the argument even more forthrightly:

> In these post-Einsteinian days the notion of prophecy cannot be
> dismissed as altogether absurd. The old Newtonian conception
> of past and future has crumbled under the criticism of modern
> mathematics, and time is no longer the one-way street we were
> once taught to believe it was.[2]

The fact that in this century a certain number of people engaged in philosophical and scientific speculation could turn to
astrology with serious interest, may perhaps mark the beginnings
of a new enquiry into the basis of the theory (if not, as Jung
believed, astrology's return to the universities). The fact that the
majority of scientists still dismiss astrology as absurd rubbish may
well be meaningless.

After looking into the subject, one may come to the conclusion
that prediction is impossible; or that character analysis is faulty;
or that astrology is practised by many cranks and some fools; or
even (as in the case of M. Gauquelin) that the results obtained by
astrologers have nothing to do with astrology. But one cannot just
dismiss the subject.

[1] C. G. Jung, *The soul and death* (Routledge & Kegan Paul, 1960).
[2] *The Times*, January 2, 1932.

VI

Astrologer and Client

I have been writing of those whose interest in astrology has become, for one reason or another, specialist. The effect of specialist interest on the man-in-the-street has generally been small. Newspaper editors, television and radio producers on the whole continue to refer to astrology only during the 'silly season' (although the BBC's news programmes, 'The world at one' and 'The world this weekend', have recently taken to inviting Katina Theodossiou to comment on current affairs, and have broadcast her commentary 'straight' and without comment). When that admirable magazine *Which?*, published by the Consumers' Association, decided to deal with astrology, it turned to the newspaper columns (although the report did point out briefly that no astrologer took these seriously). A reporter from *Time*, when planning an article on astrology, spoke on the telephone for some while with the president of the International Society for Astrological Research, only in the end to comment sadly: 'But you're not cranky enough for us!' The finished article contained no reference to ISAR. This experience has been shared by the Faculty of Astrological Studies in England; some journalists are content to 'expose' the absurdities of astrology, but less prepared to write about its serious aspects. It is true, of course, that these often demand considerable space if they are to be properly explained, and a 'good lively piece' may seem not the place for such explanation. Nevertheless, more and more people are becoming amateur astrologers: more and more people are becoming professional astrologers; and more and more people are consulting them.

How do clients find an astrologer? A very great number, of course, through the advertisements in various astrological or demi-semi-astrological magazines, such as *Fate,* or *Old Moore's Almanack.* More recently astrologers have permeated the advertisement columns of more reputable publications – even *The Times,* which for many years would not permit astrological advertisements to appear. My wife broke this particular barrier in August 1967.

The Times had telephoned Ingrid Lind, who for some time had been vice-president of the Faculty of Astrological Studies, to ask whether a potential advertiser was 'a qualified astrologer'. He was not, Miss Lind reported. But did *The Times* imply that if he had been, his advertisement would have been accepted? The answer seemed to be in the affirmative. Miss Lind contacted my wife, who attempted to insert an advertisement in *The Times* personal column. The Classified Advertisement department replied coolly that they 'regret to inform you that your advertisement commencing "Astroanalysis by qualified astrologer . . ." is one of a nature we prefer not to accept for insertion in our columns'.

After a telephone conversation with the advertisement manager, the advertisement was accepted. But when my wife tried to reinsert the advertisement four months later, the answer again was a cold one: 'Unfortunately I have to inform you that it is no longer possible for us to accept this advertisement for insertion in our columns. Nevertheless, may I take this opportunity of wishing you a happy and prosperous New Year.'

There was some more skirmishing, and eventually again *The Times* capitulated, objecting to the word 'astroanalysis', but accepting the simple announcement: 'Astrologer: Julia L. Parker, D.F.Astrol.S., Box —.' Roger Elliot, another London astrologer, had had his advertisement inserted in *The Times* daily for some months before the newspaper's advertisement department contacted him to say that it was unacceptable; but after a week's argument, the advertisement was again permitted to remain, and *The Times* now says that it will continue to accept astrological advertisements 'provided that no claims are made'.

The monthly magazine *Nova* (which runs an astrological feature to which it devotes a whole page) declined to accept an astrological advertisement ('*The Times*,' one of its advertisement representatives remarked, 'accepts *all sorts* of advertisements!'). Astrologers were referred by *Nova* to the Advertising Association, which in turn referred the secretary of the Faculty of Astrological Studies to the British Code of Advertising Practice Committee. The committee informed her that the question of astrologers wishing to advertise was usually left to the discretion of the individual newspaper or periodical concerned.

> Our information, wrote the committee's representative, is that as the law now stands, to advertise an astrological service directed at individuals is an offence under Section 4 of the Vagrancy Act 1824 as interpreted in later decisions. It is apparent that this law is not being enforced on any scale, if at all. The British Code of Advertising Practice, however, has conformity with the law as one of its prime requirements, and we cannot therefore for so long as the law remains unamended positively recommend acceptance. On the other hand, we recognise that there are many thoroughly reputable practitioners in this field, and we feel it would be unfair if we were to require rejection of their advertisements by media on the basis of conformity with the Code, when the law in question is to a large extent, if not entirely, a dead letter.

The committee pointed out fairly firmly, however, that it has power 'to control any gross abuse of the present situation by unscrupulous astrological advertising'.

The position in America seems similar: but on the whole the non-astrological press is more ready to reject astrological advertising out of hand: the *New York Times* will not countenance it, for instance; and the *Village Voice* also refuses individual advertisements, although its editor has allowed an advertisement to appear inviting readers to subscribe to an astrological computer service – because no one, he believes, could possibly take it seriously!

It is ironical that magazines should accept advertisements for the least reliable astrological services, while rejecting others from serious astrologers. As ironical as the position of *Nova*, which caters to the popular demand for the astrology of a popular column, while refusing to allow serious astrologers to announce their presence.

In general astrologers seem not to need to advertise; their business grows, if they are good astrologers, by personal recommendation. Occasionally there are small landslides; one of them, for instance, caused by Ingrid Lind's television programme for Granada TV in 1968, during which she demonstrated the bases of various statements about four people she had never met. The enquiries that followed were not remunerative, mainly because viewers did not realise the scale of charges concerned. They may have expected 'end-of-the-pier' prices instead of the fees charged for a single consultation by, say, a doctor or psychoanalyst.

Ingrid Lind sends out, in reply to queries, a neatly printed leaflet, which embodies an order form. This makes her standards perfectly plain. Her charges range from twenty-five guineas for 'the fullest psychological study of natal and progressed Chart' through a technical study of the chart at fifteen guineas (recommended 'to those who are interested in the technique and wish to know the astrological reason for each statement') and a 'portrait analysis of natal Chart and study of progressions' at ten guineas, to a 'brief analysis' at five guineas. Obviously, Miss Lind's is not the same appeal as that of newspaper astrology columns.

So for the most part, clients are 'serious' – either because they have had experience of astrology (some of them had been brought up with it, with enthusiastic parents who had consulted their own Birth Charts), or because they have specific problems. They may feel restless, want to change their job; they may be unable to make a final decision in a love affair or a marital problem; they may be uneasy about their health. An astrologer will tell you that there is no end to the human problems he has had to examine: clients seem to look on their astrologer as in the past they might have looked on a priest or perhaps a psychiatrist.

There is no limit to the age or type of client: there is perhaps a tendency at the present day for them to be of a younger age-group than in the immediate past. Any astrologer will have had experience of being approached by teenagers who not only want to consult them (and most often cannot afford the fees), but who have a basic knowledge of astrology themselves, picked up through second-hand books. There is a far greater interest than can be accounted for merely by those who have been personally introduced to the subject.

Astrologers would say that the coming of the Aquarian age accounts for the interest of young people generally. Alan Leo, outlining the characteristics of that sign, mentions several which would seem to apply to (for instance) both the 'hippies' and the students so concerned with social injustice and a new regime in education. (It is another interesting coincidence that whereas in past ages revolutions have on the whole occurred as and when society is ready to meet them in various parts of the world, student protest has occurred in the middle and late 1960s in England, France, America, Japan. ... Of course, the speed of modern travel and the increase in communications may account for this as convincingly as any astrological theory.)

> They [Aquarians – says Leo] incline towards the uncon-
> ventional, and therefore make excellent reformers ... they are
> always kind, humane ... exceedingly fond of art, music and
> literature ... have a great love for all humanitarian under-
> takings and concerns that produce harmony for the many; this
> gives them marked social tendencies ... When living along the
> purely personal lines, they are chaotic, diffusive, deceptive,
> tricky and clever for their own ends; egotistical, and apt to use
> their inflexible wills in the direction of selfish mental desires; or
> inclined to be vacillating and capricious ... Light and life
> await those who break away from the personality and live in the
> individuality of this sign. The inner nature and *destiny* of this
> sign is expressed in the one word HUMANITY.

Leo was writing in 1909.[1]

Only a minority of clients – those predisposed to astrology as a philosophy rather than a revelatory medium – come to astrologers for any kind of expansion of their knowledge of themselves. Henry Miller has written:

> It is not to discover what is going to 'happen' to us, it is not to

[1] Alan Leo, *Astrology for all* (L. N. Fowler, 1909).

forestall the blows of fate, that we should look to our horoscopes. A chart, when properly read, should enable one to understand the overall pattern of one's life. It should make a man more aware of the fact that his own life obeys the same rhythmical, cyclical laws as do other natural phenomena. . . . Astrology might indeed be called a science of relativity whose first-fruit is the dictum that fate is character.[1]

Most astrologers would certainly accept this. But most *clients* are concerned just for the very reason that they want 'to discover what is going to "happen" to them.' Or to 'forestall the blows of fate'. Will they die before their husband? Will they inherit money? Will they fall in love, marry, have children? Should they take this job, reject that? Should they ask for a rise? If so, when? And will they get it? The astrologer must resign himself to being psychologist, career consultant, marriage guidance officer, employment agent. . . .

Different astrologers deal with their clients in very different ways. Some insist on a personal meeting at some stage – either before or after their analysis has been prepared. A meeting before anything is written down has, of course, its dangers; it is then impossible to refute the allegation that whatever the astrologer later writes or says may have been based on information gleaned in conversation, or simply from the client's personal appearance and behaviour, rather than from the Birth Chart. This may indeed to some extent be true: if only to the extent that the doctor who diagnoses an inflamed appendix may base his diagnosis at least in part on having been told by the patient where the pain is. The analogy is precise: astrologers do not pretend to be superhuman.

But in fact cases of clients accusing astrologers of faking their results are very rare. Where they occur it is usually easy to see the limitations of the astrologer concerned. Whether it is because astrologers as a class have a knack of putting clients at their ease, or because in truth what is discovered in the charts is generally accurate; or whether we are all, in general, too lethargic to complain to anyone about anything unless the circumstances are fairly radical;

---

[1] *Henry Miller, his world of Urania,* op. cit.

it is a fact that the serious astrologer gets no more frequent attacks on his probity than the doctor.

If the client has a personal problem, the meeting with the astrologer can be of enormous psychological importance. This is often for reasons unconnected with astrology, of course. A woman whose daughter is pregnant, who dares not tell her husband, can bring the girl's birth data to an astrologer, cry on his shoulder for an hour or so, receive advice based on common sense, and go away the better for the encounter, without the stars having anything much to do with the matter. The advice the astrologer may give later, based on the information contained in the charts of husband, wife, daughter and boy friend, may be good or bad; but the chances are that the release of tension the woman has experienced will have helped a great deal in bringing her to some decision in the matter, or at any rate to a greater equilibrium.

Astrologers have again and again told me of clients in tears, pouring out the inmost secrets of their hearts; secrets often obviously kept from everyone else in their lives. Some astrologers find it easier to cope with this kind of thing than others. Dorothy B. Hughes, an American teacher of astrology who runs the Cellar School in Seattle, 'found that people would tell an astrologer things they probably wouldn't tell a clergyman or psychiatrist. It was most difficult for me to believe the situations that some people have got themselves into!'

Of course there are cases in which the best astrologer can only hope to persuade the client to put his affairs in the hands of another expert – lawyer, doctor, psychiatrist. A schizophrenic may have to be decisively shaken off, and his doctor informed; a distressed client who telephones every two hours may have to be firmly discouraged. Most of the professional astrologer's life is spent positively trying to help his client; and whatever his method – conventional or occult – the results seem on the whole to be good.

The anonymous author of a lengthy article in *Time* magazine summed up:

Sensitivity, intuition and maybe even clairvoyance make the difference between . . . tomfoolery and 'good' astrology. The good astrologer senses the mood of his client, perceives his problems and finds the most positive way of fitting them into the context of the horoscope. Then he looks ahead, shaping predictions so that they amount to constructive counsel. . . . There are many troubled people who refuse to accept personal responsibility for their lives, insisting that some outer force is in control. For these, a first-class astrologer can seem a necessity – and perhaps he is.[1]

This is, for someone determined not to accept the astrological theory at any costs, an extremely accurate observation.

It is doubtful whether the clients of professional astrologers are brought to them to any extent by the newspapers. Indeed, it is not uncommon for a client to say, right away, to an astrologer: 'Of course, I know newspaper astrology is rubbish.' The journalists played their part in the resurgence of astrology, especially during the war. But their place in astrology today is minimal, and they are unlikely to do any damage: the advice they offer is so general that in the first place very few people take any notice of it, and in the second anyone who did so would be unlikely to do himself an injury. But the professional astrologer could, obviously, wreak havoc with the lives of his clients, through carelessness or wickedness or ignorance. What protection can be offered by the law? At present, probably rather less than is offered against the pedlar or the confidence trickster or the fraudulent dealer in stocks and shares.

For hundreds of years (and indeed to some extent today) the astrologer was open to prosecution and punishment under various Acts of Parliament – that of 1563, 'Against Conjurations, Inchantments and Witchcrafts', for instance (although Queen Elizabeth I constantly consulted John Dee – as his diary shows; so it is unlikely that this Act was widely employed against the professional astrologer).

Queen Mary had passed, in her ninth Scottish Parliament, a similar Act; both were repealed by the Parliament of James I in 1603, to make way for an Act 'against Conjuration, Witchcraft, and dealing with evil and wicked Spirits'; and this in its turn was

[1] *Time*, March 21, 1969.

repealed in 1736, and replaced by an Act 'for punishing such Persons as pretend to exercise or use any kind of Witchcraft, Sorcery, Inchantment, or Conjuration'.

This last Act made it impossible to charge or try anyone for witchcraft; but continued to provide protection against the craftier users of magic:

> And for the more effectual preventing and punishing of any Pretences to such Arts or Powers as are before mentioned, whereby ignorant Persons are frequently deluded and defrauded; be it further enacted by the Authority aforesaid, That if any Person shall, from and after the said Twenty fourth day of June, pretend to exercise or use any kind of Witchcraft, Sorcery, Inchantment, or Conjuration, or *undertake to tell Fortunes*,[1] or pretend, from his or her Skill or Knowledge in any occult or crafty Science, to discover where or in what manner any Goods or Chattels, supposed to have been stolen or lost, may be found, every Person, so offending, being thereof lawfully convicted on Indictment or Information in that part of Great Britain called England, or on an Indictment or Libel in that part of Great Britain called Scotland, shall, for every such Offence, suffer Imprisonment by the Space of one whole Year, without Bail ... and Once in every Quarter of the said Year, in some Market Town of the proper County, upon the Market Day, there stand openly on the Pillory by the Space of One Hour.

This humane Act (one of the most enlightened of its time, pillory notwithstanding) was replaced in its turn by the Vagrancy Act of 1824, which is still in operation – apart from the sections dealing with spiritualism, replaced by the Fraudulent Mediums Act of 1951.

Dealing with 'idle and disorderly Persons, and Rogues and Vagabonds', the 1824 Act is scarcely complimentary to astrologers; except inasmuch as it has scarcely ever been employed against them. After a few sharp words about people who refuse to maintain their families ('by Work or by other Means'!), common pros-

---

[1] Author's italics.

titutes and those begging or gathering alms, the Act goes on to
state that

> every Person *pretending or professing to tell Fortunes*[1] or using
> any subtle Craft, Means or Device, by Palmistry or otherwise,
> to deceive and impose on any of His Majesty's Subjects . . . shall
> be deemed a Rogue and vagabond, within the true Intent and
> Meaning of this Act.

So far, so good. But obviously the interpretation of the Act
provides several problems. What precisely is meant by 'the telling
of *fortunes*'? Obviously a certain amount of prediction is involved.
It is interesting to remember that speaking at an Astrological Conference in England in 1938, 'a well known barrister' (unfortunately not named by *The Times* reporter) gave it as his
opinion that it would be perfectly possible to prosecute a professional weather forecaster under the Vagrancy Act with, in the
strict sense of the law, a good chance of success. Again, it is true to
say that most astrologers implicitly believe in their craft, and could
not strictly be said to be using it 'to deceive or impose on' their
clients (even if their predictions were in fact wrong).

The legal history is extremely confused. There are cases (Penny
v Hanson, in 1887, for instance) in which an astrologer has been
convicted simply for promising to deliver the goods, and not doing
so; but this is the kind of prosecution one might bring against a
vacuum-cleaner salesman who collected the money but failed to
deliver the cleaner.

Rex *v*. Stephenson (1904) is more interesting, although the defendant was in fact a palmist, and was indicted for 'attempting to
obtain money by falsely pretending that he had the power and
ability to foretell the future' by means of palmistry and a crystal
ball. An attempt was made to introduce evidence that 'palmistry
was a well-recognised science'; but it was ruled that such evidence
was not admissible. It would be interesting to hear an argument in
court about the scientific merits of palmistry – or of astrology;
alas, the situation has never arisen.

It was in 1914 that the first notable modern case was brought –
against Alan Leo. The police had evidently had their eye on him

[1] Author's italics.

for some time. He had been cautioned by them in 1911, and in February 1914 a Detective-Inspector Hugh McLean had written to his address, under a false name, asking for a list of charges for horoscopes. By return of post he received a booklet (*The stars and how to read them*) and the information that horoscopes could be had for between five shillings and five guineas (for the latter sum Leo would send detailed progressions for ten years). Inspector McLean promptly sent off a postal order for ten shillings, and received a horoscope in return, which was read to the Lord Mayor and the court, and a public gallery at the centre of which sat Mrs Leo, accompanied by Annie Besant, the successor to Madame Blavatsky, the theosophist.

The horoscope does not seem to have been outstandingly convincing, although the moderate successes promised to the inspector in the late spring may have encouraged him in the preparation of his case. He told the court that Leo had been casting horoscopes for a quarter of a century, though he declined to confirm that Leo had said that he had had over 20,000 testimonials, 'some of them from persons of the highest position in this country'.

It is unfair to accuse any defendant of getting out of a case the easy way; but one cannot help regretting that Leo did not have to make a fight for it. In the event, his Counsel very properly slipped him through a convenient loophole. When McLean's letter had been received at Leo's office, the latter had been abroad. There was no evidence that he had written the horoscope; and in fact he denied having done so. The prospect of sending Mr Leo money for horoscopes prepared by someone else was scarcely a good advertisement; but it was sufficient to extricate him from the case, and the Lord Mayor dismissed him – refusing, however, to allow him his costs. 'I am fully convinced in my own mind that there is no doubt it *is* endeavouring to tell fortunes,' he remarked crossly.

The police only had to wait a few months for their revenge. On August 28, 1917 Leo was again before the courts. This time he was convicted and fined £25. But the newspapers were full of the first bomb attacks on London, and the case was only very briefly reported in one edition of *The Times*. Later that year, Leo died.

Since 1917, there has been little legal activity against astrologers. The following year it was held that 'an intention to deceive' had to be provided before a conviction could be obtained under the Act; but in 1925 (Irwin *v.* Barker) another authority decided that 'it is *not* necessary to prove a deceitful purpose or fraudulent intent'. In between those two cases, there was one in New Zealand in which a court ruled that 'the offence of undertaking to tell fortunes is complete when a person *whether honestly believing in his power to do so or intending to deceive,*[1] undertakes to tell another person's fortune'. And this seems to be the present state of the law.

The courts have almost completely disregarded newspaper astrologers, although in 1936 there was a case against R. H. Naylor, brought by Mr Maurice Barbanell, the editor of *Psychic News.* Phyllis Naylor alleges[2] that Mr Barbanell was annoyed because mediums were clearly open to prosecution, while astrologers seemed to be getting away scot-free. However that may be, he acted as common informer, and brought an action against Naylor for his column in the *Sunday Express* of February 9, 1936. A City of London alderman, Sir Louis Newton, first heard the case; and it was then taken on appeal to the King's Bench Division, before Lord Chief Justice Hewitt and Justices du Parq and Goddard.

Barbanell had accused Naylor of 'pretending to tell fortunes' in a column 'which purported to relate what would be the fortunes of people' born on a particular date. The charge was dismissed, Sir Louis holding that 'the article being addressed to the public generally, and stating or forecasting the future of all persons born on a certain day, did not purport to tell the fortune of an individual', and so was not within Section Four of the Vagrancy Act, under which the case had been brought.

Justice du Parq enquired whether there was not a distinction between purporting to tell the fortune of a *person*, and making generalisations for a number of people born on a particular day? Gilbert Beyfus, K.C., for Barbanell, tried valiantly to steer round the question. If Naylor had sent his predictions separately to each of his readers, he pointed out, then an offence would have been committed; the fact that the fortune-telling was done openly and

[1] Author's italics.
[2] Phyllis Naylor, *Astrology, an historical examination* (Robert Maxwell, 1967).

on a large scale, made no difference. The point was that Naylor professed to tell the fortunes of people by the positions of the stars at their birth; that the Act had been passed to protect the foolish, and that the article was the very sort of thing it had been directed against. But their lordships were unimpressed. 'The article in question,' said the Lord Chief Justice, 'is addressed generally to all readers of the articles, and the purported forecasting of the future for persons born on a particular day is too vague and uncertain to amount to the professing to tell the fortune of an individual.' The appeal was dismissed.

The verdict does not appear to have been reported very fully to readers of Mr Naylor's column; and indeed if Mr Barbanell did not in fact win his case, he must have been moderately satisfied, surely, to have heard newspaper astrology dismissed in such round terms.

The law as it stands does seem to be confused. As Beyfus, K.C., pointed out in Barbanell v. Naylor, 'any person who pretends to read the future by any pretended science not known to the other party comes within the Act'. The word 'pretended' is interesting, and would surely admit some argument. Would it indeed be impossible to convict a weather forecaster under the Vagrancy Act? Would a court permit eminent astrologers to be questioned about the empirical bases of the science?

And what of the astrologer? The conclusion seems to be that if he really and obviously defrauds a client in a big way (say, by providing at a high fee 'astrological advice' based on nothing more solid than his own imagination) he could be prosecuted under the Theft Act (1968), which makes it an offence *dishonestly by deception* to obtain property or a pecuniary advantage. Obviously, if the astrologer, by producing evidence, can prove satisfactorily that his advice was based on traditional astrological interpretation, an action would fail, which seems fair.

An occult astrologer might perhaps suffer under the Fraudulent Mediums Act, which made it an offence to act as a spiritualistic medium or to exercise powers of telepathy, clairvoyance, or other similar powers with intent to deceive, for reward. It would be much more difficult to convince a court of one's honesty if one had provided an astrological analysis based in the main on *occult* astrology. One can imagine how the average court might react to the Sabian symbols, for instance.

As for the civil law, an action for damages could succeed in an appropriate case. All would depend on the skill shown, and demonstrably shown, by the astrologer concerned. A client might object that he had been given bad advice which had led to a disaster in his personal life; or a company might perhaps allege that an astrologer retained to give business advice (and there are plenty of cases of this) had advised share dealings which had resulted in immediate bankruptcy. In such cases an action for breach of contract and negligence would depend entirely on the prosecution establishing that the astrologer failed to use the care and skill which he held himself out to have, or which an astrologer would normally be expected to display. 'The prospects of a successful claim on these lines would seem to be extremely slight,' Professor Alec Samuels, a distinguished professor of law, drily observes. Certainly evidence of astrological skills would have to be given, and the case could hardly fail to be a sensation.

A sub-committee of the Faculty of Astrological Studies spent some time investigating the position in 1969, and published a memorandum in the *Astrological Journal*, which concluded that on the whole astrologers seemed to have little to fear from the law as at present enforced. But obviously there would be something to be gained from clarification of the position; and the Code of Advertising Practice Committee pointed out that repeal of the principal enactment of the Vagrancy Act as it applies to astrologers would be an advantage – if only because it would then enable that committee to advise newspapers to accept the advertisements of qualified astrologers.

Astrologers sometimes have something to gain from the rather equivocal state of the law as it stands. The first famous American astrologer, Evangeline Adams, was prosecuted between the wars under the State of New York laws. But at her trial she gave so accurate a reading of the Birth Chart of a 'Mr X' (who turned out, by coincidence or design, to be the Judge's son!) that the court dismissed the case against her, ruling that 'she has raised astrology to the dignity of an exact science'. Her fortune was made.

Recently, some attempts have been made by 'official' astrological organisations to enforce – or at least to present, for enforcement is difficult in a field where the whole course of operations is so amorphous – a code of ethics. This is not entirely new: in 1647 the astrologer, alchemist and magician William Lilly wrote 'an Epistle to the Student in Astrology' which, aptly enough, is presented to each graduate of the Faculty of Astrological Studies with his diploma:

My friend, whoever thou art, that with so much ease shall receive the benefit of my hard studies, and dost intend to proceed in this heavenly knowledge of the starres: in the first place, consider and admire thy Creator, be thankful unto him, and be humble, and let no naturall knowledge how profound or transcendent soever it be, elate thy mind to neglect that Divine Providence, by whose all-seeing order and appointment all things heavenly and earthly have their constant motion: the more thy knowledge is enlarged, the more doe thou magnify the power and wisdome of Almighty God: strive to preserve thyself in his favour; for the more holy thou art, and more near God, the purer judgement thou shalt give . . .

Having considered thy God, and what thyself art, during thy being God's servant, now receive instruction how in thy practice I would have thee carry thyself. As thou daily conversest with the heavens, so instruct and form thy mind according to the image of Divinity: learn all the ornaments of virtue, be sufficiently instructed therein: be humane, curtius, familiar to all, easie of accesse: afflict not the miserable with terrour of a harsh judgement; direct such to call on God to divert his judgements impending over them: be civil, sober, covet not an estate; give freely to the poor, both money and judgement: let no worldly wealth procure an erroneous judgement from thee, or such as may dishonour the art. Be sparing in delivering judgment against the commonwealth thou livest in; avoyd law and controversie: in thy study be totus in illis, that thou mayest be singularis in arte. Be not extravagant, or desirous to learn every science: be faithful, tenacious, betray no one's secrets. Instruct all men to live well: be a good example thyself; love thy own native country; be not dismaid if ill spoken of. God suffers no sin unpunished, no lye unrevenged: Pray, if it stand with God's will, that monarchy in this kingdom may continue, his Majesty and posterity reigne: and let the famous city of London be ever blessed, and all her worthy citizens.

Which really leaves very little unsaid. The Faculty's own Code of Ethics, expressed perhaps less nobly, is however fairly comprehensive. It must be signed by every holder of the diploma, and consists of three articles:

1. I will at all times endeavour to act in such a way as to enhance the good name and standing of Astrology, explaining its true nature, as I understand it, to all interested persons and defending it against unjust aspersions and misinformed attacks.

2. I will similarly seek to promote the welfare and good name of the Faculty of Astrological Studies by all appropriate and honourable means.

3. In all my astrological work, whether professional or otherwise, I will abide by the following rules, viz.:

(a) I will undertake no natal work unless the time and place of birth are stated with reasonable accuracy, or if these are not available, I will explain clearly and unequivocally that any work supplied in such circumstances can only be regarded as inadequate and general.

(b) In all professional work I will charge a fee commensurate with the dignity of astrological science, except in cases wherein the enquirer, being a genuine seeker after help and not impelled by idle curiosity, is unable to make payment. In such cases I will give information and advice gratuitously.

(c) I will in every case make an original and individual study of the case before me, and will not use any form of reduplication, nor will I use in my work extracts from others' writing without due acknowledgement.

(d) In work stated to be astrological I will not insert anything that is not founded upon true astrological science. Should I desire to impart advice or information derived from other sources, I will write this upon a separate sheet with an express statement that is not based upon astrology.

(e) I agree to respect in the strictest manner all confidences reposed in me, unless my duty as a loyal and law-abiding citizen of my country compels me to act otherwise.

(f) I will use discretion in making any public statements regarding political matters or persons prominent in public life, and will avoid all such as are contrary to good taste and the practice of a decent reticence.

(g) I undertake to make no improper or unethical use of the Diploma and my status as a Holder thereof and a Member of the Faculty; and as far as in me lies I will conduct all professional astrological work, should I be engaged therein, in accordance with high professional standards.

(h) I will hold for the general good and not for my private use or advantage any discoveries that I may make or conclusions that I may reach, save only such as might, if divulged in public, conduce to results undesirable in the general interest.

Finally, I . . . admit the right of the Council, in the event of wilful and grave violation of this Code of Ethics, to withdraw my Diploma and erase my name from the Register of Members of the said Faculty.

The Code of Ethics of the American Federation, while not so lengthy, corresponds to its English counterpart; although it has one interesting additional clause:

I agree to assist in any way I can in the elimination of the charlatan who may be masquerading under any form of title that can be construed to mean a connection with Astrology designed to mislead the public or trade upon their credulity in any way.

The American Astrologers' Guild makes three additional points: that members should 'satisfy themselves to the best of their ability that the purposes of a client are of a legitimate character'; that they should avoid the use of the words 'predict' and 'prediction' without making it quite clear that the words are not used in a fortune-telling sense; and that they should 'make every possible effort to contravene false or exaggerated representations of astrology'.

Unfortunately all these organisations can do is set out their codes and hope that their members will hold to them. There are no real sanctions: the news that an astrologer has been deprived of his diploma by the Faculty of Astrological Studies would be unlikely to receive the same publicity as the news that a doctor had been struck off the roll; and indeed the Faculty, the Guild or the Federation could not by any means prevent anyone from making lucrative living from gullible clients (except, perhaps, by invoking the law).

This is one reason why these organisations are right to take any opportunity of obtaining publicity of the right sort. Only by attempting to organise some kind of 'closed shop' would it be possible to ensure respectability; and quite apart from whether or not there is any truth in astrological theory, it is obviously better that it should be employed honestly.

VII

Craft and Art

There is an enormous range of astrologers working at the present time. In Europe and America it includes at one end of the scale the cheapjack who promises 'a reading' for ten shillings, and whose work is no more than a slightly lengthened version of the paragraphs one can read in a popular magazine; and at the other, the full-time professional consultant who had learned his art in theory and in practice.

Astrology is certainly one field in which (except perhaps where computerised horoscopes are concerned, and these are at present very limited in scope) the value of the reading is directly in proportion to the fee. The reason is simple: it is merely a matter of the time needed to calculate and interpret a chart. An astrologer who has taken the courses of the Faculty of Astrological Studies and is starting work, will probably find it extremely hard to interpret more than one or perhaps two charts a week. So that one is bound to be suspicious of an advertiser who promises 'Your annual forecast – comprehensive, accurate guidance' for ten shillings; or even of John Pendragon, who offers to readers of *Fate* help with 'your apparently insoluble problem' (provided you send him 'full birth date, with hour and place, also recent snaps and handwriting of all persons involved') for four guineas. Even allowing for the fact that Mr Pendragon has been working for many years, his fee seems too low to inspire complete confidence.

The worst sort of 'astrologer' is one who has had printed (or more likely duplicated) a number of sheets based on a very rough idea of the subject, and whose work consists in placing these in an envelope and licking the stamp. Mr Pendragon is concerned rather more with the occult than with astrology – indeed, he tells me that he 'understands several systems of astrology, but uses it only as an adjunct to clairvoyance'. As his advertisement suggests, he uses graphology too – 'as an adjunct to seership; [he] does not regard graphology as an Occult "science", but as part of material psychiatry of the orthodox class'. He does not feel that his fees are less than those of the average British astrologer; they are 'elastic, depending on the nature of his work and the clients' circumstances. Fees vary from four guineas to twenty guineas on the average.' So it may simply be that his advertisement is misleading.

From the point of view of the conventional astrologer it is unfortunate that Mr Pendragon advertises as 'an astrologer'; but he is not the only clairvoyant to do so. If asked to name the most prominent British astrologer of the present moment, a very great number of people would undoubtedly name Maurice Woodruff. And indeed he is prominent and successful: with a flat in London, a house in the country, another house in America – with regular astrological columns in the *TV Times* and elsewhere, television programmes in England and America, appearances at the Mayfair Theatre, London, and many other public lectures and demonstrations.

Yet he is not, and has been known to admit it, a serious astrologer. There is nothing in his newspaper or magazine work to suggest that he is not completely conventional: although there are predictions for 'Taureans with brown/hazel eyes (next week predictions for blue eyes)' which suggest that his interests are more clairvoyant than anything else. And this is, of course, the case. His mother was a society clairvoyant of the 1920s and 1930s. She was a lady of considerable interpretative powers, and on one occasion, it is said, informed a man that it would be unnecessary for her to provide detailed predictions for his wife after July 31, because she would be dead by then. She was.

When Mr Woodruff was seven he discovered that he shared or had inherited his mother's clairvoyant powers. Later he took a course of ten lessons in astrology. This seems to have been the extent of his academic astrological study. But his success is undoubted: 'My accountants will not let me say what my fees are,' he told me; his secretary quoted fifteen guineas for 'a consultation', writing on the notepaper of Maurice Woodruff Promotions Limited. He is evidently convinced of his own talent, and his conviction is certainly based on his clairvoyant powers rather than on astrological knowledge. When a private client is due for a consultation, he 'just draws out their Chart for the week', and then *adjusts it* according to his clairvoyant instinct', which takes precedence over the astrological facts.

His astrology for the *TV Times* appears also to be based as much on clairvoyance as astrology; he says he 'gets a feeling for the great masses of Leos', for instance, and divides them into 'early', 'middle' and 'late' Leos (apparently believing that no conventional astrologer is capable of this). The column, and his other activities, brings him in, he says, three to five thousand letters a week, and his influence is very considerable. He uses this in various ways. His one spectacular public miscalculation was when he predicted an overwhelming success for the Conservative party in the 1964 General Election. But he did this, he says, 'to help the Conservatives'. How much he did in fact help them is open to question: the Labour majority was of only five seats.

Mr Woodruff's publicity hand-out (headed 'Clairvoyant *and Astrologer*') claims that he was 'the first astrologer to be invited to cast a horoscope for young Prince Albert of Monaco; the first to cast a horoscope for young Prince Andrew of England; the first astrologer in Great Britain to cast a horoscope on record'. In addition, in 1968, he became the first British astrologer to have a television series of his own. This programme, for Independent Television, was shared by Marjorie Proops of the *Daily Mirror*, and it is doubtful whether any format could have been chosen which would more thoroughly have infuriated serious astrologers. There was at no point any attempt to draw up a chart for those guests to whom, or about whom, Mr Woodruff spoke, or for whom he predicted. As he put it:[1] 'We selected a different birthsign each week, and only mentioned the characteristics of that

[1] In a letter to the author.

sign. At the same time, Marjorie tried to get from me how all these guests born under the same sign were alike according to those characteristics, and this is where the astrological part of the programme stopped. All the predictions that I made for the guests were clairvoyant predictions, having nothing to do with astrology'. It is a pity this was not made clear on the programme.

Mr Woodruff's interest in the occult is paralleled by that of various non-astrologers such as the American Bruce King, a former clothing salesman known professionally as Zolar, who sells crystal balls in five sizes ($2 to $50) complete with 'six simple lessons in crystal gazing', and has on his books fifty other occult objects from Xolarscopes to aphrodisiac perfumes.

Those astrologers who seek to interest the scientists in statistical evidence look askance at those whose interest is mainly occult, and who find the whole astrological theory inseparable from the occult. Many of the latter must have been affected by theosophy. It is to theosophy that a small but active number of astrologers owe their interest in reincarnation, for this is a tenet of theosophical teaching. It is interesting that it reads parallel to the Brahmanic and Buddhistic doctrines of karma, deeply ingrained in Indian astrological lore. Karma expresses the inexorable law of moral causation; *ill* actions on earth bring their inevitable punishment in one's next earthly life. It is a convenient argument as far as it answers the bewilderment caused by the uneven distribution of happiness and unhappiness, justice and injustice, in life as we know it; and its use in astrology conveniently answers many of the questions that arise in that relationship also. But those to whom astrology offers a faintly ridiculous proposition anyway, are unlikely to be reassured by the discovery that the astrologer of their choice is also a believer in reincarnation. It is perhaps for this reason that the Faculty and other bodies are eager that their members should not stress any aspect of occultism when writing their reports. But at least theosophy is a respectable religion; and astrologers certainly owe it much.

It is not from the theosophist that the client has anything to fear; it is from the out-and-out fraud, who has acquired a certain amount of knowledge of astrological terminology from casual reading, and is prepared to use it for profit. Can this kind of fraud be positively dangerous? In the hands of a totally unscrupulous confidence trickster, as dangerous as any other. But in general, emotionally less dangerous perhaps than the fraud of the unscrupulous fraudulent clairvoyant who can (as is well known) play on the emotions of the recently bereaved, the lonely, the emotionally unbalanced. It is more difficult for a conventional astrologer to do this – more difficult even for the astrological fraud whose misdoings simply consist of selling a worthless Birth Chart or a set of predictions for ten shillings.

Mass-Observation in 1941 found 'an enormous concentration in the holiday resorts like Blackpool and Southend [of] people like Miss Alis Paul of Otford, Kent, who has an enormous postal business of horoscopes at £1 each, or Mrs Forncett Osborne, who sends "inspirational messages by post" from Farnborough'.

The damage the astrological fraud does is of course in proportion to the wealth of the person he defrauds; and I would not defend him. Nevertheless, it may be thought that he is less of a danger to society than many other people working in the same general area; he is in a sense a pick-pocket; but the pocket is being willingly held open for him, and on the whole his pickings are fairly slender.

Unfortunately it seems all too likely that many of the people who most need a serious astrologer's help are directed to the advertisers who promise analyses at ten shillings or a pound; and they are likely to be, also, those who can least afford a higher fee. The Faculty of Astrological Studies appears in the London Telephone Directory under 'astrology', which leads a good number of enquirers to its secretary and a list of diploma-holders in England and abroad. For the average client, however, it is still very much 'the luck of the draw'.

But at least the situation is improving. There are more serious astrologers about, and the chances of applying to a good one are better. Unless and until the general public knows more about the subject, a complete safeguard will be impossible; and there will always be the back-street astrologer ready to do a cut-price job, as there will always be clients content with one.

The serious astrologer, on the other hand, must in some way come to grips with a really enormous body of astrological information. Until about twenty years ago, he could only do this by becoming an apprentice. Katina Theodossiou, for instance (who is one of the world's most successful astrologers), initially became an assistant of the late R. H. Naylor (John Naylor's father) when he was astrologer to the *Daily Express*. Naylor, having examined her Chart, told her quite firmly that she would be an astrologer. Her interest in the subject at that time was slight; she simply wanted a career in journalism. But Naylor taught her to set up a Birth Chart, and in order to supplement her income she began to help him in writing occasional paragraphs, and continued to teach herself by reading his astrological textbooks.

Similarly, Charles Carter learned his craft from the shilling manuals of his elder, Alan Leo, whose fuller textbooks are still in the libraries of most astrologers. One or two astrologers issued mimeographed astrology lessons in monthly parts. But the texts of astrological textbooks available between the fourteenth and nineteenth centuries are sufficiently complex to suggest that an amateur might have had some difficulty in learning from them. An astrologer would have been most likely to learn his craft from the mouth of a teacher. It was not until the early years of this century that a layman of moderate intelligence could perhaps expect to pick up an astrological textbook from which he could teach himself to be an astrologer. And even now this is no easy matter. It is perhaps significant that the major astrologers of the last century were men of leisure – either because they had private means, or because they provided themselves with those means.

Alan Leo, for instance, although he had proved himself as an astrologer by the time he was thirty-five, only afterwards in the early 1900s had the leisure in which to write the first really thorough, straightforward and comprehensive astrological textbooks of our time. *Astrology for all, How to judge a nativity,* and succeeding volumes which included *The progressed horoscope,* and *Esoteric astrology,* are substantial works. The average reader coming to them with no knowledge of the technique of astrology may find it an uphill fight to learn the craft from them. The mechanics of setting up a chart are complicated enough to need simple expression in contemporary language (the matter of interpretation is different, and an antique style in that direction is no positive disadvantage). So a textbook of simple astrology needs, probably, to be rewritten for every generation. It was done fifteen years ago by Margaret E. Hone in *The modern textbook of astrology*, written specifically as a classroom textbook; and Jeff Mayo's *Teach yourself astrology* has more recently provided a much simplified course by which it is possible at least to learn the basic craft.

Live classes in astrology spring up, and die again, from time to time. The Theosophical Society of England formed an Astrological Lodge, for instance, at the time of its own foundation in 1916; but there were no formal astrological classes, and there are still none in England – although the Lodge and, on a higher standard, the Astrological Association, hold regular lectures on various aspects of interpretation and theory. Some astrologers give individual private lessons to students.

In the United States there are a few more or less formal schools – such as the Cellar School of Astrology founded in 1962 in the basement of her home in Seattle by Dorothy B. Hughes. Ten or twelve students a week then attended classes; by 1968 between 90 and 100 students came to classes held seven times a week. Local Astrological Societies in the US also sometimes hold classes; and most American astrologers seem more eager than their English colleagues to pass their knowledge on personally to groups of students. Harriet Friedlander, of the Pittsburgh Astrological Association, for instance, feels obliged 'to teach anyone who has a sincere interest in astrology'. 'I abhor the large number of "do-it-yourself" kits available today,' she says; 'and I compare this to putting a scalpel and a book of instructions into the hands of an amateur and telling him to perform an operation.'

The principal English teaching body, the Faculty of Astrological Studies, holds two examinations of its students, the final one for a diploma which carries with it the right to print the letters D.F.Astrol.S. after the successful student's name, and the Faculty's encouragement to practise. (Incidentally, it has been for some time the American practice for an astrologer to print the initials of any organisation to which he may belong after his name; which may mislead some into believing them to possess a kind of official qualification. John Smith, A.F.A., simply means that Mr Smith is a member of the American Federation of Astrologers.)

The diploma of the Faculty is increasingly recognised within astrological circles as signifying that a student has a good basic grounding in astrological techniques, although everyone emphasises that this is merely the beginning of what can be (and should be) a lifetime of study in the subject. The Faculty was started in the late 1940s, under the aegis of the Astrological Lodge of the London Theosophical Society – at that time the only properly constituted astrological body in the country. Charles Carter, then President of the Lodge, and Lorenz von Sommaruga, a science student of London University who was interested in the subject, felt that a proper teaching body should be established which could lay down a course of study reliable enough to be regarded as authoritative, with regular examinations ensuring that students reached a satisfactory standard of technique. Carter became the first Principal of the Faculty, formed a governing body (the Council), and chose teachers. Two classes, for beginners and more advanced students, began to teach not only calculation and general theory, but the history and technique of interpretation.

The Vice-Principal of the Faculty was Margaret E. Hone who, becoming interested in astrology as a girl, had joined the Lodge in 1934. When it became clear that a system of lectures accompanied by personal note-taking was a cumbersome and on the whole unsuccessful means of teaching the subject, Mrs Hone embarked on the writing of her *The modern textbook of astrology* which would cover the examination syllabus, and could be used by students unable to attend classes. Although it owed much to its predecessors, as must any book of its kind, it introduced several relatively new ideas – perhaps most radically, the system of 'keywords' on which students could base their interpretation of a Birth Chart.

For instance, the key-words Mrs Hone suggests for the Sun are *power, vitality, self-expression*; for Aries, *assertiveness*; for the Ninth House (summarised) *foreign travel ... more profound mental activity*. The student applies this by learning the key-words parrot-fashion, and setting them together in a stilted sentence; so that an interpretation of the Sun in Aries in the Ninth House would read, perhaps, 'Your power and vitality are used assertively in matters of travel and deeper study.' Later, the student is able to write more freely, and to loosen and broaden the scope of his remarks to suit various circumstances.

The key-word method is intensely irritating for anyone whose interest in words is more than basic; but undoubtedly for examination purposes it is valuable, enabling a student more easily to retain a broad notion of a great number of more or less complex attributions of signs, Houses, planets.

Within a few years of the foundation of the Faculty, it was noticed that attendances at classes in London were falling off, while at the same time there was a demand from abroad, and from various parts of Great Britain, for a postal course; so in 1952 Mrs Hone devised and wrote courses of study for external students, and it soon became clear that this method of teaching was for several reasons superior to open class methods.

In 1956 the Faculty's school was closed, and all students became 'external', sending their work to a tutor by post for comment and correction. By this time Mrs Hone had designed badly-needed printed forms for calculation and setting out of Birth Charts; and by this time too the Faculty had severed its connection with the theosophical Lodge – the religious connotation as well as the emphasis on various aspects of the occult (reincarnation, for instance) was felt likely to put off as many students as it gained.

A steady growth of general interest in Astrology is mirrored in the progress of the Faculty, which, less than twenty-one years after its foundation had enrolled its one-thousandth student. In 1957, Mrs Hone (who had become principal, with Ingrid Lind as vice-principal) retired as Tutor, and Jeff Mayo succeeded her. In 1969 he became also the Faculty's principal, on Mrs Hone's final retirement. Both Mr Mayo and Miss Lind had contributed to the list of popular books on astrology which encouraged the general interest, and brought the Faculty additional students. Other general books (such as Louis MacNeice's coffee-table picture-book *Astrology* – that fine poet's last book) had also fostered interest, and by 1969 the Faculty had registered students in seventy-five countries from Iceland to Australia, Japan to Zambia, Thailand to Hawaii. In 1954 there had been only eighteen students; by 1965, there were 75; by 1966, 91; by 1967, 144; and a total of 221 students was recorded during 1969, after 638 prospectuses had been sent out on request. While in the early days students were on the whole middle-aged or elderly, in 1968 over half of the students were between the ages of thirty and forty-nine, one third of them under thirty. The youngest student was sixteen, and the oldest, eighty-four.

The two courses, Junior and Senior, consist of mimeographed instruction letters from the Tutor, which lead the student through Margaret Hone's two textbooks. During the two years of the courses, the test papers are completed by the student and returned to the Tutor and his assistants for correction and comment. There are certain 'between-term tasks' which mark the student's progress, and the junior course culminates in a Certificate Examination. In the past it has been the custom to fail students only if they are obviously not getting to grips with the subject. The certificate is an encouragement to the student to embark on his second year of study. It has no professional status or value.

The diploma is a different matter. There is a serious attempt to ensure that the final examination is properly conducted, although this is necessarily difficult when it is impossible to gather all the students together under one roof. When one sits an examination in one's own home, one has room for manoeuvre. But the Faculty insists on the appointment of an independent invigilator, to whom examination papers are sent; who must invigilate personally, and ensure that only the proper textbooks are used at the proper times. There is a move to attempt to set up a system whereby only diploma holders can act as invigilators; but this is difficult to administer.

About eight examiners mark the five final papers, awarding their marks separately and without consultation; the candidates' names are omitted from their papers, and no examiner is aware of the marks awarded by another. An average of the two sets of marks given for each paper is taken, and decides the issue.

The first paper is designed to ensure that the candidates have at least an accurate general knowledge of astronomy. It is fair to say that the paper would be child's play to a student astronomer; but it is perhaps the least important of the four papers as far as astrology is concerned (except, of course, as regards the movements of planets within the solar system). It could be argued that it is broad enough to test an intelligent interest in and knowledge of the subject. The student may be asked such simple questions as, 'what are the causes of Spring tides?', or he may be invited to draw a rough diagram of the solar system. But he may also be asked to define the perihelion or the mean obliquity of the ecliptic, or to explain the phenomenon of retrograde motion of planets.

As far as general astrology is concerned, he may have to write an essay on the astrological significance of one of the outer planets; or to discuss the way in which an astrologer should work in collaboration with a psychiatrist. (There is, incidentally, a move to propose that in the near future the course should include at least a recommended reading list of psychological textbooks, or perhaps a brief course in the subject.)

The second paper is more technical. One examination paper (that for 1951) included as mandatory questions:

1. Discuss the truth of the following statements:

(a) Trines and sextiles predominating in a map do not make for a strong character.

(b) A T-square is 'an excellent dynamic' in any map.

(c) A Grand Trine 'was considered very evil by medieval writers, and unfortunately this view appears to be often correct'.

2. Imagine that an important sporting contest between two men is to take place, the date and place of the contest being known. If you were in possession of the birth data of both men, say how you would marshal all possible evidence as to the outcome of the contest. To which pieces of evidence would you attach most importance?

Other questions in this paper deal similarly with interpretation: with how one might elect a map to predict the best time to start a journey; how one would interpret three similar transits to three different clients. . . .

The questions in the third paper on calculation and general theory are designed to ensure that the student can adequately cope with the more or less complicated mathematics concerned in the various aspects of astronomy – taking into consideration calculations for southern as well as northern latitudes, the niceties of the international date-line, of differences in time standards for various countries, and so on.

The fourth paper ensures that the candidate can set up a Birth Chart properly, and list its constituents. He is given the birth time and place of a client, and asked to set up a chart, inserting the House cusps, the planetary positions and aspects (transposing these from Placidian to Equal House systems); and then he is asked about the aspects operative for a particular year, to progress the Moon for some months, and to note the effectiveness of the slower-moving planets.

Finally, from a Birth Chart and progressions provided, the candidate must write a character analysis, answering specific questions. These refer, always, to a known person: perhaps a relative, perhaps a friend, of one of the examiners, so that apart from the theory having to be correct, it is possible to judge just how helpful the would-be astrologers might be to a real client. (It is, incidentally, fascinating to look through perhaps twenty character analyses of someone one knows, all written by people to whom the subject is completely unknown; it is surprising – at all events to a sceptic – to see to what extent the character of the subject is properly caught.)

It is fairly clear that a student capable of going through the five papers of the Faculty's diploma examination, and obtaining a pass mark, should be able to use a considerable amount of astrological skill and knowledge; and that however good or bad an astrologer he may become, at least he will be in no sense a fraud.

The Faculty's course and concluding examination appear to be unique. After nineteen years of deliberation, the American Federation of Astrologers devised a set of examinations for a 'Certificate of Proficiency', and these were taken for the first time by some of the astrologers attending the Federation's 1960 Convention at Long Beach, California.

Since then, examinations have been a part of the AFA's annual

Conventions. There are three grades – student, teacher, and professional (strange, perhaps, that a 'teaching' examination should precede the 'professional' one); 'inasmuch as only local and State authorities can give *licences*,' comments the AFA, 'we give Certificates of Proficiency.'

The International Society for Astrological Research does not, it appears, intend to become a teaching body; but its Council is examining the possibility of setting up an examining body which would provide a diploma of some sort signifying that an astrologer had reached a certain standard of proficiency. It is thought that this diploma might perhaps be interchangeable with the Faculty's; and the rough outline of the proposed papers seems to suggest that the examination would be on the same lines. It would include the setting up of a horoscope, interpretation, knowledge of the history of astrology and its relationship to other sciences, and finally 'the examinee's ability to be articulate about the nature of astrology, its theoretical bases, its methodology and its purposes'.

The AFA looks forward to 'the future when our examination programme has been well established and more widely known to the general public, when people wanting professional astrological work done will ask practitioners if they have passed an examination to give evidence of their proficiency as an astrological practitioner'.

This is the nub of the matter: there will be no real value in examinations until the general public recognises that (as with any other professional body) it will on the whole get better value from those people who have successfully sat them. The Faculty is conscious of the need always to raise standards, and is gradually marking papers more and more severely; presumably this will eventually bear fruit, and while there will no doubt always be cheapjack astrologers just as there are back-street abortionists, the public will gradually recognise the value of employing – supposing an astrologer is to be employed at all – someone who has learned his job.

VIII

Opium of the People

A survey conducted in 1968 by the Opinion Research Centre revealed that every morning two-thirds of the adult British public reads the astrology columns of the popular daily newspapers. In France, the figure is 58 per cent; in Germany, 56 per cent. A very great number of people evidently pay some attention to the generalised statements made every day by Lord Luck, Francesco Waldner, Orion, Katina, or their continental equivalents.

When one thinks of almost 600,000 people on a Monday morning in England taking special pains to 'keep confidences given recently', or following the injunction to 'take a chance on something – you'll be right!', the mind boggles. Yet it seems that 58 per cent of the seven million people who regularly read their horoscope column and believe what they are told, come from 'the professional and managerial class'; and men and women in the age-group twenty-one to twenty-four are almost twice as likely to take their horoscope seriously as the middle-aged.

And newspaper astrology is of course the least acceptable aspect of that art or science. It is difficult to accept the theory that any considerable proportion of 'believers' would go so far as, for instance, to alter travelling arrangements because Lord Luck told them to do so. Any reader must surely realise that a paragraph of four lines purporting to make an accurate forecast which must affect one-twelfth of the population will be valueless?

But it seems that a good proportion of these readers goes on to discover at least a few of the complexities of the subject. One or two, at least, of the astrological writers in the magazine press (where more space is available) do occasionally point out that astrology does not begin and end with the characteristics of the subject's Sun-sign; and the astrological magazines go into some detail, sometimes in terms unlikely to be readily understood by a casual reader. The sale of the more or less professional astrological magazines is relatively small; *Horoscope* (produced in America, but circulated in England as well as in the US) sells a quarter of a million copies every month, and five or six thousand of these go, in America, to what the editor calls 'professional astrologers'.

The more popular *Horoscope purse books* – giving more or less detailed forecasts for each day, in a series of twelve books, one for each Sun-sign – sell over eight million copies a year, evidently to a readership drawn from the people who read their morning's prediction in the daily paper.

Astrologers who write columns for newspapers and magazines are the only ones to defend this practice. Their defence is not surprising, for there is a good living to be had from astrological journalism. An editor will pay at least £30 for a week's predictions, and these are often syndicated to several newspapers – Eva Petulengro, a clairvoyant astrologer whose headquarters is in Brighton, has a column in at least fifteen newspapers, including the *Western Evening Herald* of Plymouth, the *Hanley Sentinel* and the Nigerian *Spectator*. It has been calculated that English newspapers and magazines spend something like £20,000 a year on astrological columnists. In America the figure must be in the region of £150,000.

But neither is it surprising that serious astrologers condemn newspaper astrology, which has probably been mainly responsible for the fact that it is difficult – almost impossible – for anyone to present astrology as a serious art in this country. It is patently absurd to pretend that newspaper astrology could have any scientific basis, or even any theoretical basis; and since newspaper astrology is as near as most people get to the science, it has become very difficult to discuss it seriously.

Many astrologers decline for this reason to write astrological columns, although others have accepted – Katina Theodossiou, for instance, who is a serious and accomplished astrologer. Her appearances on the radio in England, when she has compared the charts of politicians, or forecast the complete success of the first moon-landing (because of the admirable personal horoscopes of the astronauts concerned) have been impressive. She will only weakly defend her newspaper columns on the grounds that astrology is after all 'based completely on the twelve signs' – a proposition that a number of astrologers now dispute.

English newspaper astrology began effectively in 1930 with R. H. Naylor's column in the *Sunday Express*. Naylor was an extraordinarily successful journalist and a very intelligent man with a flair for writing in a slightly cynical, sophisticated style. A Mass-Observation investigator who studied the astrological columnists in 1941 wrote of him:

> He is well-educated, left-wing in an unusual way. He has an exceptionally clear understanding of morale factors [this was, of course, during the darkest period of the war] is strongly anti-bureaucratic, anti-Conservative and anti-Communist, but with an approach to what is going on in the world which is to a considerable extent Marxist. He is in fact possessed of a temperament which is individualistic, rather unstable, and opportunist, but with some ideas of his own which equip him to be a modern mass astrologer.

Naylor was fortunate in having an early and spectacular success. The editor of the *Sunday Express* commissioned him to examine the Birth-Chart of Princess Margaret, who was born on August 21, 1930. There was a great deal of interest in the article; but its main interest is now retrospective. Princess Margaret would, Naylor wrote,

> have extreme originality of mind, an unconventional vein, a keen interest in everything that is up-to-date, original and novel ... From Venus will come a vivid emotional nature, which insists on following the dictates of the heart rather than the head ... Events of tremendous importance to the Royal Family and the nation will come about near her seventh year [King George VI unexpectedly succeeded to the throne in fact a few months before the Princess's seventh birthday], and these events will

indirectly affect her own fortunes. . . . She will marry rather suddenly, about the 24th or 26th year.

Princess Margaret in fact married in her thirtieth year; but it was during her twenty-sixth year that she issued to the press a statement about her relationship with Group-Captain Peter Townsend, which had caused much press speculation. Naylor's prediction was not perhaps very far out – although it cannot have meant much to readers in 1930, and the interest shown in the article was no doubt aroused as much by the general attitude of devotion to royalty as by the then extremely rare public appearance of an astrologer.

At all events, the editor was so delighted by the extent of that interest, that he commissioned another article from Naylor, who wrote a second piece about the general characteristics of those readers born in September. This provoked even greater interest, and the editor proposed a series.

It was in his first article of this series, which appeared on October 5, 1930, that Naylor wrote that British aircraft were likely to be in serious danger. And on that very Sunday came the news that the airship R-101, *en route* from England to India with a distinguished group of passengers, had crashed in France. Not unnaturally, the newspaper widely publicised Naylor's melancholy success. He was allowed a full-page for his next week's predictions and soon became the first nationally-known astrologer.

Other newsapers were not long in copying such a success, and by the time war broke out most national newspapers had their own astrologer. Some of them, like Edward Lyndoe, who wrote for the *People*, were extremely able journalists, if at that time relatively inexperienced astrologers. Lyndoe, wrote Mass-Observation's reporter, 'writes in a distinguished, snappy, hearty style, very informal. He treats his readers rather like Max Miller treats his audience in a music hall (and with something of the same effect).'

Newspaper astrologers have perhaps done something to draw people towards astrology, if·they have also repelled them. Clients who come to astrologers through the newspapers tend to want to be told about the tall, dark, handsome stranger. They generally

read the columns because they want to be amused – and perhaps
to some extent reassured. Newspaper astrologers on the whole tell
people what they want to hear. They tell their readers to do what
they were going to do anyway – to make opportunities, to be
cautious in money matters, or whatever. What Mass-Observation
said in 1941 continues to be true today. The astrological column

> gives a day-to-day *explanation* of what is going on in the uni-
> verse, a very rough code, a suggestion that there is some sort of
> pattern for events to follow. It thus deals, to some extent, with
> the feeling of insecurity which now [1941] prevails, and with
> the feeling that the whole of civilisation has gone haywire and
> that there is no reasonable pattern in the universe. . . . [Astrol-
> ogy appealed] to the lack of deep ideological or theological
> belief among the majority of the people, and the lack of large-
> scale emotional outlets . . . Astrology has arisen as a symptom
> of our times, to meet the need of our times, but to meet it
> without regard for effect, as a mere dope or with a profit motive
> unrelated to the long-term national interest. Its general impact
> is antagonistic to intelligent and co-operative war effort, but so
> long as other steps are not taken, it has a considerable sedative
> and soothing value.

After the war astrology would not last long, in Mass-Observation's
view; increasingly broad education would surely undermine it,
and it would in the end dwindle in effect, and die. The opposite
has been true, however: and it is doubtful whether astrology has in
its mass effect ever been as strong as it is today. But the reasons
may well be those suggested in 1941. There is still an intense
feeling of insecurity, and occasional outbursts of mass non-violent
hysteria, of 'large-scale emotional outlets' (from pop-concerts in
Hyde Park and poetry-readings at the Albert Hall right through
to the mass involvement of viewers in television soap-operas) are
symptomatic rather than curative.

As far as the astrological journalist is concerned, the climate has
never been more comfortable; and nothing in astrology is as easy
as the preparation of a weekly or daily astrological column. It
simply involves the setting-up of twelve charts, one for each of the
signs. The columnists do not always even roughly agree. Here, for

instance, are five predictions for Leo, which appeared on the morning of March 10, 1970:

This morning somebody is likely to show you a fatal flaw in current plans. There's nothing to do but start again. —Jeane Dixon, *Daily Sketch*.

You must co-operate to the fullest extent with a work partner today. Beware of exaggeration; you could land yourself in a tricky situation. — Orion, *Daily Mail*.

Private life will be much more lively. Friends will be helpful. — Francesco Waldner, *Daily Mirror*.

Things run smoothly at work and in business, but it is the personal side of life that sparkles now; go-ahead period in romance. — Lord Luck, *Daily Express*.

You can tie-up an important deal, purchase or task today. Take stock of a budding relationship which you may wish to develop. Or not. [sic]. — Diana, *Sun*.

There are very faint signs of agreement in some areas, but a reader with even a moderately critical attitude could hardly fail to dismiss astrology from his mind, on evidence of this kind. And a very great number of people do so. Some sort of superstitious attraction, together with the deeply inbred instinct of which I spoke earlier, makes the astrology columns important to the rest. Several editors have dropped astrology columns from their newspapers only to have been forced by the extent of their readers' protests to reinstate them. As far as a large proportion of readers is concerned (perhaps mainly women), the astrological column seems quite as important as the leader column.

The style of most astrological journalists could perhaps best be described as telegraphic; for the space allowed to them is small. Occasionally, in magazine journalism, a writer can spread himself. *Nova* allows its astrologer (who calls himself Astra Nova, and happens also to be a theatrical agent) a whole page; he has been able to develop a style of his own which is consistently amusing; he scatters his page with technical terms, giving an air of authority without being too confusing:

Mars in your opposition sign of Sagittarius this month is hideous for matrimony, while Jupiter in Libra is sensational for affairs of the heart — sort that one out.

The mutual aspects of planets are decidedly complex, so you will just have to settle for another trying period when delays and frustrations prevail. And if you think that's all a bit nasty, there is worse to come – for by the end of July both Uranus and Jupiter will be in your opposition sign of Libra – the seventh house of your solar horoscope, the house of marriage and open enemies.

This reminds one rather of Nat Gubbins in the *Daily Express* before the war:

> *Cancer* – for you Dame Fortune's smile is always a cynical leer. This week she will be thumbing her nose at you. All your bad luck in the past will seem like Paradise to what will hit you between now and next Sunday.

There has been much discussion about the possibility of working out a system of mass prediction which might be of use to magazine and newspaper readers. The real difficulty is that no general magazine editor would be likely to allow an astrologer sufficient space to try one out; an easy table would have to be provided by which the reader could discover his Ascendant; and even then the prediction possible would be very vague.[1]

More often than not, and despite Naylor's success, newspaper astrologers have been spectacularly wrong in predicting national and international events; another blow for mundane astrological theory. During the war, naturally, there was great interest in knowing how things were likely to go; and astrologers often made general predictions about the various theatres of war. In September 1941, *Picture Post* turned its attentions to these forecasts. Its article, and a subsequent one, was prompted by the publication in the *New Statesman and Nation* of an article based on the Mass-Observation findings, which revealed that 'nearly two-thirds of the adult population takes "some interest" in astrological prediction as it is practised in various newspapers, particularly Sunday newspapers'.

Picture Post suspected that astrology was perhaps even more important than the Mass-Observation report suggested: 'Newspaper astrology,' wrote its reporter, 'has provided the main

[1] But see p. 190.

antidote to the harshness of this war's reality. It has taken the place
of the big drums, flags and mob oratory of the last war.' A large
claim, which on the whole was unsubstantiated. The reporter then
went on to examine two years of forecasts by five astrologers,
scoring points for successes (often very generously: Nostradamus
II, of *Old Moore's Almanack*, was awarded points for predicting
the war when, in August 1939, he wrote: 'The outlook is extremely dark, but a ray of light appears, notably in the horoscope
of Mussolini.'!)

Gypsy Petulengro of the *Sunday Chronicle* emerged from the
test ahead of his competitors; and the front page of the *Sunday
Chronicle* duly publicised the fact – omitting, however, to point
out that although the Gypsy had indeed scored 13 points, the total
possible score would have been 45; so that his result was less than
sensational. When a *Picture Post* reader pointed this out, the
editor retaliated by quoting Petulengro's column for the Sunday
before Hess's unexpected arrival in England. The Gypsy's column
had stated: 'Hitler's right-hand man will die this week.' 'That was
a pretty good plunge,' wrote the *Sunday Chronicle*'s editor,
J. W. Drawbell, 'but what he actually wrote in his copy was
"Hitler's right-hand man will be *lost* this week". The word "lost"
puzzled the sub-editor, who queried it. After discussion it was
difficult to define what was meant by "lost", and the word "die"
was substituted.'

A week or so later, *Picture Post* covered a Foyle's literary lunch-
eon at which there was a splendidly contentious clash between
R. H. Naylor and Gypsy Petulengro, the former stating that no
modern astrologer would make 'the absurd claim that the stars
influenced mankind'; while the Gypsy said that he firmly believed
that 'the stars ruled the destiny of mankind and nations'. 'Only in
denouncing their critics as an ill-informed, ill-natured collection of
busy-bodies and spoil-sports are the newspaper astrologers generally agreed,' said *Picture Post*, summing up.

However, the fact remained, and remains, that newspaper and
magazine editors cannot do without their astrological columnists.
A pool taken by the Opinion Research Centre and published in
the *Sunday Times* in 1968, concluded that 68 per cent of
the population read their horoscopes, and 19 per cent be-

lieve that 'there is something in it'. Of the male population, 53 per cent read the horoscope columns; but of that percentage only 11 per cent believe that any attention need be paid to what is said. Of the 77 per cent of women who read the columns, 26 per cent of them pay more or less serious attention. The proportions break down interestingly into class sectors: 70 per cent of the 'unskilled working class' follow their stars; 58 per cent of the 'professional and managerial' class also read the astrology columns; and, rather surprisingly perhaps, no less than 77 per cent of the population between the ages of twenty-one and twenty-four regularly read the forecasts. The readers within that age group seem in fact twice as likely as the middle-aged readers to take their horoscopes seriously.

These figures are reflected in the heavy sales of astrological magazines: magazines such as *Your Horoscope Guide*, by Eva Petulengro, and *Prediction*, edited by Olivia Malthouse. No astrological magazine could survive by relying on the serious interpretation and explanation of the astrological theory. The popular astrological magazines are riddled with the occult, with magic and superstition. One issue of Eva Petulengro's magazine, for instance, has contained articles on ghosts, the interpretation of dreams, and 'growing some flowering plants to attract the good influences of the planets ruling each of the Zodiacal signs'! *Prediction*, on a slightly more serious level, might interpret the Charts of Victoria and Albert, carry an article about the Tarot ... but also examine faith-healing and ghosts. The advertisement columns reflect this approach. Most of the advertisers are in fact clairvoyants or mediums, Red Indian seers or palmists or 'psychical readers'.

Of all 'astrological' magazines, the best known must be *Old Moore's Almanack*, which was founded in 1697, and has been published every year since – for the last half-century by Foulsham's of Slough. Its circulation in England is a registered 1,300,000. It appears also in Australian, Canadian and American editions.

The almanack is on sale at the recommended price of sixpence at most newsagents, and for as much as they can raise by various other street and door-to-door distributors round the country. It undoubtedly has a strong hold on the imagination. Most people have seen it about since they were children, with its familiar archaic cover:

> *Dr Francis Moore's Almanack ... Prophetic Hieroglyphic Engravings ... Weather Guide ... Sun and Moon Tables ... Fairs ... Flat and Chase Race winners ... Your Birthday Forecast ... Pools Forecast ...*

Whatever the value of the Almanack astrologically, the advertisements are fairly scurrilous. From two addresses in Polperro one is offered images of Joan the Wad and her consort Jack o' Lantern. One pound will bring one the Talisman of Solomon the King; ten shillings, a *genuine* four-leaf clover. A thirty-five shilling touchstone will ease oppressive thoughts, and while a medicated cream without hormones is beautifying one's breasts, one may consult a Magic Crystal, bought in a case with a guide containing full instructions, for a mere fifty shillings.

On its astrological side, *Old Moore* opens with a general summary of what the coming year will bring: '1970 – The Year of Confrontation'. This is written, as are the more detailed predictions for each month, and more or less detailed predictions for each Sun-sign (significantly headed 'Your personal *fortune* and guide') by the same professional astrologer, whose identity Foulsham's decline to reveal. He does not seem to be spectacularly successful, and where his forecasts are accurate, this tends to be because they are general. For 1970, for instance, he predicted that the pound would periodically be shaken up by foreign speculation; that the Russians would step up their avowed aim, world conquest; that 'trades unions everywhere will use every means for getting better terms for their members'; that farm workers would agitate for higher wages; that bickering would continue between the Jews and Arabs. On the other hand, in the monthly predictions the astrologer does give the sources of his opinions, so that anyone with a working knowledge of astrology can follow his arguments.

One will not find the kind of political (or personal) astrology printed in *Old Moore* in the more serious astrological magazines, which circulate among professional astrologers – such magazines as the *Astrological Journal* of the English Association, *Les cahiers astrologiques* in France, or *Kosmobiologie* in Germany.

The *Cahiers*, which was founded in 1938 and is consistently serious in approach, has often been the first to publish news of the latest astrological developments, the latest experiments; and while until recently it was only available in French, during 1970 an English edition appeared. *Kosmobiologie* was founded in 1928 by Reinhold Ebertin; but it existed – and exists – in the main to publish the arguments and opinions of Ebertin and his followers, 'cosmobiologists' who often disagree fundamentally with the principles of other European astrologers.

The *Astrological Journal* circulates to members of the Astrological Association as its house journal. Edited by John Addey, it was published first in 1958, and prints not only theoretical articles and examinations of various Birth Charts, but technical and speculative articles and reviews, as well as often controversial correspondence. It is a magazine on a high level.

The United States does not seem at present to have a periodical of equal standard. The most consistent is probably the *Bulletin of the American Federation of Astrologers*, a duplicated 'lunar monthly' for Federation members, first published in 1939. Often there are interesting articles by well known American astrologers; but – partly because of its appearance, and partly due perhaps to somewhat slack editorial control – it has an amateur air.

The *Astrological Magazine* of India, a monthly, is edited by Bangalore Venkata Raman, and has been published for over half a century. It is very different from its Western counterparts, simply because of the different attitudes of Eastern and Western astrologers. (The terminology, too, is different.) Mr Raman includes in his magazine, for instance, an airways guide for each month, which day by day points out the astrological significators for journeys. On September 20, 1967, for instance, he warned that travellers should expect 'Marana Yoga throughout the day and night. Avoid all journeys especially towards the north'.

There are hints for farmers: 'September 18, Asterism good only for purchase of cattle and putting up water lifts. Otherwise keep to routine.' And there is personal advice – a sort of kindly astrological aunts' column: 'When will I meet my guru again?' asks one correspondent, sending his own and the guru's birth date. Or, 'Is there any indication for divorce or reconciliation with the present wife, or second marriage?'

Many of the notes in the magazine are such as Western astrologers would not, or could not ethically write. The feature articles are serious, but again different in tone from those in Western magazines. There are different astrological terms, a different layout of Birth Charts, and so on.

A potentially most valuable astrological magazine which began publication in 1968, is *Kósmos*, published by the International Society for Astrological Research, whose headquarters are in Ohio. The magazine sets out (as does the Society itself) to be international in character. It succeeds, although the standard of its contents has been variable. Its editor, Julienne P. Sturm (who is also President and Executive Secretary of the Society) at first had an insufficiently firm editorial hand, so that some of the articles in the first three or four issues were coy and winsome (about the activities of ISAR's mascot, a puppy born at the time of the Society's conception; or reprinting the reactions of a group of young school-children to an astrological talk). Within the last year, however, the magazine has printed some very interesting data.

Mass-Observation's 1941 report stated:

There is not clear in the general mind of the ordinary reader of newspapers, the distinction between the 'official' astrologer and the newspaper horoscope astrologer. The general attitude is that of semi-seriousness, lacking the full belief of a religion. There is throughout astrology a strong emphasis on the future. ... The ordinary person can still find in astrology a means of integrating and explaining all sorts of happenings, and so persuading himself or herself, as it more often tends to be, that *she* is born under a lucky star and that no harm can come. ...

It is just this attitude that sells the popular astrological/occult magazines; and against which the serious journals are so clearly directed.

IX

The Professionals

For the two hundred years or so up to the time of Alan Leo (who by 1898 had become a full-time professional) it would have been extremely difficult for anyone to make a reasonable living as an astrologer. Leo succeeded partly because by the time he had acquired the necessary techniques, the general interest in astrology in England was reviving; and partly because he mass-produced astrological analyses by a method still used by a number of hard-worked professionals. He became, with the help of a staff (by the turn of the century he employed nine people), a sort of one-man computer. He had been writing analyses for some time, and had filed away separate sheets of paragraphs describing the effects on the personality of certain astrological indications.

By the time he was well established, and advertisements were bringing in a number of clients, he was able simply to calculate the Birth Chart, and then instruct his assistants to remove from the files the sheets setting out the effects of Sun-sign A, Ascendant B, Mid-Heaven C, and so on – clip them together, and post them off. The resemblance to a computer is obvious; although of course the scale is different. Katina Theodossiou fed in over 40,000 separate items of astrological information when she programmed a computer for an American firm, in New York. Leo's system, like the modern computer's, must break down at the point where the astrologer's personal knowledge of the client is necessary for problem advice, or the comparison of charts for marriage, for instance.

Leo charged one shilling for his vestigial test horoscope, and it has been said[1] that within three years of inaugurating his system, he had sent out over 20,000 horoscopes. Few professionals today could rival this output and indeed the demand for bastard horoscopes of this type has much diminished. The top-ranking astrologers, however, are able to make a very comfortable living, and might be able to do so simply by serving individual clients – apart from their many other interests.

Certainly a professional in every sense of the word, John Naylor deals with individual cases, but also has a multiplicity of journalistic enterprises. Mr Naylor followed his father, R. H. Naylor, into astrology. He originally studied to become an electrical engineer, but during the war he suffered from tuberculosis, and during the months of enforced idleness, he studied astrology. After his cure he became a full-time astrologer.

It takes him, he says, about an hour and a half to prepare one analysis, and he has been known to prepare as many as five in eight hours, which at twelve guineas a time would make for a reasonable income even without his journalistic activities. These include the preparation of the year-book *Your stars*, which he publishes himself, and which sells 40,000 copies in this country; and *Your luck*, which sells 30,000 in England. Both handbooks sell 60,000 copies in America. Corgi Books have distributed over two and a half million of Mr Naylor's books in the US and 100,000 in the UK. So perhaps it is not surprising that he felt justified in devoting a couple of pages in *Your stars for 1969* to a violent attack on the Labour government's 'punitive taxation policy'; there was only one glancing reference to astrology in the article, which was called 'Taxation won't solve our problems'.

Mr Naylor's charges for 'special personal services' are set out in a printed leaflet, on which a secretary types in red lettering (no doubt necessarily) the words ALL FEES PAYABLE IN ADVANCE. For a personal consultation the charge is three guineas; for a problem analysis, two guineas. Delineation and forecast comes in two grades: one for seven guineas, one for twelve.

'An increasing number of thinking people,' writes Mr Naylor, 'are ordering these typescript notes which will give a clear picture

[1] Ellic Howe, *Urania's children* (William Kimber, 1967).

of the indications regarding Character and Abilities, Business Relationships, Your Career . . . Also a five-year forecast, with one year in detail, and answer to special queries or problems.' For a further forecast ('Many clients order a further forecast or one year's directions each year') the charge is another six or ten guineas; and 'for the parents anxious to help their child towards a happy and useful life, an outline of the indications regarding Character, Education, Marriage, Health, Family Relationships, the Future, is of great help' – seven guineas. In a final note, Mr Naylor reminds one that the date, hour and town of birth are necessary; but that if the hour is not known, a photograph, a 'list of dates and nature of several important events during your lifetime', should be enclosed instead. This is to enable him to 'rectify' the Birth Chart.

Mr Naylor's twelve-guinea report comes neatly typed and bound in a printed cover. On the inside cover is a note explaining in very simple terms the nature of the Birth Chart, which is later drawn in full. There follows another printed page setting out the positions of the Sun, Moon and planets in straightforward language: 'The Zodiacal sign Pisces is on the Ascendant or Eastern Horizon . . . the Sun is in the sign Gemini; the Moon is in the sign Pisces', etc. Then comes the Birth Chart itself (though without the angles drawn in), and a diagram setting out the major aspects.

The analysis is interleaved at each section, and ends with a final printed page detailing the aspects of life and experience associated with each House (Fifth House: children, love affairs, hobbies; Twelfth House: enemies, imprisonment, secrets), and a key to the symbols used. There is also a duplicated but personally signed Special Note:

This concludes my attempt to analyse some of the indications in your horoscope. I hope that what I have said will prove accurate and will give useful help in planning out your life and affairs.

Your horoscope and case history are always kept carefully filed and ready for immediate reference. If I can ever be of further service to you, either in giving specific advice and guidance on problems which crop up from time to time, or in preparing further notes when these expire, I shall always be happy to hear from you.

If you are sufficiently interested, and wish to make fuller use of astrological guidance, it is always possible to obtain more detailed extensions of the foregoing notes. A more detailed forecast can be made for any desired further period, showing the influences operating month by month – or even day by day.

Please address your correspondence to me and mark it PERSONAL, and it will then receive my immediate and confidential attention.

It is easy to see why Mr Naylor is one of the most successful professional astrologers in the country. Apart from its intrinsic interest and merit, his work is properly presented; decently bound, and typed; he has tried to show that his interest is a personal one. Alas, other professional astrologers are not as careful. Analyses arrive badly typed, uncorrected, unbound, clipped together with a single pin.

Mr Naylor considers that the primary function of astrology is predictive. Prediction quickly and usefully applied can be of the greatest help in the spheres of medicine and economics in particular, he alleges; and certainly there is evidence to support him.

As to the *particulars* of prediction, he is less assertive. One hundred per cent efficiency in prediction would be supernatural; he is happy simply to aim at a percentage efficiency. The rôle of astrology, he feels, is not to 'tell all', but 'to issue guide-lines'. He is happy for a client simply to know that a coming phase in his life will be either positive or negative. He says that he keeps an eye on the psychological effect upon his client of what he writes.

'People criticise astrologers for always looking on the positive side,' he says, 'but this is psychologically very valuable and necessary. One must be cheerful.'

Ingrid Lind, an ex-professional singer, came more recently to astrology than John Naylor. Her interest in the subject stemmed from a similar interest on the part of an aunt, 'an instinctive Theosophist', who believed firmly in reincarnation (as Miss Lind does), and felt that the frustrations she suffered in her life were the result of a former incarnation as a rake. This aunt left Miss Lind a library of astrological books when she died at the end of the Second World War, and a gradually increasing interest led Miss Lind to take the course of the Faculty of Astrological Studies, whose diploma she received in 1952. By now she has written close on 5,000 individual analyses, and is 'utterly convinced of the basic validity of astrological technique'.

She has done a certain amount of 'public' work. She wrote an article for the *Guardian*[1] in which she studied the Birth Charts of Lord Butler, Sir Alec Douglas-Home, Quintin Hogg and Reginald Maudling. When she looked at these, she was puzzled to see that Lord Butler's immediate future seemed to be pleasant and tranquil, whereas the other Conservative party leaders seemed to go through an extremely difficult time until at least 1967. In the event, a short time after her article appeared, Lord Butler retired from active political life and returned to academic life.

Miss Lind is mainly interested in the psychological aspects of astrology. 'If there is a framework of potentials out of which the individual cannot step, then let him accept this and make maximum use of his life,' she says. 'As St Paul said, it is silly to "kick against the pricks"; for some the lesson of life is to handle success; for others, the lesson may be to cope successfully with frustration.'

The work I commissioned from Miss Lind was less efficiently presented than Mr Naylor's, being an unbound sheaf of papers stapled together at one corner. It included the usual Birth Chart containing relevant details, and a duplicated typed foreword in which Miss Lind explained her attitude to interpretation.

At the end of the report she included some extra duplicated sheets in which she gave some information about the important signs predominating in my chart: 'Geminians are intelligent, quick-witted, lively and versatile ... Pisceans are sensitive, idealistic and emotional ... Virgo individuals are shrewd, discriminative, diplomatic, reserved ...,' etc. I cannot but feel that this might lead to some confusion. Miss Lind makes it clear that 'the total YOU is a blending of these Signs, and no element in the

[1] October 15, 1963.

QA–K

character shown in the Chart cancels another out, however con-
tradictory they may seem to be'. I am not sure how helpful this is
to a client; nor how helpful he is likely to find a list of 'some
suitable occupations' which include no less than twelve careers
under Gemini and Pisces (including anaesthetist, medium, wine
merchant, journalist and secret agent).

But of course the styles of various astrologers appeal to one as do
the styles of various novelists or critics; and if on the whole *I* found
Miss Lind's work somewhat less impressive than that of Mr
Naylor (and both of them rather less interesting than that of Mr
Charles Harvey, who concentrates almost totally on the psychological implications of a Birth Chart), this is not to say that other
people would do so.

As far as I am concerned, the occult interest which permeates
Miss Lind's work is antipathetic. She is one of those people so
convinced of her own belief, and so naturally poised within her
own position, that she evidently finds it extremely difficult to conceive that anyone else is not sensitive to the forces with which she is
so familiar. When, for instance, I attempted to explain how
difficult I found it to take naturally and easily her references to the
occult in general and reincarnation in particular, she pointed out
that it was equally difficult for her to understand my position.
'You see, most of the people I am in contact with naturally accept
these things,' she said.

Miss Lind had a considerable success during 1968, when Granada Television made a film examining her astrological powers.
Although this was not a serious programme in the sense that far
too little time was allowed for discussion, and what discussion took
place was fairly vestigial, it was at least the most serious attempt to
date to treat astrology on television.

For the programme, Miss Lind was presented with the birth
data, and nothing else, of four individuals. I am assured (and
believe) that she knew nothing about the people concerned other
than where and when they were born, their sex, and whether they
were married or single. She drew up the charts, and was allowed
three months in which to consider them (usually, she considers a
chart and writes her reactions down immediately on paper). In
the programme, she was filmed talking about the subjects; and

they were independently filmed, talking about themselves. The films were then inter-cut.

The first subject was a man who, Miss Lind thought, would be a strong, active, courageous type, with an urge to prove himself, and with 'plenty of dramatic intensity'. She felt that he would have been 'destined for rather sensational events', which may have come to head during the war, when she thought he would have served in the navy, seen action in a position of command, and probably been decorated. He would have had 'what might be called "a splendid war" '. At the end of this, he would have got out of the service, gone into business, and probably made plenty of money – but doing what he liked to do. Domestic life would always take second place to his business, although his home life would be happy.

The man in question then described the action, in the Far East, for which – as a naval officer attached to a submarine flotilla – he had won the V.C. After the war, he had formed a company engaged in commercial diving, and eventually a second company specifically to work in connection with the North Sea gas enterprise. He felt he was not very good with money, but very good at organisation; he was away from home a very great deal, but regarded this as inevitable, and said that his wife recognised that his home life must always take second place to business.

The second subject was a woman who, Miss Lind thought, was dedicated to a career, which seemed to involve administration; she might perhaps look after an hotel – there was a strong indication that she 'looked after' people. Her health could suffer because of over-involvement with other people's worries, and although her early home background would have been happy, there were indications of difficulties in her domestic life.

The woman was in fact a welfare officer; her husband felt that the responsibilities of her work were affecting her health. Her parents had been divorced when she was seven; she had married at twenty, but was divorced; was now happily remarried, but felt that she was domestically 'not an easy person to get along with'.

The third subject Miss Lind felt to be a commanding personality – clever, original, way-out, with enormous self-confidence and the ability to project himself well. The focus of his life would

be his 'big' way of expressing himself. His career should be in
sensational entertainment.

The subject described himself as 'one of Britain's top showmen
– another Barnum'. He was indeed extraordinarily extrovert: 'I
give the public anything of a sensational nature,' he said; he had
organised the public showing of Leatherslade Farm, the great
train robbers' hide-out; he had exhibited people who were buried
alive, marathon piano-players, a vanishing vicar, a vampire who
lived in a coffin. Much of the impact of his character was visual,
and Miss Lind's description of him was recognisably accurate.

The final subject was more sketchily presented: she had, said
Miss Lind, the feeling of 'being at the top', which might be the
product of a family background; she felt the need to escape and
run her own life, but might make some mistakes doing it. She was
perhaps typical of the people born between 1941 and 1943, who
tended to seek way-out things, wanted to 'break out of the feeling
of materiality'.

The subject, the wife of a man with whom she ran a shop in the
King's Road, Chelsea, said that she had been brought up 'in an
aristocratic family' with no need to worry. She now felt however,
that she needed to get away from the city, and often went to
Glastonbury to experience the feeling of remoteness there, and of
legend. She hated the thought of being confined within a material
world.

Miss Lind prefaced her remarks, in each case, with a physical
sketch of the subject, which if not spectacularly accurate was at
least never totally inaccurate; and it was noticeable that the subjects often used precisely the same phrases, when describing themselves, as Miss Lind.

A short discussion displayed the usual anti-astrological
prejudices. A psychiatrist admitted that there had been 'what appeared at first glance to be one or two – not many more than that –
one or two interesting "hits" '; but after that the discussion was
even-tempered, at least, and was perhaps (from the producer's
point of view) almost too placid. The psychiatrist accused Miss
Lind of being right about the V.C. but of not specifically describing the submariner's present occupation of deep-sea diving. To
which Miss Lind replied that she was not a magician, and could

not possibly make statements as specific as those the psychiatrist demanded.

The programme probably did some good; if it was no more than an illustrated party game (for Miss Lind was only asked, really, to demonstrate a feat of astrological conjuring, not to answer serious questions or suggest ways of combating special problems), at least it was seriously conducted, and on a certain level, convincing.

Other television programmes in England dealing with astrology, usually in passing, have been heavily biased. Light relief, rather than serious thinking, has been expected of the astrologer. When Patrick Moore, the well known amateur astronomer, presented a programme in the series 'One pair of eyes', he and the programme's producer seemed to me faintly dismayed and surprised that my wife, who appeared in the programme, should show a real interest in her subject, should appear reasonably normal, should have studied astronomy and the history of her subject, and should possess neither a set of bead curtains nor a crystal ball.

In Mr Naylor and Miss Lind one has the middle-of-the-road 'general practitioners' of astrology; the equivalent of the sound osteopath, with perhaps slightly unconventional methods, but an admirable general knowledge of medicine in general. Mr Woodruff on the other hand perhaps more closely resembles the fair-ground faith-healer whose panache and general good humour make him good value for money.

But of course in the background, unknown to the general public, there are astrologers like the late Charles Carter, spending their lives not as practising astrologers, but in correlating astrological material and writing textbooks; or in forming new theories of astrology and seeking evidence to support them.

John Addey, for instance, is one of those astrologers who has been concerned recently to discover some proper scientific basis for his subject; he has evolved a theory which he feels is so important as to lead perhaps to a radical rethinking of much current astrological theory, and which he supports by statistical and other evidence considerable enough to make it at least of substantial interest. After working for some years, he first presented his findings in an article in *Astrology* in 1958, 'The search for the scientific starting-point'; followed in 1961 by an article in the *Astrological Journal* which he entitled 'The discovery of the scientific starting-point': the titles speak for themselves.

Addey studied initially the Birth Charts of 970 nonagenarians, and later the nativities of 1,280 sufferers from paralytic polio-myelitis; subsequently, he has applied the methods he has evolved to the birthdates of 4,465 clergymen and to 7,302 doctors of medicine. He has shown, to his own satisfaction, at least, that all astrological effects are based on the harmonics of cosmic periods, or as he sometimes says, 'the harmonics of symbolic circles of re-lationships'.

His ideas are not easy to explain, and indeed are complex enough to make a summary both difficult and in the end tan-talising. But they are undoubtedly important – perhaps as import-ant as any astrological theories expressed in the past two or three hundred years.

In each solar year of $365\frac{1}{4}$ days, the Sun appears to move once around the circle of the ecliptic, passing at a fairly constant speed through the 360° of the Zodiac. As far as astrologers are con-cerned, it starts on March 21 at 0° Aries, and ends at the same point a year later. For the layman, the point the Sun reaches at any given day is represented by the date; for astrologers, by the degree of the ecliptic.

If one takes the dates of birth of a large group of people – say, clergymen or doctors – who have something in common (their predisposition to their careers) – and studies the position of the Sun on those dates, one can hope to find whether that type of person tends to be born at a certain time of year; the evidence will be provided by the *distribution* of the Sun around the circle of its annual path. In studying the position of the Sun in the Charts of the 7,302 doctors, it was found that the distribution of their dates of birth seemed to follow a certain pattern which could be de-scribed by superimposing waves of different length around the circle of the ecliptic. (Addey points out that of course all such distribution-patterns may be described in this way, no matter how random they may be; but that the test of the signficance of the distribution is measured by conventional statistical processes well known to statisticians.)

In the case of the doctors (and similar wave-patterns were observed when other groups of like-minded people were similarly studied) Addey began by showing that there was a wave of 30° in length which 'described' their birth-date positions. That is to say that a wave was distributed about the ecliptic with twelve peaks, corresponding to the twelve signs of the Zodiac. Addey did not expect there to be a 'wave' of any kind when the experiment started; he simply observed that one existed – and that more doctors tended to be born at the 'peak' of the wave than in its trough; the graph of the distribution of births actually revealed the steady rise and fall of the wave. If the number of births which occurred in the negative half of the wave was subtracted from the number of cases in the positive half, the difference was 346.

The significance of the words 'the difference' may not be immediately apparent. But if one were to spin a penny 7,302 times, one would expect (more or less) an even number of 'heads' and 'tails'. If the penny came down substantially more often 'heads' than 'tails', one would begin to suspect that some other factor than chance was operating. And if one spun, say, five or six pennies seven or eight hundred times, and the same trend towards 'heads' was observable, one would suspect . . . well, what? Certainly that some outside force was intervening, whether material (a disparate distribution of metal due to the design of the coin, perhaps) or psychic.

The key-word of the argument is 'significance'. Statistically, a 'difference' of 346 in a total of 7,302 *is* significant – to the extent of 5,000–1; and when Addey goes on to claim a similarly significant 'difference' when examining other totals, one has to take some sort of notice.

But his experiment with the doctors' Birth Charts did not end with the discovery of the 30° wave. He found that if he imposed the 30° wave on to another of 60° in length, and if the total number of cases in the negative half of this wave were then subtracted from the number of cases in the positive half, the difference was 262; a statistical significance of over 3,000–1 against chance. It is this 60° wave which is the basis of Addey's belief that he has rediscovered a theory which may have been prevalent in the ancient days of astrology – a theory far more integral, flexible and penetrating than that of today's astrologers.

The six waves, each with a positive and negative phase, correspond to twelve signs of the Zodiac, equally negative and positive in character. But Addey feels that modern astrologers (and 'modern' in this context is obviously a relative term) place far too much emphasis on the number twelve – twelve signs, twelve houses, twelve main aspects – whereas in fact this number is only slightly more important than other numbers. In the nativities of the doctors, for instance, the pattern is a wave of $2°$ in length – the 180th harmonic of the ecliptic, as Addey puts it. The alternative degrees of the Zodiac 'tend to show high and low totals'. In every one of the twelve conventional zodiacal signs, even-numbered degrees outnumber odd-numbered degrees, and the total difference is 256 cases; another statistical difference in excess of 300–1 against the effects appearing by chance.

> These high statistical levels of significance [Addey points out] can be multiplied many times from this one set of data alone, and this is only based on the Sun's position in the ecliptic. There are many other circles of relationship – the relation of the planets to the Zodiac, to each other, to their daily revolution of the heavens; all of which show their characteristic harmonic patterns for each class of horoscope.

Addey and his co-worker Peter Roberts have examined their theory again and again. At the least, they have produced certain apparently significant patterns from the study of a large number of Birth Charts – patterns which would not seem to have been capable of revelation by any other current astrological methodology, although they tie in with some other results obtained by other means – notably by Michel Gauquelin.

Addey claims that his discovery 'will not only increase the scope and accuracy of astrology a hundredfold, but also make its demonstration in statistical terms a simple matter'.

Katina Theodossiou, whose forename is the trade mark of various enterprises, has turned her attention recently with great success to various forms of business enterprise. She is a well known newspaper astrologer, defending her columns with enthusiasm.

She advises various business houses, and most recently has helped to set up the most elaborate of the growing number of firms producing horoscopes by use of a computer.

Katina had felt for some time that it should be possible to use a computer in astrology, and was approached by a group of New York businessmen who suggested that it should be possible to programme a computer so that it could perform the necessary arithmetical calculations and arrive at the positions and angles of the planets; and put together information which would result in a complete horoscope in reasonable detail.

With two mathematicians and six IBM-trained programmers, she worked for over fifteen months for about eighteen hours a day, devising the material with which the computer should be programmed. In the end she had prepared something like 40,000 separate paragraphs applicable to various zodiacal circumstances. Each paragaph had to be applicable also to any type of person; and each had to be capable of joining to each in every conceivable permutation of the total. The semantic problems were enormous, and the work obviously extremely arduous – although before anyone claims that it is definitive (and Katina would certainly not claim this herself) it should be remembered that it has been calculated that a conservative estimate of possible astrological combinations in one chart is in excess of 539,370,750 plus thirty o's!

The financiers concerned in the business in New York were, one gathers, increasingly disturbed by what they regarded as an unusual amount of time spent in the preparation; they were no doubt ultimately comforted by the success of the project when the computer got under way – the financial success, at any rate. By the beginning of 1969, about 10,000 horoscopes a week were being turned out by the machine, providing an income of $120,000 a week. At the time of writing, a branch of this enterprise has opened in London, although apparently with less immediate success.

The astrological value of this and similar systems is extremely doubtful. Although it is claimed that only $1\frac{1}{2}$ per cent of the total number of clients take advantage of a firm 'money-back' guarantee, it is fairly obvious that no computer can give at present as complete consideration to a chart as a human astrologer; and there have been more or less violent attacks on computer systems by various conventional astrologers – perhaps the most lively being that mounted by Olive Adele Pryor at the 1968 Seattle Convention of the American Federation of Astrologers.

Nearly two years ago [she said] a group of computer experts invited me to a conference regarding the delineation of a horoscope by computer. These men were ethical, and wanted to know if a helpful 'in depth' job of delineation could be done by computers – no flim-flam thing, but a real public service. Computers had been used for the maths necessary to erect a Chart, so this presented no problem; but delineation is an art, and that is another story. When these experts realised that astrologers dealt with ten planets, twelve signs, twelve sign rulers and twenty-four decanate rulers; with three types of houses; that much depended on the grouping of the planets, etc.; the dignity, debility and exaltation, etc. of the planets in different signs; they quickly figured out that no computer could carry the number of digits which would be required for the answer, and therefore the accuracy of the analysis of the Chart would be questionable.

(In fact computers existed in 1966 perfectly capable of dealing with the necessary computations; Miss Pryor was misinformed.)

An acquaintance, a businessman, came to Miss Pryor a few months after her discussion with the 'computer experts', and gave her his chart; she saw immediately that he was probably a diabetic, as indeed proved to be the case. A year later he sent for a computer analysis advertised by post. The analysis was subsequently printed in the AFA *Bulletin*. Miss Pryor commented that 'it is lacking in specific detail, and, as you will see, could and did work a great deal of harm to this man, who himself was an astrologer and quite a good one. Many of the computer's conclusions are inaccurate and verge on the fraudulent ... at best they are irresponsible.' She pointed out that the analysis put forward 'phases of special interest' in the client's life between his sixty-third and seventy-seventh years; he died in fact in 1968 at the age of fifty-six. There was a fairly detailed reference to his health, but no mention of possible diabetes – though this was quite plainly indicated in his chart. Miss Pryor would have expected his fatal illness, and could have placed it accurately in time; but there was no hint of any danger in the computer's analysis, and she had reason to believe that the subject was influenced by the computer analysis in not taking more care of his health before his death. Miss Pryor actually accused the firm concerned of 'using the US mails to defraud'.

Spirited though her attack is, it begs several questions. Would a human astrologer really have more readily seen the signs of a fatal illness in the Chart than a computer? If so, why did the client ('himself an astrologer, and quite a good one') not do so?

There is no indication which computer service Miss Pryor was accusing of skimping; there is no doubt that the service programmed by Katina Theodossiou is the most thorough of those currently in use; beside it, the Astroflash system in use in Paris is extremely limited. Astroflash (or Ordinastral, as it is called in France) was programmed by the distinguished French astrologer André Barbault – a witty writer and an astrologer who is much admired. He programmed the computer with much less information than that fed by Katina into the American system. Under the aegis of Roger Berthier, who conceived the idea, the computer was eventually set up just off the Champs Elysées, where clients could watch the horoscope being tapped out in front of them. The business had begun in Le Mesnil le Roi in 1967; by February 1969 it was processing eight hundred horoscopes a day at ten francs each. Subsequently, Astroflash opened in Grand Central Station, New York (where at the time of writing it continues to prosper). In November 1969 it opened a stall in an amusement arcade in Piccadilly Circus. But the clientele of the amusement arcade proved unwilling to pay £2 for a horoscope, and with computer time costing the licensee, Mr Bruce Eckert, £90 a day, the stall soon closed. Mr Eckert subsequently told the *Financial Times* that when he was in Paris negotiating for a licence to use the system, he had fed his own birth data into the Astroflash computer. 'If you are contemplating signing any contracts at this time,' the machine remarked, 'don't.'

The Ordinastral or Astrolash analysis provides a well drawn

Birth Chart and detailed planetary positions; but explains that 'your portrait was drawn up from the positions of the Sun, Moon, Mercury and Venus and ... the sign of the Ascendant'. It is, therefore, really extremely limited; and additionally, the English translation of the French original is stilted and sometimes illiterate – if amusing. I was informed, for instance, that I had 'long dreamed of a delicate affection of a slightly baroque nature'.

Various smaller and astrologically insignificant schemes have made their appearance from time to time, and made considerable sums of money for their sponsors. One quite large scheme, started in London in 1969, was so thinly based that it took no account of the necessary allowances for British Summer Time, and therefore quite often got *everything* slightly wrong. Other schemes provided perhaps some amusement, but of a fair ground nature. At Harrods' 'Way In' boutique and subsequently at Selfridges, in 1969 and 1970, one could deposit one's birth date (not time or place) at a counter, with seven-and-sixpence, and after some hic-coughing from an impressive piece of machinery (which looked like a computer but was really only a printing machine) receive a short 'Electronic Personality Probe'. This had been devised (I was assured by a gentleman whose face, as far as I could judge from a telephone conversation, was straight) by astrologers and a team of psychologists with a view to offering serious astro-psychological help to clients!

Computers may in future be able to provide the answer to large-scale astrological queries, by correlating evidence on a vast scale. If the astrological theory can indeed apply to weather, earth-movements, other natural phenomena (or for that matter to the movement of stocks and shares), a computer could obviously be used to make such information quickly and accurately available.

Human astrologers are working, as I have said, in business. Katina Theodossiou became interested in business astrology soon after the war. She was asked to set up a chart for a businessman who was considering a merger. She did so, and with the help of a Belgian astrologer who had been doing business astrology, worked on the problem. This gave her a taste for business astrology in general. Gradually, she began doing her own research. She sub-scribed to the *Financial Times*, the *Stock Exchange Gazette*; and after a while the movement of stocks and shares began to make astrological sense. She acquired the *Stockbrokers' Directory* and found out more about the identity of companies – when they were formed and incorporated; she chose nine or ten and watched them carefully. She now works in an advisory capacity for over fifty companies, some of them bearing internationally known names. There is an initial basic fee of 100 guineas for a consultation at which she collects the information she requires about the company and its officers; she then works on various charts and eventually gets a good general picture of the company's astrological personality. She is then in a position to give advice on particular contingencies, for which her fee may be from 25 guineas upwards.

It is difficult to produce evidence about this aspect of astrology. Astrologers are ethically bound not to reveal clients' names, and the clients themselves are not eager to do so (presumably fearing the effect of the revelation on the price of shares). Businessmen are simply not willing to confirm that they employ an astrologer – even if rival businessmen (as is sometimes the case) are retaining the same man! In fact, an astrologer is often retained semi-privately by a member of the board of a company, and the accounts will show his fees as paid to 'a business consultant'. He will sometimes be brought the astrological data of two or three companies with which mergers are under consideration, and will have to inspect the charts of the members of rival boards, and of the companies themselves, before advising on a take-over. He will have to advise, also, a propitious time to make contact, and for the signing of papers. Attempts to discover the birth data of board members and executives, and the times of signing of contracts, are perhaps an unlikely aspect of business espionage!

All this no doubt sounds ludicrous and lunatic to anyone who has had no experience of business astrology; and although I am prepared to concede a sort of joint company personality discernible from the charts of the board, I find it difficult to understand the astrological conception of a company chart based on the time of incorporation.

But the general attitude of astrologers to business astrology is varied. Denis Bartlett, for instance, has met regularly with stockbroker friends over a number of years to discuss general moves of the market, and believes that these are in fact geared to the weather and its cycles – dull weather will result in a heavy, sluggish market; good weather in a lively, expansive one.

Of course there are other theories. During the first world war, a Mr J. A. Crabtree of Walsall did a great deal of research on world trends in business – among other things, studying the iron prices in the United States from the time of the Napoleonic Wars up to 1900. He discerned three cycles – 'price cycle' active for forty years; a 'prosperity cycle' for ten years; and a 'trade cycle' which seemed active over forty months.

Mr L. I. Hunt, a businessman who has studied business forecasting since 1930, claims that by using Crabtree's cycles it would have been possible accurately to forecast the depressions of 1921 and 1931, and the better periods of 1925–7 and 1935–7. Hunt himself claims to have predicted various slumps, and also the period of general prosperity in 1956–7. 'Crabtree's Cycles,' he wrote, 'have proved to be a good general long-term guide to the state of the country's economy, and on the whole rather more reliable than some Government (and other) economic forecasts.'[1]

In an article written in 1965, Mr Hunt predicted a minor boom in 1966, followed by 'a serious depression centreing on 1971'. His prediction does not seem at the time of writing to be impossibly wrong.

Crabtree's cycles were not in fact astrological in nature; but when Mr Hunt began to study astrology in 1953, he examined the actions of Saturn and Uranus in particular; Saturn has a cycle of $29\frac{1}{4}$ years (similar to Crabtree's 'price cycle'), and Uranus a cycle of 84 years. Mr Hunt found that on the whole, taking into consideration the action of Jupiter as well, the main aspects of the two planets corresponded with the Crabtree Cycles, and with major fluctuations in world business activity observed over some years.

He concluded that 'it is abundantly clear that, whatever may be the underlying reasons for it, there has been a significant relationship between the movements of the three planets studied and the periods of prosperity and depression which have occurred during the past forty-five years'.

[1] *Astrological Journal*, vol. VI, No. 4 (Autumn 1965).

X

The Planets and the Weather

A correspondence between the weather and the movements of the Sun and Moon is too obvious not to have been formulated as soon as man had the power of thought; and the connection between the phases of the Moon and the sea tides is perhaps not much less subtle. Power over terrestrial weather was eventually attributed to other planets as well.

The Egyptians noticed that the waters of the Nile rose only once a year, and the Egyptian New Year was set at that time, when the dried earth was revitalised by the apparent intervention of two heavenly bodies. The Babylonian *Anu–Enlil* has a section devoted to weather forecasting: 'If a dark halo surrounds the moon, the month will be cloudy and rainy'; 'If there is thunder in the month of Shebat, there will be a plague of locusts.' It is obvious that it did not occur to man to look elsewhere than to the skies for the signs of the weather which so obviously originated there. If there was to be any signal of what weather was to come, it must be written in the firmament.

One of the fullest early books of instruction in weather forecasting by the use of the planets however was printed in London in 1555 (by 'Thomas Gemini'!) Its title is as charming as it is lengthy:

A PROGNOSTICATION *of right good effect, fructfully augmented contayning playne, briefe, pleaſant, choſen* rules, to iudge the weather for euer, by the *Sunne, Moone, Sterres*

Cometes, Raynbowe, Thunder, Cloudes, with other Extraordinarie tokens, not omitting the *Aſpects* of *Planetes,* with a brefe Iudgemente for euer, of *Plentie, Lacke, Sicknes, Death, Warres* &c. Opening also many *naturall cauſes* woorthy to be knowen, to theſe and others, now at the laſt are adioyned, *diuers generall pleasaunte Tables:* for euer manyfolde wayes profitable, to al maner men of any vnderſtanding: therefore agayne publiſſed by Leonard Dygges Gentylman, in the yeare of oure Lorde. 1555.

The book is a strange mixture of shepherd's lore and astrology:

> If thyck clowdes reſemblying flockes, or rather great heapes of woll, be gathered in many places, they ſhewe rayne [says Mr Gemini convincingly. Or (and I 'translate')] some have observed evil weather to follow when watery fowls leave the sea, desiring land; the fowls of the land flying high; the crying of fowls about waters making a great noise with their wings; also the seas swelling with unaccustomed waves. If beasts eat greedily, if they lick their hooves; if they suddenly move here and there making a noise, breathing up the air with their open nostrils, – rain followeth.

He also makes a brave attempt to explain natural phemonena: 'Of earthquakes, in the most quiet time: Plenty of winds, entered into holes, cones or caves of the earth, which absent from above the earth causeth quietness; the violent bruiting out of them (the earth closed again) is the earthquake.'

But most of the book, as far as natural phenomena are concerned, is plain common sense: Dygges explains eclipses, hail, thunder, quite accurately. And his astrological explanations, whether or not they are dependable, are plain and straightforward:

> The conjunction, quadrature or opposition of the Moon with Saturn in moist signs bringeth a cloudy day, cold air, according to the nature of the sign; if she go from Saturn to the Sun, by conjunction or otherwise, harder weather ensueth. . . . Jupiter in Cancer bringeth calm pleasant weather . . . Venus in Leo, drought . . . Mercury in Libra, winds. . . .

With the coming of the Age of Science, weather forecasting 'by the stars' was only considered a little more ridiculous than the shepherd's warnings which are still used in the country (and which the most advanced meteorologist will accept as more accurate, over local areas, than 'official' forecasting). But more recently, the attitude has begun to change. Sir Bernard Lovell, not a particular friend to astrologers, has written:

> In the last few years, some strange and inexplicable links appear to be emerging between lunar phase, rainfall, meteoric impact, magnetic storms and mental disturbances. It almost seems as though we are moving through a series of scientific fantasies to a proof of ancient beliefs.[1]

And it is many years now since J. S. Haldane pointed out that 'the universe may be not only queerer than we suppose, but queerer than we *can* suppose'.

The influence of the Moon on the earth is certainly not restricted to the movement of the tides; it also embraces the earth's magnetic field and the upper atmosphere. In various parts of the world, meteorologists and scientists have worked on the influence of it and the planets on our weather. Sometimes, they have been utterly hostile to traditional astrology. Sydney Makepeace Wood, an American scientist, for instance, started an article on the subject by stating unequivocally: 'The perpetration of witch-doctor mummery and fantastic nonsense by the astrologers has been a factor in the neglect of the study of tidal and magnetic effects of the planets upon the Sun by those best qualified to give it helpful thought and attention.'[2]

However, some attention has been given to the subject. During the war, for instance, C. A. Mills (Professor of Experimental Medicine at the University of Cincinnati) wrote a paper in the *Bulletin of the American Meteorological Society* entitled, 'Some Possible Relationships of Planetary Configuration and Sunspots to World Weather,'[3] in which he found that 'Sunspots, with the accompanying variations in solar radiation, appear to be the chief

[1] *Sunday Times,* May 15, 1964.
[2] *Illinois Engineer,* March 1949.
[3] *Bulletin of the American Meteorological Society,* April 1941.

indicators of extra-terrestrial force directly affecting our weather, but the sunspots seem to be dominated in turn by planetary forces working upon the Sun'.

The difficulty is that these forces, and their effects on earth's weather, appear to be extremely slight, and so very difficult to study – for the method of investigation naturally has to be statistical. The *effects*, indeed, are so slight and so general (according to the British Meteorological Office) as to be of no value, at least at present, in the forecasting of weather for such relatively small areas of the earth as that covered by the British Isles.

One general view is that the atmospheric 'tides' may be caused by the phases of the Moon in the same way as the tides of the sea. The lunar sea tide is about two-and-a-half times the solar sea tide; and the atmospheric tide is in the same ratio. The heat of the Sun causes certain fluctuations in atmospheric pressure – but the Moon radiates little heat, and so the fluctuations it causes in the Earth's lower atmosphere can only be by gravitation, and the lunar tide observed at Greenwich Observatory has been as faint as 1/100 Hg mm (mercury) – far too minute, it is thought, to have an effect upon the weather.

Yet the Moon's effect upon the *upper* atmosphere seems to be considerable. At Huanacayo, in Peru, there has been measured a lunar tide of forty miles in amplitude in the Appleton (F) ionised layer of the stratosphere. Its effects on the lower atmosphere are not by any means fully understood, but may be important. In this connection, John H. Nelson, working for RCA Communications in the United States, predicts by astrological means storms in the ionosphere which interfere with short-wave radio communication – with an accuracy (recognised by his employers) of 93 per cent.

There have been a great number of monographs on the Moon's effect on rainfall. In 1962, for instance, D. A. Bradley and M. A. Woodbury of New York University and Glenn W. Brier of the Massachusetts Institute of Technology, announced the discovery of a remarkable correlation between the phases of the Moon and rainfall in the United States. E. E. Adderley and E. G. Bowen of the Radiophysics Department of the Commonwealth Scientific and Industrial Research Organisation in Australia arrived independently at similar results for the southern

hemisphere. They concluded that lunar phase alone could account for about 20 per cent of variations in total daily rainfall, and
almost 65 per cent of fluctuations in US rainfall overall. No causal
explanation for the Moon/rainfall relationship was established.
The statistics, dramatic as they are, aroused very little interest
when they were published in England in the *New Scientist* and
Science: perhaps because they had appeared first in an astrological magazine.

Statistical evidence connecting the Moon and rainfall was
nothing new. In 1937, Dr Luis Rodes, Director of the Observatory
of the Ebro, near Tortosa in Spain, had published a monograph
based on the study of twenty years' rainfall statistics. He had found
a slight increase in precipitation when the Moon approached
Earth to its nearest point. In France, Mineur had discovered that
rainfall maximums at Parc St Maur and Nantes, over no less than
170 years, occurred on the third day of the lunar month. In Greece
over 39 years, Carapiperis had notes that thunderstorms occurred
more frequently during the first and new-moon quarters, as well as
when the Moon was at its perigee.

The Moon/rainfall relationship is the lunar influence probably
most examined; but other correlations have been made. In North
Wales Herbert Henstock observed a relationship between the
minimum night temperature and the lunar phase; when he drew
temperature curves for several years, he noted a regular fall in the
minimum night temperature at or near the date of the full Moon
at each lunation. The drop was sudden, and limited to two or
three nights at about that date. Henstock obtained data from
American, Canadian, South African, Australian and Indian
meteorological stations, and found a similar effect. The fall in
temperature varied from four to forty degrees, was greater in
summer, but independent of latitude and height above sea
level.

The Moon is our nearest neighbour, and it is not surprising that
anyone working on the effect of the planets on terrestrial weather
should start with her. However, there is evidence that the distant
planets also have their effect. Astrologers have pointed this out
over hundreds of years (just as Empedocles, in the first century
B.C., mentioned in passing that the Moon was made of glass, some

time before the astronauts returned with samples to prove him
right!)

But the statistical evidence produced by scientists who have,
more recently, examined the planets' influence on Earth's
weather, is not particularly encouraging, if only because of its lack
of clarity. V. A. Firsoff pointed out[1] that while a good match
could be made between radio fade-outs and planetary positions,
an equally good match could be made between the same planetary
positions and matinée performances at the Folies Bergères. Nevertheless, it appears that the main sunspot period (which averages
$11\frac{1}{2}$ years) may relate to the period of revolution of Jupiter (12
years), and sunspots are known to some extent to affect our
weather. Mercury's position in relation to the Earth has been
correlated with temperature changes, and it seems that (considering figures collected over a period from 1883 to 1941) Earth's
temperature may be affected from 2° below zero to $1\frac{1}{2}$° above
normal, varying in proportion to Mercury's distance from the
Earth (which is from $38\frac{1}{2}$ million to 36 million miles!).

In 1911 the Proctor of the Royal Society in London, Professor
Albert Schuster, first advanced the theory that sunspots were
perhaps caused by a force (either tidal or gravitational) exerted by
the planets on the surface of the Sun, which is delicately balanced
between the forces of gravity and the opposing outward thrust of
radiation. More recently, K. Takahashi of the Japanese Meteorological Research Institute calculated in 1956 the tidal oscillations
on the Sun precipitated by Jupiter, Venus, Earth and Mercury,
and concluded that solar activity must certainly be affected by
tidal oscillations.

The American meteorologist C. A. Mills has correlated devi-
ations from the normal mean monthly temperatures at eight US
weather stations – at Boston, New York, Baltimore, Cleveland,
Cincinnati, St Louis, Chicago and Minneapolis – for the half-
century from 1890, and found

> some evidence [of planetary effects], although the multiplicity of
> such influence always at work prevents any high degree of cor-
> relation between weather changes and the position of any one
> planet. Earth temperatures tend to be above normal when the

[1] 'The planets and the weather', *Country Life,* March 24, 1960.

various planets are in the same direction from the Sun as the Earth, and below normal as they pass around on the opposite side of the sun.[1]

Even Mercury, he noted, the smallest of the planets, seemed to affect Earth's temperature; and the distance between the planets and Earth also seemed not to have a proportional effect on this influence. Which ties up with the remark of John J. O'Neill, late science editor of the *New York Herald Tribune,* that

> the hypothesis of the astrologers that forces are transmitted to the earth without attenuation with increasing distance, and do not vary with respect to the difference in masses of the Sun, Moon and planets on which they originate, was totally inconsistent with the old style of Newtonian mechanics, but today is in complete accord with the much more recent Einstein photoelectric theory, which demonstrates that the effect of a photon does not diminish with distance, and which has been universally adopted by scientists to supplant the Newtonian mechanics in that field.[2]

Mills concluded:

> The degree of tendency for unseasonable warmth to occur as some of the planets come into the same heliocentric longitude as the Earth, and for periods of cold to come as they pass around on the opposite side of the Sun, is sufficient to warrant close study of these relationships.

Since Mills made his examination, some of the elements affecting the Earth's weather from outside what one might call our own environment have been more fully understood. Corpuscular radiations, for instance (electrically charged particles) are known to reach the Earth from the Sun, and are reduced when Venus is between us and it; the planet apparently acting as a magnet. These radiations cause a heating of the Earth's stratosphere and a consequent drop in ground level temperatures.

What of course needs to be done is a comparison of traditional astrological weather-lore and the most recent knowledge we have

[1] *Bulletin of the American Meteorological Society,* op. cit.
[2] *Horoscope,* March 1960.

of how the planets appear to affect our weather. But since Mills published his first findings, we seem to have got no further. Meanwhile other theories have been suggested and examined, many of them concerned with the planetary cycles.

It is difficult to discover the attitude of professional meteorologists to the cycle studies which have been made. The British Meteorological Office, for instance, will provide instances and point out experiments which have been published; but are less eager to comment on them, and quick – indeed, instantaneous! – to deny that any results of such studies could have a practical use in weather forecasting in the foreseeable future. The effects of cycles (as of the Moon) are 'too general' to be of use – although one would think that a very great number of people would be at the least happy to hear that there was a good chance of a fine summer in 1975, say, quite apart from any practical utility of such a statement.

Weather cycles do not appear to be restricted to relatively short periods. Sydney Makepeace Wood has pointed out that there are meteorological cycles several hundred years in extent, which are even more reliable for use in weather forecasting than short-term cycles. 'The weather of today, for example, may in general be like that of one year or two years ago, but it is much more likely to be an almost exact duplicate of the weather of several hundred years ago.'[1]

Professor Schuster spoke of the Bruckner cycle – of thirty-four years – in the weather; every thirty-three years the Sun, Venus, Earth and Mars return to the same position relative to each other and the Sun. Wood sees the thirty-four-year cycle as 'a consequence of the merger' of these two cycles. He quotes the example of the rainfall in the Chicago area as an example of how the Bruckner cycle affects the weather.

The Chicago rainfall averages about 33 in. a year. In 1934 this fell to 22.78 in.; it was a year of drought. In 1901, thirty-three years earlier, it was also low – 24.52 in. In 1867, it was 22.41 in. And, incidentally, in 1967 (twenty-one years *after* Mr Wood's article was written) there was a bad drought in the Chicago area. Perhaps more difficult to check is Mr Wood's assertion that there is

[1] 'The planetary cycles', *Illinois Engineer*, February 1946.

a 737/8-year cycle (which, for instance, brought a record high-water level to the American Great Lakes in 1838, as to the Nile in 1100). He goes on to discuss yet more cycles: one of 46/48 years, one of 87 years, one of 178 years.

'The further we explore the structure of our home, the solar system,' he concludes, 'the more clearly we perceive the closeness of [the planets'] interrelationship and that of all organic life as we know it.' A statement which places him firmly in line with the astrological theorists he despises.

Much more recently than Wood, W. E. Davis (of the Meteorological Office, Strike Command, High Wycombe) has been working on an attempt to devise an optimum weather index applicable in summer to all places in the United Kingdom, so that it would be possible to compare the summer weather at different places for different years.

In his published theory, he examines the year-to-year variations for Kew from 1881 to 1967, and discovers that there is a distinct variation between the optimum index for odd and even years. Using an index scale of measurement, he claims in fact to have discovered a series of cycles which demonstrates that 'the probability that the index of the summer of 1971 at Kew will exceed 825 (only 14 of the 88 previous summers have exceeded this value)' i.e. the probability that the summer of 1971 will be a very good summer indeed 'is 75 per cent, the pure-chance level being 16 per cent. The probability that at least one of the summers 1969, 1971, 1973 exceeds 825 is 87 per cent – the pure-chance level is 41 per cent.'[1]

Without presenting Mr Davis's argument fully (and it is couched in meteorologists' jargon, at least as difficult to the layman as astrologers' jargon) it is easy to see that he is making the kind of 'forecast', based on the kind of experimentation, which provokes groans of pity when astrologers make them. He concludes, in fairly unequivocal language:

Even with such a cursory examination of the changes in the optimum index, it is possible to make some forecasts about the summers to come, on the assumption that the oscillations will

[1]'Weather', *Journal of the Royal Meteorological Society*, August 1968.

continue. The odd years should reach their maximum in 1971, with the even years showing a broad maximum over the years 1966–74. On this basis, there are grounds for suggesting that at least one of the summers of the years 1969, 1971, 1973 may be exceptionally good and some of the even years 1968, 1970, 1972 and 1974 may show high values.

Almost any of the writers with whose experiments and findings I have just been dealing might be horrified if the word 'astrology' were mentioned in his hearing. When I first contacted the British Meteorological Office in connection with current work on weather cycles or the influence of planets on terrestrial weather, I had several times to assure various people that it would be made quite clear that the Office in no way 'uses astrology' in its weather forecasting. The astrologers would no doubt claim that this is obvious when one examines the percentages of successful forecasting of meteorologists and specialist astrologers. But in any event, it is clear that, as far as meteorologists are concerned, astrology is a touchy subject. Yet what is astrology about if not the alleged effect upon the Earth of the neighbour planets? The Meteorological Office is far from ignorant of what has been done on these lines. Its official library contains a collection of well over 250 books and pamphlets about lunar and planetary influences on the weather.

Not all the work in this general area is about weather: some of it, for instance, is about cyclones, hurricanes, earthquakes. Dr R. Tomaschek, a German scientist, had for instance examined the Charts of 134 earthquakes of equal or greater magnitude than 7, during the years 1904, 1905 and 1906. From the results of his examinations[1] it emerges that the placing of Uranus in the Charts was significant. There was a probability of much less than 0.0001 of its position being random. Uranus is regarded by astrologers as a planet of tension, of explosion, of the sudden and unexpected.

Subsequently, Dr Tomaschek worked on the Charts of the 1924 Tokyo earthquake (in which a million people died) and that of 1950 in Assam, and later wrote of the 1960 Agadir and Chile earthquakes that they 'concur with the evidence provided by previous earthquakes, and support the assertion that a correlation

[1] *Nature*, July 18, 1959.

exists between earthquakes and cosmic configuration'.[1] He concluded that he was dealing with a factor which was 'not a relationship of cause and effect in the usual mechanical sense'.

Astrological weather-forecasters (as opposed to meteorologists, although they are often good amateur meteorologists) work in their own ways, some of them using traditional means, some their own theories. A few have been extremely successful – among them the Bartlett brothers, Denis and John, who between 1934 and 1955 ran a professional weather-forecasting office in Fleet Street.

Their parents had been theosophists, and they naturally grew up with a general interest in astrology, although with no desire to use it. They started out as conventional forecasters; but the poor results they were able to obtain by conventional means disappointed them and they threw themselves into every kind of experiment, finally ending up with their own method of applying astrology to meteorology. This is based, according to Denis Bartlett, on a massive grasp of weather statistics: of 'the norm' for the weather in any place at any time of year, for not only a month, but a week or even perhaps a day – but the norm affected by certain astrological factors.

Conventional astrology, according to Denis Bartlett, is 'completely useless' as applied to meteorology. In forecasting he uses his own graphs based on a hundred years of weather statistics, and on a great personal knowledge of the idiosyncrasies of the weather. He applies these to any given time or weather situation in conjunction with whatever planetary configurations – squares, oppositions, or conjunctions – may be occurring. Sun and Moon in conjunction or opposition tend to bring high tides; Sun and Jupiter in conjunction lead invariably to high pressure in the North of Britain, with east winds off the east coast; Mars and Saturn in conjunction bring cold weather – as in the bitter winter of 1947. Sun and Mars in conjunction make for heat: as in the second week of August 1911, on one of the hottest days on record.[2]

[1] *Astrological Journal*, vol. IV, No. 2 (Summer 1963).
[2] On August 9, 1911, a temperature of 100° F was recorded at Greenwich – the highest temperature ever recorded in England for August, and the second highest ever recorded in the country.

Naturally, all this sounds (and is) over-simplified, but its application obviously works; the simple proof of this is the success over many years of the Bartlett brothers' business. From the day in 1936 when they forecast the first day of early snow for the Shell Company's winter oil advertising campaign, through years of forecasting the tricky English weather for film companies on location, up to the Investiture of the Prince of Wales in 1969, they have been in constant demand – as Denis Bartlett is today, some time after his official retirement. He claims that during the war, indeed, the late Duke of Atholl distributed his forecasts unofficially to generals, and that these so convinced Winston Churchill that the brothers were given commissions in the navy's Meteorological Branch, and their official and unofficial forecasts were used in many wartime actions.

Another notable astrological weather forecaster is L. Furze-Morrish, who in Australia, with P. A. Jacka (who is not an astrologer) has been working for some time in this field, and claims 70 per cent to 80 per cent correct results at least in temperature and cloud forecasts.

Aspects from planets to sensitive points in the heavens correlate with variations in the weather [he says]; fine weather and generally high pressure systems correspond with Jupiter's aspects, cloud and low pressure systems to Venus, and to some extent Neptune, which seems to bring light cloud, mist or overcast of a thin type. Saturn lowers temperatures, also possibly Uranus. Mars raises the temperature. For instance, on July 28 and 29, 1969, Jupiter made a certain aspect with Mars in a certain point from about 4 p.m. on the 28th until about 4 p.m. on the 29th (local time). Though it is winter here [North Caulfield, Australia] and the mean temperatures for July are about 46° at 9 a.m. and 55° at 3 p.m., the temperature rose to over 60° on the evening of the 28th, and remained high all night and next day. On the evening of the 29th, there were two Venus aspects, and at that time the temperature fell and rain started with heavy overcast. There was also a Saturn aspect coming up.[1]

Mr Furze-Morrish admits that 'for some reason every now and

[1] Letter to the author.

then the aspects fail to work'; that 'occasionally something appears to throw out our forecasts – why, I do not know.' And indeed, there is obviously much work to be done before any kind of totally reliable system of astrological weather forecasting can be devised. But surely, it is a field meteorologists might at least glance towards?

Meanwhile, it continues to prove a means of pleasure and profit and incidental amusement. Margaret Hone, for instance, used to hold a summer party every year in the garden of her house near Chichester. Struck by her friends' comments that she always chose good weather for her parties, and obviously commanded the weather, she thought about her system of timing, and realised that – being a keen sailor, and having many friends who had their own boats – she invariably chose weekends when the tide was high at noon or thereabouts, so that her guests could get up the creek nearby.

High water at midday, at the time of the spring tides, occurs when the Moon is in conjunction with, or in opposition to, the Sun: that is, either full or new. The weather had always been good at this time. On the other hand a friend, who chose a later date, with high water at about six and the Moon in a square aspect to the Sun (at quarter-Moon in the sky) used regularly to be rained right off her lawn!

XI

Astrology and Medicine

The traditional connections between astrology and medicine go back a very long way in human history, but they became to some extent particular in the Hermetic cult which originated before Herodotus. 'Hermes Trismegistos' was the name the Greeks gave the Egyptian god Thoth, who reputedly wrote treatises on theology and the occult, philosophy and astrology. It is only during the early part of this century that it has been fully realised that the popular, occult and astrological Hermetic writings are much earlier than the 'learned' writings from the same source (the theology and philosophy), and reflect ideas and beliefs common during the years of the early Roman Empire.

In these, the seven planets correspond to seven human types. The zodiacal signs are related to various parts of the human body – Aries concerns the head and face, Leo the spine, back and heart, Pisces the feet, and so on. But the Hermetic theory goes further than these general indications and relates different ailments to the sub-divisions of 10° of which each sign has three. Stomach troubles are indicated in the first decanate of Virgo, lung troubles in the second decanate of Cancer, etc. The occultists attached various curative functions to, for instance, the stones and colours associated with the various zodiacal divisions. But as far as 'pure' medicine was concerned, astrologers confined themselves to showing that various illnesses could either be confirmed or signalled by observing astrological indications within the relevant signs or section signs.

Not unnaturally, modern 'traditional' astrologers have modified Hermes. Charles Carter, for instance, in his *The principles of astrology*,[1] drew together most of the theory along which those astrologers interested in health were working in the 1920s, and continue to work – most consultants, writing a report, will at least refer in general terms to their clients' health prospects. Carter gives the traditional correlations of planets, signs and physical weaknesses full attention. He lists first the 'physical rulerships' of the planets – that is, the areas of the body on which each planet seems to have a specific effect:

> The Sun – general vitality and constitutional strength; the heart and back.
> The Moon – the nutritive and assimilative system; the stomach.
> Mercury – nerves and respiratory system.
> Venus – kidneys, throat, skin.
> Mars – muscular and excretory systems; nose and nasal passages; skull and face.
> Jupiter – the blood and liver.
> Saturn – the bones.
> Uranus and Neptune – these both work chiefly through the nervous system, but little is known with any certainty as to their physiological rulerships.

Mr Carter goes on to give the 'traditional sign-rulerships': these are frequently to be seen also in old astrological prints:

> Aries – head and face.
> Taurus – neck, throat and larynx.
> Gemini – shoulders, arms, lungs, nervous system.
> Cancer – stomach.
> Leo – spine, back and heart.
> Virgo – bowels and fingers.
> Libra – kidneys, lumbar region, skin.
> Scorpio – urinary organs and lower bowel.
> Sagittarius – hips, thighs, buttocks.
> Capricorn – bones, knees.

[1] Charles Carter, *The principles of astrology* (L. N. Fowler, 1921).

Aquarius – ankles, circulation.
Pisces – feet.

Astrologers will quite often assure a Geminian that he is likely to find his shoulders, arms and lungs vulnerable; that he may have some difficulty with his nervous system. I would not care to say that the astrologer is necessarily always right, although I have known cases in which he has been.

Mr Carter finally notes that 'so far as diseases can be ascribed to single planets', the following are characteristic maladies:

Mercury – neurasthenia, epilepsy, nervous excitability.

Venus – diseases resulting from easy and self-indulgent living; most forms of kidney trouble.

Mars – all feverish conditions, inflammation, sudden acute and painful complaints, usually resulting from strain, exhaustion, overwork, or carelessness.

Jupiter – diseases of excess and plethora such as gout; abnormal growths; complaints commonly arising from rich living, which need treatment by fasting, hard exercise and self-denial.

Saturn – diseases are chronic and inhibitive rather than painful (unless Mars is involved as well, as in rheumatic fever). They generally result from poor living: exposure, hardships, or hereditary troubles. Rheumatism is usually mainly shown by an affliction to the ascendant from this planet. Melancholia.

Uranus – sudden attacks, usually hard to foresee and to cure. The nerves are usually affected. Paralysis is mainly Uranian.

Neptune – extreme physical sensitiveness. Morbid fears, delusions and other obscure psychic conditions. Liability to nervous worry.

By studying these traditional indications, the professional astrologer is able not only to warn a client of the kinds of illness to which he may be prone, but (in the section in which the progressed Birth Chart is considered) to warn the client *when* he may be subject to, say, a chill (indicated perhaps by a transit of Saturn to the Sun).

Charles Carter researched into astrological indications of ill-health. Sometimes the number of cases he examined was too small to be statistically valuable, but sufficient to confirm the traditional indications. For instance, he examined the Charts of ten diphtheria cases, and knowing that traditionally the disease is characterised by activity in Taurus and Scorpio, and to a lesser degree in Gemini and Sagittarius, examined the positions of the Sun, Moon, seven planets and Ascendant in each Chart (100 positions in all). He discovered that 49 positions fell in the four signs mentioned, and of these, 30 were in the first two (Taurus and Scorpio). Nearly twice the average, in fact.

In this sphere, as in many others, there are disagreements between astrologers, each sure that his conclusions about the indications of a particular illness are the right ones. In the final analysis, every astrologer must be persuaded by his own findings; whether he can persuade others, is another matter. One non-conformist is William J. Tucker who, in a monograph entitled *Astromedical diagnosis,*[1] takes several side-swipes at Mr Carter.

The lay reader is likely to find Mr Tucker's particularity a little off-putting. He suggests, for instance, that the planet ruling the day of the week a man was born 'will spotlight many salient features of any given individual's medical history'; a statement which almost every other professional astrologer would regard as rubbish. However, much of what he says is more interesting. He alleges, for instance, that he has been able, after observing the Birth Charts of patients, to work out astrological formulae which help doctors to diagnose 'puzzling cases'. Of appendicitis, he writes: 'I believe that the inflammation of the appendix is invariably caused by a spread of intestinal catarrh, since I find that the stellar causation is always an affliction between Jupiter (which is always associated with catarrh) and Mars (which is always associated with inflammation)'; he gives four examples of the Birth Charts of appendicitis victims to confirm his opinion. An insufficient number, of course; but he claims that they are only typical of many he has seen. 'Influenza epidemics,' he writes,

[1] William J. Tucker, *Astromedical diagnosis* (Ohio, Schary Publishing Co., 1958).

setting out another theory, 'have been found to recur every 33 weeks, which happens to be exactly the period between each successive adverse phase of Jupiter with Mars ... hence we have reason to suspect from the start that adverse configurations between Mars and Jupiter lie at the root of influenza epidemics.' Mr Tucker suggests that the 1918 epidemic of Spanish influenza was prompted by a square between Mars and Jupiter occurring at the same time as the conjunction of Saturn with Neptune. I confess I find this difficult to accept; although one must remember that while the glib employment of the old 33-week/month/year cycle sounds implausible in this context, doctors have over some years recognised that there does seem to be a four-year cycle of influenza virus type A, which they have been unable to explain.

However, the evidence Mr Tucker produces is on the whole unsatisfactory, even if it is only vestigially representative of more evidence in his files. He gives no birth-times for his patients, so that it is impossible to check their charts. Or is it possible that he has worked out the charts for midday in each case? If so, most astrologers would surely dismiss his evidence.

He evidently feels strongly that medical men in all departments of practice could benefit from a knowledge of astrology. He even suggests that the police surgeon would profit by it. It should be possible to tell from the Birth Chart of a murder victim whether in fact he *was* murdered: not because murder, the action of the assassin rather than the victim, would show; but because *accidental* death should be clearly apparent. A Birth Chart, he says, summing up, would enable a doctor to see from what ailments a patient is liable to suffer, and prescribe a regime best suited to avoid those ailments. A doctor might for instance look to see 'whether there are several planets placed in the Zodiacal signs of both Virgo and Pisces. If there are such planets, a predisposition towards tuberculosis is to be expected, and a special examination ... should be made in order to elicit in what periods the threat will materialise.'

Of course. But only if the indications are indeed correct; and valuable though such a means of diagnosis would be (often, presumably, showing astrological 'symptoms' of disease before any physical symptoms appeared) there is obviously a great deal more experiment necessary before a practical system can be worked out, if in fact one is possible.

There are various books on astrology and health: not only giving the traditional indications, as Mr Carter and Alan Leo, before him, have done, but taking matters a stage further. Vivian E. Robson, for instance, in *Astrology and human sex life*,[1] concentrates on 'revealing for the first time the intimate link between the stars and your sex life'. The book 'details the sexual characteristics of you, your family and your friends' in chapters which not only show (with the examples of the charts of Oscar Wilde, Tchaikowsky, the Marquis de Sade and others) the astrological indications of sexual deviation, but go on to indicate the chances of sexual compatibility.

It is a more serious book than my quotations from the dustcover might suggest: and serious study is going on in this field. In *Correlation 3*[2] there was a short note on the work being done by C. Gosselin and the International Astrological Research Unit (of which he is secretary) into the criteria by which sexual deviation may be recognised in a Birth Chart. The 'sample' was small: 72 cases only. These were obtained by advertising in 'certain magazines' (*Kinky Happening, Pussy Cat,* and *Intro Circle*), and offering to exchange a completed questionnaire for a 'free advice horoscope' based on a Sun-sign delineation. One cannot help feeling that this may have put a large number of sexual deviants off astrology for life.

The result of the enquiry, Mr Gosselin says, was that

statistically significant and highly statistically significant patterns were found within the limits of the sample replying. It should be noted that the possession of such patterns is not a categorical concomitant of deviancy, but the general predisposition is shown. The absence of such patterns does not preclude deviancy, but it should be less likely.

The pattern revealed 'the presence of one or more aspectual T-squares' in the charts of sexual deviants (the nature of the deviancy is not revealed). The planets most frequently involved in the

[1] Vivian E. Robson, *Astrology and human sex life* (Foulsham, 1963).
[2] *Correlation 3* (Astrological Association, 1967).

T-squares were the Moon, Pluto and Saturn; the theoretical occurrence of T-squares is one in four; the sample showed two in
three. A pattern was recognised in 66 per cent of the charts when a
probability was 25 per cent (the age range of the sample was 17 to
71). The findings have some bearing on Vivian Robson's book,
though they do not completely substantiate the claim of the *Tetrabiblos* that sexual abnormalities are attributable to afflictions between Venus, Mars and Saturn. ('Should Saturn be absent and
Mars be with Venus along,' remarked the authors, 'or even although Jupiter also be with her, men will become highly li-
centious, and attempt to gratify their desires in every mode.')

Today it is probably true to say that somewhere, someone is
working on every possible connection between astrology and
medicine. The same issue of *Correlation* which published Mr Gosselin's comments on astrology and deviancy, contained also a pre-
liminary note on a study which Charles Harvey is making of
astrology and genetics, with special reference to haemophilia. And
there are points at which astrology and medicine are beginning to
meet.

The effects of the Moon on the mentally disturbed and on
menstruation have been known to some extent for centuries. It has
been suspected – it still is suspected – that the connection between
the period of menstrual cycle and the period between two new
Moons is coincidental; and yet large samples (of between 10,000
and 20,000 cases) have tended to show a statistically considerable
indication of, for instance, an increased frequency of menstrual
periods during a waxing Moon.

As far as 'lunacy' is concerned, there are available statistics,
some of them prepared by various world police forces, which
confirm the popular idea that mental and emotional disturbance
does increase towards the time of the full Moon. There seems to be
a growing medical opinion that mental disorder may be affected
by slight modulations in the earth's magnetic and electric fields
which appear to be brought about by the phases of the Moon.
'Electromagnetic phenomena can be shown to be associated in
some ways with biologic processes,' writes an anonymous con-
tributor to an American medical magazine. 'The terrestrial environment is rich in electromagnetic phenomena (and secondary

effects from these); and the terrestrial electromagnetic environment is subject to variations induced by other electromagnetic
events in the solar system.'[1]

There seems no reason why, if indeed electromagnetic fields
affect the mentally disturbed, they should not affect also the
normal, the healthy. Obviously, these effects would be greatest
when the human being is at his weakest, perhaps in childhood, but
certainly in the first stages of development in the womb.

'When the sperm nucleus reaches the egg nucleus these two lie
side by side as their content is combined,' writes Geraldine Lux
Flanagan in *The first nine months of life*.[2]

> In this half-hour an immeasurable number of traits of the new
> baby are decided within the pin-point egg. These include the
> features of the human species and also the individual trade-
> marks such as male or female sex; the colour of eyes, hair and
> skin; the configuration of face and body; the tendency to be tall
> or short, fat or lean, ruggedly healthy or prone to some diseases;
> and undoubtedly also the tendency to certain qualities of tem-
> perament and intelligence.

This offers a fascinating field for speculation. It seems at least
possible that if cosmic forces are at work (and if the astrological
theory has elements of truth, then they must be) this is the moment
at which their force must be strongest. Would it be possible, by
timing as nearly as possible the moment of conception (perfect
timing would be of course impossible), to ensure that one's child
was male, fair-haired, handsome, tall, ruggedly healthy, intelligent . . .?

Work on the outskirts of this field is being done by Dr Eugen
Jonáš in Czechoslovakia, and was reported in 1967 in an interview
published in the *Astrological Journal*.[3] During his work as a psychiatrist, Dr Jonáš had noticed that some women with sensitive
nervous systems were unusually active, sexually, at intervals of

[1] *Hospital Focus* (New Jersey, Kroll Pharmaceutical Co., 1967).
[2] Geraldine Lux Flanagan, *The first nine months of life* (Heinemann,
1963).
[3] F. Rubin, 'The lunar cycle in relation to human conception and the sex
of offspring: an account of the work of Dr Eugen Jonáš', *Astrological
Journal*, supplement 1967.

thirty days, regardless of the menstrual cycle (to which a regular recurrence of sexual vitality might have been attributed). He also became interested in the problem of deformed, defective and underdeveloped children, of which he had wide experience at the State Clinic at Nagysurany.

In order to follow up these interests, he studied gynaecology, obstetrics and biology, and also read widely in the ancient works of Egyptian, Greek and Indian writers, in which there were numerous references to astrology. Reluctantly, he noticed that these seemed sometimes to be borne out by his own observations. So he began to look closely at the activity of the female nervous system and the problem of the conception of deformed or 'non-viable' children, in relation to the positions of the planets. He has always stressed that initially he found such a connection unthinkable and ludicrous. But after observing thousands of cases at the gynaecological clinic in Pozsony, he came to the inescapable conclusion that the sex of the embryo depended on the position of the Moon; and that bodies in the solar system could affect the physical completeness of a newborn baby.

He listed to his interviewer three conclusions:

That the ability of a mature woman to conceive tends to occur under exactly the phase of the Moon (Sun–Moon relationship) which prevailed when she was born.

That the sex of the child depends on whether, at this time, the Moon is in a positive or negative field of the ecliptic.

That the viability of the embryo is influenced to a great extent by the positions of certain celestial bodies at this time.

He was able to give some specific illustrations of these contentions. He even produced a case which showed that his theory would work under unusual circumstances. On his advice, a sterile woman reluctantly received her husband during menstruation (at the time of her maximum fertility, according to Dr Jonáš) and conceived a child at this first new attempt!

Dr Jonáš attempts to explain the nature of the mechanism connecting the Moon with fertility and the determination of sex perhaps need not be fully described here. It is important, however, to note that he has made attempts to confirm the theory over the past eleven years, and has had an 87/94 per cent accuracy in 'predicting' times of fertility. He has also investigated the relation-ship between planetary positions at conception and the 'viability' of children.

At the very beginning, he studied the positions of the planets at the time of conception of twenty imperfect children, and dis-covered that *in each case* this had taken place when the Sun and major planets were in opposition. He was of course prompted to continue his observations, and found that during 1960, out of a total of 80,000 births at Nyitra, Nagyszombat, Postyen and Pozs-ony, 112 were 'non-viable' children. His calculations showed that when hereditary diseases were excluded again the conception of non-viable children had always occurred when the planets were in opposition. He felt that this sample was large enough to make further observation justifiable, and work has been carried on since. Occasionally, practical advice has been given. A Mrs Patrovics, of Nyitra, for instance, had had three deformed children con-secutively; her fourth child was born deformed in the sixth month of pregnancy. Dr Jonáš prepared her Birth Chart, suggested four periods during which it should be possible for her to conceive a normal child. She conceived at one of these times, and gave birth to a healthy child.

Dr Jonáš suggests that the explanation of the connection be-tween the planets' positions and deformity in children may lie in the extreme sensitivity to radiation of spermatozoa at the time of conception. 'It is conceivable,' he told his interviewer, 'that the harmful effects of our solar system's major planets become con-centrated at certain times, and affect life on the Earth to a greater extent.'

Not surprisingly Dr Jonáš's work has been the subject of con-siderable debate in Czechoslovakia (and indeed elsewhere, where it has been made known). When Dr Jiri Malek was appointed by the Czech Academy of Sciences in 1957 to examine Dr Jonáš's theories, and arranged for him to introduce them at the first National Conference of Biological Rhythms in 1964, there was some scandal. Not even ten thousand examples confirming Dr Jonáš's view would, one delegate affirmed, convince *him* that the theory could be valid. But the general view seems to have been that of Dr T. A. Valsic, head of the anthropological and genetics department of the Comensky University of Pozsony. He disbelieves the theory; but is 'of the opinion that every young scientific worker should be given a chance to prove his idea, especially when he advances a fundamentally new concept'.

That chance has certainly been given Dr Jonáš at the Astrobiological Society of the Slovak Academy, which is officially supported; and if his work there is done as thoroughly, and supported as well by scientific evidence, it will be difficult for scientists outside Czechoslovakia to ignore his theories.

At the present time there does not seem to be any noticeable expansion of the use of astrological theories in the field of psychology. Since the death of Jung, no comparable mind has attributed much importance to astrology, although various working psychologists and psychiatrists use it. Psychologists sometimes have a working knowledge of the subject themselves; others will send patients to a consultant astrologer. Dr Fritz Riemann of Munich is one psychiatrist who uses astrology as part of his equipment. He believes that it is always advantageous to spend two or three initial sessions with a disturbed patient in examining with him his Birth Chart. 'The patient realises, then, that he isn't just a failure – a poor neurotic,' Dr Riemann says, 'but that his real problem can be solved in relation to his destiny.'

He instances one particular patient who had deep feelings of guilt and inferiority, and a tendency to suicide. An examination of her horoscope convinced her that these emotions resulted from specific planetary configurations against which she could fight. She was not a failure because of her own guilt. She made an excellent recovery. She would have done so, perhaps even if Dr Riemann had used the Birth Chart of Groucho Marx, pretending that it was hers; the chart was simply a weapon which was used to renew her confidence and change her point of view. However, he also finds a study of a patient's Birth Chart helpful to himself; knowing his own chart, he can avoid the various pitfalls of the psychiatrist-patient relationship; and from the patient's he can also see when particular pressures on the patient's psyche are likely to arise. He can discern the areas *where* those pressures may arise, making a shortcut possible right at the start of analysis.

Dr Riemann also suggests, practically, that a general use of horoscopes by psychiatrists could overcome the problems which arise when a patient has to change psychiatrists in mid-treatment; a proper basis not only of knowledge but of trust could be established.[1]

This is yet another area in which a great deal more knowledge is necessary before the right kind of regular and general use of the horoscope could become customary. International exchange of information and opinion is, above all, necessary in all these fields.

[1] For further consideration of a posssible relationship between astrology and psychiatry, see Appendix I.

XII

Astrology in America

It has been estimated that there are approximately 10,000 full-time and 175,000 part-time astrologers in the United States; but while the latter figure may well be correct, the former is probably an over-estimation. The American Federation of Astrologers has a membership of only 1,300, and many of those are from outside the US. But there as elsewhere, astrologers are extremely contentious, and spend a great deal of time criticising and gossiping about each other and each other's organisations. They share a dislike, on the whole, of being associated with too large a group of their contemporaries. So membership of any of the larger bodies may have no relevance to any total number of astrologers in the country.

Comparatively few American astrologers learned their craft through such bodies as Professional Astrologers Incorporated, of Los Angeles (which claims that over half its students go on to be professional consultants). The majority learned from other, older astrologers, or from books, so that it is very difficult indeed to arrive at any accurate estimation; and doubtless many of the 10,000 professionals fall into the category described by Paul R. Grell (the Federation's Executive Secretary) as 'commercially minded people and "quick dollar" artists'.

It is difficult to assess the damage done to the reputation of astrology by these 'quick-dollar artists'. Certainly no harm is done by the zodiacal cocktail glasses, zodiacal writing-paper, zodiacal posters (many of them demi-semi-pornographic), and the zodiacal beauty parlours with twelve hair styles, one for each sign! Only marginal harm is probably done by the hippies' preoccupation with astrology – which is more fashionable so far in America than in England, although the imported version of the hippy musical *Hair* still contains as one of its hit numbers the song, 'The age of Aquarius':[1]

> *When the Moon is in the Seventh House*
> *And Jupiter aligns with Mars,*
> *Then peace will guide the planets*
> *And love will steer the stars.*

A naïve belief in the 'order of the stars' may be at the back of the generally increased interest in astrology; although this is shaken almost weekly by scientific arguments about theories of the universe, even these may contribute. A feeling that 'the centre cannot hold' must draw a certain cast of mind towards a system which seems to depend on the fact that there *is* a centre (symbolic if not actual) that can and does hold. A Yale chaplain, quoted in *Time*, asserted that 'a widening interest in astrology is a beautiful example of the lobotomised passivity that results from the alienating influence of modern technological society'. On the other hand, Marshall McLuhan, concentrating on the psychic elements of the subject, believes that it consists of 'tomorrow's science dreamed today'.

The proliferating radio and television shows in the US scarcely uphold either view, for they make little attempt to be serious about astrology. It is difficult to see how they could do so without losing the wide popular interest which programmes must have in a sponsored system (and, increasingly, to be fair, is considered necessary in our own non-sponsored system). There is no reason to suppose that a television or radio show based on 'real' astrology could not be devised; but the easy way out can commend itself to those performers who combine a maximum of personality with a minimum of astrological knowledge; and serious astrologers might well indeed be extremely difficult to work with in a television studio, if

---

[1] The Broadway production of *Hair* had, incidentally, a resident astrologer – Maria Crummere – who chose the opening dates for the productions in New York, London, Munich, Stockholm, Copenhagen and Los Angeles.

only because they would be unlikely to agree to any format which might short-circuit the calculations they consider essential, or might simplify the complexities of a Birth Chart. So US programmes consist on the whole either of 'personality shows' or of the equivalent of the newspaper astrology columns.

Oddly enough, the interest in astrology in the US probably dates from the radio series of Evangeline Adams, whose story is a fairy-tale success which commends itself to every would-be astrologer. Miss Adams began studying astrology in the 1890s, and in 1899 arrived (carefully on time) in New York, and checked in at the Windsor Hotel on March 16. That evening she calculated the chart of the hotel's proprietor, who, she found, was 'under one of the worst possible combinations of planets – bringing conditions terrifying in their unfriendliness'. Early next morning the hotel was burned to the ground, killing the proprietor's daughter and several members of his family. He told his story to the press, and Miss Adam's reputation was made. She opened a studio above Carnegie Hall, to which J. P. Morgan, Mary Pickford, Enrico Caruso, Maggie Teyte, and even King Edward VII, came for consultation.

Two years before her death in 1932 (which like Charles Carter in England, she predicted accurately, politely declining a three-week lecture tour which would have started a few days before her death) she started a radio programme which was broadcast three times a week. Within a year, she was receiving 4,000 letters a day; and when she died thousands of clients came to see her body lying in state in her studio. The *New York Times* was unimpressed: 'Radio and astrology dancing to victory hand in hand make a sufficiently odd couple; but that is not all. This incongruous fellowship has flourished in an age of intellectual emancipation. . . .'

A protégé of Evangeline Adams' was Carroll Righter, one of the best known American astrologers of the present day on the broadly popular level. Miss Adams was a friend of the Righter family, and when Carroll Righter was fourteen she calculated his chart and discovered that he had several of the indications commonly found in the charts of astrologers. But it was not until the depression years (after he had worked in law and on various civil projects) that he became a full-time astrologer, in an attempt, he has claimed, to help some of the unemployed men he met. He calculated their Birth Charts, and found that he was able to direct them into jobs which they would not otherwise have considered.

When he became ill, he consulted his own chart, and discovered that it promised him better health in the Western rather than the Eastern States; so he moved to Los Angeles, and his better health was no doubt bolstered by the fact that there was a vast and on the whole undiscriminating interest in astrology among the film people he met in California. In 1939 he became a full-time consultant, claiming Marlene Dietrich, Robert Cummings, Tyrone Power, Van Johnson, Ronald Colman and Ronald Reagan among his clients.[1] (Mr Reagan's public interest in astrology seems to have declined since his election as Governor of California.)

Personal consultations rather than written Reports (as with a great number of American astrologers) means that Righter has time to write a number of syndicated astrological columns, and a number of books – guides to business, finance, fashion, marriage. (Incidentally, two Northwest University Professors of Psychology, Lee Sechrest and James H. Bryan, took Righter seriously enough to examine his marriage counselling and that of eighteen other astrologers, concluding that the advice they offered was 'generally valid and useful'; but there is no reason to suppose that the advice of any civilised and intelligent human being would not be equally valid and useful.)

Mr Righter occupies the middle ground; and in California this may well be something to be proud of. 'In California,' a visiting astrologer told me, 'one can sell anything.' For once, legend seems to be equalled by truth. The Heliotrope Free University of California, for instance, has offered a practical witchcraft course, conducted by Witch Antaras Auriel (a barefoot figure in flowing white robes and with long blonde hair; close examination of his photographs proves him to be warlock rather than witch). The Midpeninsula Free University of California has five courses in astrology – 'Jungian', 'Advanced', 'Out of the Aquarium and into

[1] Information from *Time* article, op. cit.

the Aquarian' (sic), 'Occult Things and the New Age', and 'An Occult and Astrology Workshop'.

The interest shown in astrology by some hippies has of course led to wild accusations that it is a bad influence. These were recently emphasised (as were more general accusations against the hippy movement) after the revelations of the cases against Charles Manson and his hippy 'family' for the murder of the film actress Sharon Tate and others, under the most revolting circumstances. In the *Observer* in December 1969, Charles Foley and William Scobie reported from California ('the screwy state') on 'the dark and complex background' of Manson and his gang.

> With 10,000 people making a full-time living from astrological forecasts and another 20,000 part-timers, the occult is big business [they wrote]. Free universities created by drop-outs run courses on Jungian astrology. One has an astrological work-shop, providing a ritualistic substitute for conventional religion which makes no moral demands.

Attributing the entire US astrological population to one state, confusing astrology with occultism, seeing 'ritual' in the calculation of Birth Charts, the writers confuse the issue with wonderful thoroughness. It seems as though they would, like a great number of people, have seized any stick with which to beat the hippies; a predisposition to dominoes would have been as useful.

But it does still seem likely that of the total number of astrologers in California (and no doubt they are thicker on the ground in that state than elsewhere) a good proportion are fraudulent; and who can wonder, when consultant astrologers can charge $250 for an hour's consultation, and find plenty of clients at that price? The astrologer on this level must have considerable personality and perhaps considerable astrological knowledge. The one American astrologer I have met who charged this kind of fee certainly has an exceptionally persuasive personality, and was able after a simple glance at an ephemeris to produce a broad and on the whole accurate picture of my past life (and indeed of that of a friend) within a moment or two.

Fees of $250 an hour are, however, the exception rather than the rule. Of 287 astrologers questioned in 1959, only 11 per cent described themselves as professionals, and only 20 per cent recorded *any* income from astrology. Professional Astrologers, Inc. now advise a minimum charge of $15, but say that professional astrologers from their classrooms charge on average from $25 to $100 for a character analysis, with about $35 for a year's progressions, and about $100 for five years. But Dorothy B. Hughes of Seattle says that 'the average person in this part of the country is not willing to pay for the amount of time and study an astrologer puts into his work. Here we are lucky to get $10 for as much as three or four days' work . . . yet they will go to psychiatrists and pay $30 an hour. It is most disheartening.' So California is evidently bonanza country in this, as in many other fields.

If there are some astrologers earning vast sums of money, and others earning very little, there is a small group of middle-of-the-road astrologers charging what one might call a 'reasonable' fee. Marc Edmund Jones, for instance, stresses in an urbane yet somewhat severe broadsheet, that his advice (which is 'that of a psychologist') is charged for 'by the hour'.

> The general survey of the character with the more comprehensive charting of the directions and transits, and a buttressing of indications either by horary astrology or solar return as suggested by the nature of current problems, requires two hours. The outline of astrological potentials for the year or so immediately ahead, when the horoscope has been calculated previously and is in the files, can be prepared in an hour.

This idea is not unfair: the preparation of analyses do in fact require disparate times. Mr Jones's fee is $25 an hour; so that his initial analysis and progressions for a year cost $50. This compares with $125 charged by Dane Rudhyar (the author of *The astrology of personality* and of various astrological theories) for 'a complete Harmonoscope (from 20 to 25 typewritten pages)'. But he charges an extra $25 for rectifying a chart, and a minimum of $15 for later enquiries. Private consultations are charged at the rate of $25 for an hour and a half, and $12 an hour afterwards.

The whole middle ground of astrological activity in the US since the war was described by Marcia Moore in 1959 in a document which was published as a research bulletin by Astrological Research Associates of New York the following year. Miss Moore prepared this as a thesis for a B.A. Honours degree at Radcliffe College, and sent out a questionnaire to 900 astrologers, most of them in America. The thesis is a comforting document, if only because it reveals that the vast majority of American astrologers hold to a personal code of ethics which directs them positively towards an intelligent view of what can and cannot be done by astrology, assuming that it works; and what should not be done by astrology, whether it works or not. Their approach to the subject is scientific in instinct if not in fact.

> Astrologers need to study mathematical logic [one astrologer told Miss Moore]; this would eliminate most of the twaddle. Astrology must be separated from its inhibiting load of religion and wishful thinking, which defeats objective consideration of facts and problems. Astrologers must learn to discipline themselves in the use of scientific method. . . . It must purge itself of crackpots, vagueness, medievalism, oriental philosophy and the prevailing ignorance its practitioners now have of what the science really is.

This position is an extreme one, and one from which many astrologers would differ. 'I feel it would be disastrous if science with its present outlook and attitude developed a scientific astrology,' wrote another correspondent. 'I agree with H. P. Blavatsky when she said "Astrology in its deeper aspects is one of the occult arts".'

Many astrologers hold strongly that astrology and the occult are indivisible; and the connection between astrology and the theosophical movement is particularly strong in the US. A 'First Temple and College of Astrology' was founded in Los Angeles in 1908, and still teaches the subject; one section of the original Rosicrucian brotherhood (split by dissension after the death of its founders, Max and Augusta Foss Heindel) was much concerned with the subject; and so is the Church of Light (founded on the work of C. C. Zain and now led by Doris Chase Doane).

Some astrologers have built up for themselves, and are sometimes concerned to transmit to others, involved theories of the place of astrology in the modern world. One of them is Dane Rudhyar, whose *The astrology of personality* is scarcely average astrological thinking.

In it he examines various theories of the forces which seem to bind the universe (including Jung's principle of synchronicity and Smuts's theory of holism), and closely allies astrology ('the algebra of life') to some of these theories, examining its symbolism, and classifying the various viewpoints which may be held within the basic pattern (the astrology of the individual, the collective, the occult, and 'harmonic astrology', whose purpose he sees as the revelation of the whole being). It is a complex and somewhat opaque book. 'The statements,' as Huckleberry Finn said of *Pilgrim's progress*, 'is interesting but tough.'

While some astrologers argue that astrology in the 1960s should rely completely on established scientific techniques and standards, Mr Rudhyar argues that

> it is this relying which, to my mind, would denature astrology. There should be other ways of making astrology more sound as a consistent system of thought. . . . What I have contended always is that without a basic philosophy, astrology does not mean much that is valid for the development of human individuals. Without it, horary astrology is unabashed fortune-telling. Some day, a new *cosmobiology* may be built as a modern science, but this will apply to the whole biosphere rather than to individual persons.[1]

But Mr Rudhyar is in the minority. Almost 80 per cent of the astrologers in Miss Moore's study placed astrology firmly as 'a science' intent on developing 'more knowledge of the operations of natural law as it works through man, the world and the cosmos' – and the emphasis for most of them was on *man*. Only 30 per cent thought that astrology was 'a discipline of thinking basically different from modern science' (roughly, Mr Rudhyar's line); and there was a general agreement that astrological techniques were too difficult to be widely popularised, so there was obviously a case for ignoring complaints that astrologers were insular – this was probably inevitable.

[1] *Kósmos*, February 1969.

Miss Moore concludes that

> the ideal of astrology from the beginning has been to interpret
> the whole of life and to orient man toward that Reality which is
> source and sum of all disciplines and points of view. It should
> ultimately represent a synthesis of approaches to truth, based on
> the concept that man and cosmos are integral wholes within
> which each part has its rightfully ordained function.

Certainly this summarises the general attitude of the middle
strata of astrologers. Of over thirty astrological associations I contacted in the US not one asserted any kind of interest in astrology
as a means to 'foretell the future'; all, in one way or another,
asserted that astrology could be a means of helping individuals to
discover more about their personalities, and a means of balancing
their relationship with the world about them.

Every organisation has its cranks; and it is unfair to accuse
astrology of having a larger than average number of them. But it is
perhaps fair to say that America (and, indeed, possibly England)
has fewer 'serious' astrologers than for instance France, Germany,
or Austria. There are exceptions: interesting articles do appear
from time to time in the astrological press, but all too often American astrologers – even those who have been working seriously in
the field for many years – eagerly publish material which can only
raise a laugh among uncommitted readers. The *Bulletin of the
American Federation of Astrologers,* for instance, printed a detailed account of the 1968 Convention at Seattle, attended by
over 600 members, most of them professional astrologers. 'Our
speakers' (the editor stated) 'are from the very best available in all
parts of the country, the best collective group of astrological
speakers assembled anywhere. . . .' Certainly some lectures were of
interest: Ruth Hale Oliver's examination of the relationship between astrology and science (a somewhat putative one, perhaps);
Louise Ivey's account of the life and work of Dr Tim Dooley,
the American humanitarian, commenting on the astrological
influences which informed him. Marc Edmund Jones (an
influential and reputable astrologer), gave to the Convention an
amusing, rather than stimulating, talk.

But there were also lectures of a much lower standard. Olive

Adele Pryor, for instance, lectured on 'A Decade with Uranus and Neptune'. She explained astrologically the phenomenon of hippies and flower people, and the reasons for the government subsidy of 'plays by LeRoi Jones ... whose work is mostly filthy'; she ascribed to the influence of Uranus and Jupiter the acceptance by America of the 'absurd plans' of the Socialists 'until we now live in a Socialist Democracy – not a Democratic Republic, as the Founding Fathers ordained'. She went on to condemn 'men with long hair, beards, serapes or blankets for coats', and predicted for 1970 'many catastrophic fires set by arsonists, radicals', 'continued agitation by radical elements – all communist inspired and financed'; and 'further attempts to liberalise our government to the end that we will be absolutely Socialistic ... observe what this has done to Sweden.'

It may be unfair to condemn the Federation for listening to a lecture such as that; but it is difficult to excuse its publication in cold print some time later.

The International Society for Astrological Research, Inc., founded in 1968 with the aim of drawing together astrologers from all over the world, and helping astrology 'regain its position in the academic and scientific field', has a list of vice-presidents which reads like an international Who's Who of astrology: Arthur DeDion and L. Furze-Morrish in Australia; Wilhelm Knappish and the Countess Zoë Wassilko in Austria; Brigadier R. C. Firebrace in England; B. V. Raman in India; and Youko Shiojima in Japan. The Society's primary function was said, at its foundation, to be the encouragement of 'responsible astrological research and the foundation of an International Institute of Advance Astrological Studies'. During its first year it announced its sponsorship of five research projects: attempts to discover the 'astrological signatures', (i.e. the common indication in various birth charts) for 'poor spelling ability'; and for astrologers; investigation of the possibility of predicting earthquakes (a project to be carried out with the aid of a computer, and under the aegis of two professors of mathematics of the University of Miami); the house position of the Sun at the moment when marriage ceremonies commence; and the house position of the Sun at the time of formation of public corporations. The last two projects, of course, have reference to the effects on the subsequent marriage history, or the subsequent history of the corporation. In addition, *Kósmos*, the Society's magazine, has been regularly produced; and a research pamphlet is also published periodically.

The American Federation of Astrologers was founded in Washington in 1938 ('on the morning of May 4, at 11.38 a.m., EST'). Ernest A. Grant, on the occasion of the silver jubilee, noted that the conception of several astrologers in various cities of the US was 'to replace a previous, rather loosely-knit organisation in which they were all participating with a strong, well-founded, non-profit association for the advancement of astrology and its proper utilisation'.

The 'Aims and Objectives' of the Federation expands on this: they include the development of

> ways and means of eradicating illiteracy and dissociating those whose work in the name of astrology is misleading to the public [and assisting] all persons engaged in educational, scientific or humanitarian efforts, such as teachers, graduates, lecturers or writers on astrology, whose work is beneficial and who are duly qualified as adjudged by this Federation, and who are not acting in wilful offence against public policy.

The Federation also holds examinations (as do various other bodies in the US) and awards certificates of proficiency.

The certificates are of very little help in protecting the public from amateurs and crooks, however, because the public knows very little about them. Neither does the fact that an astrologer does not hold any examination certificate necessarily mean he is a bad astrologer: in Marcia Moore's survey of 1959, although 55 per cent of the sample had taken a course of some kind, 38 per cent had studied alone, and only 25 per cent possessed any kind of certificate or diploma. (No doubt the proportion has now increased.)

Another important American body is the Astrologers' Guild, which emerged from a series of informal luncheons held by a group of astrologers during 1926 at the Nara Restaurant on West 51st Street, New York. Various papers were read, and there was informal discussion; gradually more and more 'members' became interested, mimeographed notes were issued, and there was a move to a larger restaurant on West 52nd Street. And eventually, at a carefully elected moment (noon EST on April 9, 1927) the Guild itself was officially formed. In its Certificate of Incorporation it stressed aims and objectives similar to those of other astrological bodies all over the world: to 'co-operate with scientific research bodies'; to suppress the conning of credulous clients; to spread the knowledge of conventional astrology; and to encourage research and proper practice.

The Guild published for its members its *Astrological Review*, which has been running for almost the whole forty years of the Guild's history; and this shares with the American Federation's journal the distinction of being one of the only two regular astrological journals in the country. It is not, however, free from eccentricities or inaccuracies; and it too publishes material which may strike the average reader as comic. Mary Glennon Harter's Invocation at the Guild's annual Christmas Party for 1968, for example—

> Oh God-power of our varied understanding, let us now become more consciously aware of the force-fields of Thy loving vibrations. There is an old tradition that the period from December 6 with its cleansing fire element – the symbol of man aiming an arrow towards the stars – melts into the timing of January 6, when the earth element of Capricorn organises this essence into a cleansing and renewing influence. It was believed that our tiny earth ball was at a slant whereby a flood of loving good will was sent forth from the angelic realms. . . .

Not, of course, that equally ludicrous invocations cannot be heard at the meetings of various bodies in England. And the Guild is a professional body, its Code of Ethics is fairly founded, and it evidently has a concern for sound astrology at heart, even if it is weakened at times by over-credulity.

XIII

The East and Africa

There are many differences in technique and interpretation between Eastern and Western astrology; but overwhelmingly there is a difference of public attitude. The effect of astrology on the day-to-day life of the Indian is still very considerable; nor is an official interest entirely lacking. B. V. Raman, a distinguished Indian astrologer, and the editor of the *Astrological Magazine* of India, has played a leading part in an extensive campaign to reintroduce astrology into the Indian universities. Indeed, in 1967, he gave the first of a series of annual lectures on astrology at the University of Rajasthan at Jaipur.

In his efforts to modernise India, President Nehru to some extent turned his face against astrology, but there is reason to suppose that his daughter is more sympathetic, for astrology is founded as firmly in the minds of the majority of contemporary Indians as it was in the minds of Europeans before Galileo, probably more firmly, indeed, since it had for the Indians a large religious connotation – being one of the six *angas*, or aids to understanding, of the Vedic texts. And today astrology remains deeply involved with the Indian social and religious system – notably with Varnashrama Dharma, the caste system. It is important to realise that Karma, the law which is at the base of Hindu philosophy, is not as Europeans often imagine, based on absolute fatalism. The tendencies shown in the horoscope indicate the way things are going, so to speak – they support the *prarabdha karma*, the extent to which a man is moving towards his salvation.

In the first of his lectures at Rajasthan University, Mr Raman spoke of astrology and general Indian religious beliefs:

A man's heredity is his inheritance from his own deeds in a previous life. A man's character and potentialities are the summation of his own deeds in previous lives. His present life is influenced by *prarabdha karma* – the tendencies of his previous deeds that have started to function. There are others hidden in his nature; he can prevent the bad ones among them from taking shape through his choices. He can modify the future while he has to suffer the consequences of the past.

Indian astrology envisages the whole cosmos, particularly the Sun and the planets, as co-operating with the human individual in moulding his self-formation and self-realisation in the effort to reach Moksha.[1] The universe is a *karya kshetra* – the valley of realisation through deeds. Hence there is room for both freedom and cosmic law in the Indian scheme of things which is shared by Indian astrology.

The Indian (non-Hindu as well as Hindu) goes to his horoscope for direction on the course which will bring the best rewards, not only on earth but in heaven. And this course affects a man even before his birth, in the activities of his parents, by the *Shodasa Karmas* – sixteen different kinds of ceremonial carefully timed by astrological calculation.

Before the birth of a child three ceremonies have already been performed. The father and mother must at least attempt to conceive the child to order, on a date and at a precise time arranged by the astrologer. Saturday and Tuesday are bad days for conception; so are the fourth, eighth, ninth and fourteenth lunar days, and days of the full or new moon. Certain constellations are inauspicious; others equally auspicious.

Next, *Pumsavana*, a ceremony for the mother; less common now than a generation ago, this is held to fix the sex of the child. At a particular time after conception, in the third month for those who want a male child, the mother must drink a draught prepared from two unbroken buds taken from two twigs from the eastern

[1] Moksha – 'release from bondage to the sensual and the individual'.

and northern sides of a Banian tree, a single grain of paddy, and a single seed of masha, or two seeds of white mustard and curds. But the concoction is only efficacious on the proper day and at the proper time.

An auspicious date for the baptism, and even more important an auspicious *time,* is chosen by the astrologer. The first letter of the name is chosen on the basis of calculations referring to the constellation under which the baby is born. The astrologer fixes times for the first feed of rice, the first haircut, the beginning of the child's education.

From babyhood astrologers are at the child's elbow. A wealthy family will bring an astrologer 'under contract', and consult him with great regularity and particularity. A poor family will have to make do with the astrologer-on-the-corner – the equivalent of the public letter-writer. He will be consulted, for a given fee, when the situation seems to demand astrological advice. Obviously, the influence of astrology on Indian everyday life is immense; it is reflected in the personal columns of the newspapers.

> *Alliance sought by rich young businessman earning 1,500 rupees monthly and worth six figures, from beautiful vegetarian Brahmin girls under 25, knowing music, tailoring, domestic duties. Reply with horoscope.*

> *Wanted, a fair Brahmin lady virgin, 19, height 5 feet 3 inches, under star Moolam, to marry a well-to-do boy of 38 . . .*

'Send horoscope' corresponds to 'photograph please' in the Western matrimonial columns; and it seems if anything to be more important. Officially, unless the horoscopes agree, there is no question of a marriage, or even the beginning of negotiation. Astrologers are not immune from bribery, however, and a rupee or two in the right palm has been known to result in a quick manipulation of a Birth Chart.

Strictly speaking, there are various essentials to be considered. Mr Raman (in a lecture delivered in New York a few years ago) set them out:

> The astrologer first studies the longevity of the bride and bridegroom, and if it is found that long life is not indicated, the

horoscope is rejected. Then he will find out whether the girl's horoscope brings any good luck to the husband and his family. The astrologer is also expected to trace from the horoscope any predisposition to hereditary diseases or immorality or widowhood. After satisfying himself about the character, health and general mental soundness of the girl, he will check similar characteristics in regard to the boy, mostly from the point of view of sex compatibility, psychological or temperamental compatibility and physical or health compatibility.

Indian astrologers recognise three 'natures': *Deva*, or divine; *Manusha*, or human; and *Rakshasa*, or devilish. These are revealed by a study of the Birth Chart; and it is rare for a *Deva* to be allowed to marry a *Rakshasa*; although to some extent this depends on sex – a *Deva* or *Manusha* man should not marry a *Rakshasa* girl; but a *Deva* or *Manusha* girl could marry a *Rakshasa* man! As a human soul passes through the various stages of evolution, it is possessed by various animal instincts, which are expressed through the degrees of the Zodiac as sexual urges. A Leo is unlikely to be sexually compatible with an Arian; and although this may not be a bar to marriage, it is seriously taken into consideration. After the horoscopes have been properly compared, and a marriage agreed on, the date has of course to be carefully fixed. No marriages at all take place at certain times of the year.

Astrologers are consulted, too, about building, both private and public. Before anyone moves into a new home, a date must be set. Important journeys are taken at times considered fortunate by astrologers. If an Indian falls ill, he sends first for his astrologer. If the latter calculates that the illness will be a lengthy one, it is obviously then worth summoning the doctor! Operations are performed on days that are auspicious for the patient rather than the doctor; and one surgeon – a Dr Guruswamy of Madras – has seriously proposed that hospitals should keep a patient's horoscope at the foot of his bed, along with his case-sheet.

The influence of astrology on all fields of Indian life can hardly be over-stated. It is considered perfectly normal, perfectly acceptable, perfectly proper to consult an astrologer; and often, although perhaps decreasingly, it is considered rather unnatural *not* to do so. The Indian is, of course, conditioned to accept astrology as a divine science (most astrologers are also priests of the Brahmin caste) capable of indicating the results of past Karma: a consultation can goad him to a greater effort in a predicament, or ease him from the results of catastrophe.

The professional astrologer in India will predict on every level; not only the personal, but the national and international. The late Professor Suryanarayana Rao predicted in March 1914 that a large-scale war would start in August of that year, and be sparked off by a royal assassination. Several Indian astrologers predicted the 1936 Behar earthquake, and the 1939 war; a week after the Germans occupied Paris, an Indian astrologer predicted the fall of Hitler in 1945, and the Allied victory. It seems to be generally, if wrily, admitted in Europe that Indian astrologers are extremely proficient in detailed prediction.

On another level, some astrologers (often working at stalls in the streets) work from the *Naides* or *Nadi Granthas* – palm-leaf manuscripts of very great age, containing innumerable horoscopes. One of the *Naides,* the *Satyasamhita,* has 125 volumes, each of 300 leaves it is imputed to Satya Charya, a Hindu astrologer of 30 B.C., at the Court of the Emperor Vikramaditya. On the basis of a given birth-time, or sometimes, a palm-print from the enquirer's hand, the entire life-history can be revealed. Easy or difficult childbirth, references to places where one will live or bear one's children, information about one's parents, education, future career, number of marriages, illness . . . all are to be found in the Naides. The Nadi philosophers assert that there are certain basic patterns of destiny (3,600 in every day, each pattern corresponding to 24 seconds of time; so that during each hour, 150 different patterns rise over the horizon). The relevant one will reveal much about the client.

Why has astrology continued to have such a hold on Indians? It may be that a low standard of general education has had much to do with it, but Mr Raman points out that

the integration of ancient ideals and values into the life and thought of the average Indian is so powerful that it is acting as a shock absorber. The long history of India shows the process of assimilation. Many an attempt was made in the past to foist on India new ways of living, believing and thinking. Each attempt failed in the sense that the best in it was assimilated. This assimilation makes the culture of India one of integral humanism. The philosophy of astrology is in tune with the philosophy of the people – the common factor being Karma. The universe is *Brahma* and the individual is the *Atman*. The physical aspect of the universe, *Brahmanda*, has as its counterpart the physical aspect of man, *Pindanda*. Therefore changes in the universe must have their repercussions on the individual also.

The conception is one which is difficult for a Western man to see as inevitable; but it is regarded as such by most Indians.

Elsewhere in the East, astrology is also strong. A television programme in the 'Whicker's World' series on BBC television at the end of 1967 was entitled 'Isle of Astrologers'. Alan Whicker watched the President of the Senate of Ceylon, the Hon. Abhaynatne Ratnayake, having his palm read by Professor Bulanthsinghala, who described himself nevertheless as an astrologer. The wife of the Minister of Local Government, Senator M. Tiruchelvam (a former solicitor-general), told Whicker of a detailed prediction made for her husband when he was an infant, and which substantially came true. It had even, she said, described *her*; a thin, dark girl interested in medical studies, and subject to asthma.

Doctors in Ceylon had done some research into the apparent relationship between the phases of the Moon and the frequency of births. Dr Anthonis, a London-trained senior surgeon at the General Hospital in Colombo, had found that by far the greatest number of deliveries took place on full-moon days. He suspected that there were correlations to be made between physical illnesses and the phases of the moon.

In Japan, astrology is only beginning to scrape a narrow foothold. Within the thousand years before Christ, there was keen interest at least at court. In A.D. 675 the Emperor Tenmu built an observatory especially for astrological purposes; and it is believed that he applied astrology widely to political and military affairs. Such surviving records as exist seem to suggest that Japanese astrology was borrowed wholesale from China – whence it had come, no doubt, from India – and was greatly strengthened by the importation of Buddhism in about A.D. 550. By A.D. 1113 astrology was widely used in military circles, by both generals and admirals – not only for timing military manoeuvres, but for forecasting the weather.

For eight hundred years the Japanese interest in astrology waxed and waned, but remained alive. The Emperor Meiji (1867–1912) actively discouraged it – he was busy dragging his country painfully into the twentieth century – and it is only since the 1939–45 war that an interest has revived, although there had been some signs of a renewal in 1922, when Kumamoto Arihisa, head of Kyoto Astronomical Observatory, published an indifferent adaptation and translation of Raphael, which because of his (Arihasa's) position was treated with respect.

In December 1955, Youko Shiojima published *The modern textbook of astrology* and started an 'Astro-Institute' to instruct would-be astrologers. Mr Youko Shiojima was a student of London University before the war; then became an adviser to the Imperial navy; and after the war turned to professional astrology. He holds both personal and correspondence courses, and will only accept students who are university graduates. He publishes a list of thirty-five professional astrologers he has trained, who practise in Tokyo, Yokohama, Kobe, and many smaller towns and cities.

The history of astrology in China is as long as in India, but far less well documented. The many civil wars destroyed most astrological libraries, and (as with all the generic arts in China) the continuity of history is obscured.

It seems probable that the most important period in Chinese astrological history was *c.* 246–207 B.C. (the Ch'in dynasty), when astrologers were honoured and supported officially. Later there were frequent periods of intense astrological activity, respectable and otherwise. Marco Polo found five thousand astrologers in the city of Kanbalu in the thirteenth century. They foretold the weather, epidemics, wars, famines, political conspiracies; they elected dates for journeys, the building of houses, the naming of children – much as they still do in India. Marco Polo relates how astrologers would sometimes hold up funerals for months (so that extra thick coffins had to be built for the dead!) and even then would occasionally and perversely order a specific line of exit from the house, so that a hole would have to be hacked through a wall to allow the funeral procession to pass.

Astrologers, though sometimes supported by the court, would not accept court appointments, preferring to build their own often very rich establishments. Astrological symbolism would be used to veil the most perceptive and revolutionary ideas, political, social and economic. The symbolism protected the astrologers if the suggestions failed or if their predictions did not turn out to be correct. The messages were improperly interpreted by the officials, the astrologers would suggest.

Astrology played a prominent part in the T'ai Ping Rebellion, and was used by the war lords in the early years of the republic to lay down plans of campaign, troop movements, and so on. The Empress Tzu Hsi's wild vacillations of policy were apparently prompted by astrologers; and she hurriedly shifted the coffin of an ancestress when astrologers pointed out that particular tomb as eminently suitable for her own burial. She was buried in it, at 5 a.m. on November 27, 1909, at the astrologers' behest.

After the declaration of the republic in 1912 the majority of astrologers were forced either to abandon astrology or to lower their standards – which by all accounts were at that time very high. The republic was not, officially, sympathetic; and astrologers had always, anyway, derived their considerable income through the dynastic system which now no longer existed. They now turned to teaching and tutoring in other subjects.

After the overthrow of the Nationalist government in 1949, the few astrologers left (most of them elderly) were ridiculed and reduced to silence on the mainland or driven to exile and often death in extreme poverty in Taiwan.

There are of course many parts of the world where astrology has scarcely been seriously studied. Australia and Africa are cases in point. There are one or two amateur astrologers in Australia. The newspapers and women's magazines print the usual astrological columns. But serious astrologers are few. Perhaps the most notable Australian astrologer is L. Furze-Morrish, whose astrological writing is well-known in England and America. An expatriate, he founded an Australian College of Astrology in 1967, and conducts classes in Caulfield, where he lives. He is the only major astrologer in Australia to have a regular clientele.

Arthur DeDion, another Australian astrologer, was in practice until a few years ago; and there are other serious students of astrology, among them Richard Silberstein, who is working on the possibilities of computerised astrology.

As in other countries, the Theosophical Society conducts astrological classes, and the Melbourne Lodge holds a weekly meeting of people generally interested in the subject; but these are amateurs. The Australian public, Furze-Morrish believes, is apathetic; the universities mainly hostile – and although 'a few individuals in the universities are interested' they are 'afraid to say anything openly for fear of reprisals'. This sounds melodramatic, but I believe it.

Africa is so vast a continent that it would be surprising if astrology had not a toe-hold here and there. On the west coast, among the immigrant Indians and Pakistanis, a number of apparently not very good Hindu astrologers have set up in business. But on the whole, as one astrologer in Kenya (Mr Roy Allin) points out, 'Astrology is as little known now as was the interior of Africa a century ago.' There would, in any case, be great difficulty in working among the Africans, in establishing their birth-times.

In South Africa, the position is somewhat different. There, there are several students of the British Faculty who seem to practise almost in secret; but at least they are in touch with each other and are occasionally able to meet.

The Dutch Reformed Church is totally opposed to astrology, and – the only example of positive censorship I have come across – succeeded recently in stopping the Afrikaans newspaper *Sarie Marais* publishing an astrological column. (Not that any astrologer would object to newspaper astrology being suppressed!) An Afrikaans women's magazine was similarly attacked by the Church in 1950, when it started an astrological column; but the readers showed practically no interest, so the reasons for dropping the column were no doubt equivocal.

The astrologers who do practise quietly in South Africa work on the whole among English-speaking South Africans. Most of Anne Cilliers's clients are women, many of them asking for their children's Charts to be considered.

The Afrikaaners are too firmly entrenched in their Calvinistic upbringing and attitude towards life to dare enquire into anything as soul-imperilling and Church-condemned as astrology [Mrs Cilliers pointed out in an article in *Kôsmos*]. If nothing else it engenders fear in them, especially if it should hit uncomfortably close to the mark.

In common with astrologers everywhere, the few professionals in South Africa find that they are expected to work virtually for nothing. 'I am overwhelmed with enquiries from people who want me to "have a look at their stars", as they put it, apparently thinking it will only take me a few minutes,' says Irene M. Foy of Johannesburg. Mrs Foy is a little more sanguine of public interest in astrology than Mrs Cilliers. She feels that there is considerable interest at Witwatersrand University, and although she agrees that the Dutch Reformed Church is hostile, she found that the Prime Minister, Dr Vorster, was interested enough at least to send her his birth date, and personally to acknowledge a copy of an astrological article about South Africa in relation to his own horoscope.

The country has its share of unsavoury characters and quacks. One for some time successfully advertised for clients, had their horoscopes professionally calculated and the analyses written by a distinguished British astrologer, and passed them on at a fifty per cent profit.

Interest among the non-white South Africans seems to be concentrated wholly on the newspaper columns, which seem more than usually indifferent, and generally syndicated. In the Johnnesburg *Star*, for instance, Eva Petulengro of Brighton instructs the South African Taureans to wear green, depend on the figure 3 for good luck, and watch out for the initial W at work!

XIV

Europe

Italy is perhaps the least astrologically-minded of European countries. One would have to travel to Scandinavia to find a comparable lack of interest. There is no properly organised Italian association of astrologers, although there are signs of a minor revival of interest at present.

There are the usual astrological newspaper columns (the Vatican, not having so far emulated the Dutch Reformed Church; on the contrary, there are strong rumours that the Vatican is interested in Dr Jonáš's work in Czechoslovakia, which has obvious bearing on the birth control controversy!); many of the columns are, again, syndicated, and by British writers. One Italian women's magazine now however publishes a monthly essay based on a single zodiacal sign, with instructions to readers enabling them to find their Ascendant as well as Sun-sign. This magazine, *Bellezza*, has also commissioned astrological articles of a serious nature from overseas astrologers; and its astrologer, 'Dottoressa Horus', is in fact Dr Rosanna Zerilli, a scholar who is also working on a long essay on the astrological aspects of Italian culture in the early Middle Ages, with particular reference to Dante's *Divina Commedia*, which has a great many astrological connotations.

One or two essays on astrology have recently been published in Italy. Rosita Cardano has made a study of the work of her ancestor, the scientist and astrologer Gerolamo Cardano (1501–76), whose astrological aphorisms William Lilly translated into English in 1676. They wonderfully mingle general entertainment and genuine traditional astrological lore. One finds, 'Mercury, mixing his Beams with Mars, is a great argument of a violent death'; and then, 'When Venus is with Saturn, and beholds the Lord of the Ascendant, the Native is inclinable to Sodomy, or at least shall love old hard-favoured Women, or poor dirty Wenches'; and, 'Make no new Clothes, nor first put them on when the Moon is in Scorpio, especially if she be full of light and beheld of Mars, for they will be apt to be torn and quickly worn out.'

Dr Ernst Bernhard, perhaps Italy's most distinguished Jungian psychotherapist (he died in 1965) was extremely interested in astrology. A book of his on the subject is about to be published. But most available publications are of the 'pocket-book' type. Francesco Waldner's magazine *L'astrologo moderno* is typical, giving primary instruction to amateurs, mixed with the occult and with palmistry. Nicola Sementowski-Kurilo publishes the rather similar *Nuovo trattato di astrologia*.

Astrological fees in Italy seem on the whole to be rather high: as much as 30,000 lire or 40,000 lire (between £20 and £30) for a written horoscope of something like 6,000 words; or 15,000 lire (about £10) for an hour's personal consultation.

There seems to be considerable social antagonism towards astrology in Spain – if the experience of José Murgui-Muñoz is typical. A banker who is a part-time astrologer in Barcelona, he was practically disowned by his family because of his interest in the subject. 'In these troubled circumstances,' he told me, 'I made some *strong remarks* about my only nephew.' These turned out to be accurate, with the result that the nephew nowadays ignores the advice of his parents and aunt, and turns to his astrologer uncle for guidance – a circumstance, one would have thought, unlikely to improve Señor Murgui-Muñoz's family relationships.

Professor Sesma of Madrid obtained considerable publicity a short while ago when he appeared on television twice within a few weeks, first to allege the existence of a scientifically ascertainable 'world of the heart' best revealed through astrology; and then as the newly-appointed President of the Spanish Flying Saucers' Society. Not, perhaps, the best kind of publicity.

The doyen of Spanish astrologers is Sanders Salcedo, now seventy-five, who has been a professional for forty-five years. He has published a great number of astrological books of one kind and another, including treatises on astrological history and practice, as well as *Magic perfumes and astrology,* and *Zodiacal fixed stars and sexuality.* In 1955, shortly after he had become (he says) official astrologer to King Mohamed V of Morocco, he travelled to Tangiers, and founded there the Scientific Centre for Astrological Studies, with a journal (*Practical Astrology*) with a circulation of 50,000. He is working at the moment on a lengthy study of the astrological and psychological implications of male and female forenames; and on another long study of sexuality (*'normale et déviée'*) interpreted by astrological means.

Spanish bookshops are full of prediction booklets, and newspaper astrology has a fervent following. There is also a surprisingly high sale of astrological textbooks. The Librería Francesca in Barcelona stocks translations of books by Alan Leo and Max Heindel, and a Spanish translation of André Barbault's *In defence of astrology,* published by Editorial Iberia, sold well. These publishers attempted to commission an astrological textbook – but since they demanded that the author should devise a system of astrological prediction which did not require the use of an ephemeris, the idea fell through! At the end of 1969, the Librería Francesca ordered a hundred 1970 ephemerides from London, only to be forced to re-order within a few days.

In France there is, on the one hand, considerable activity at the Centre International d'Astrologie in Paris, while the *Cahiers astrologique* regularly contains discussions (often at a level of personal vituperation not excelled elsewhere in Europe!) which at any rate indicates a burning interest in the subject among professionals. On the other hand Germaine Holley, who has practised not only in France but also in Switzerland, Belgium and America for some years, feels that France is fundamentally uninterested in the subject; that there is a lack of serious discussion and research.

Certainly astrology in France during the first half of the century seems never to have been far from alchemy, palmistry, numerology, and the Tarot. The more conventional astrologer began to emerge later than in Britain but newspaper astrology got going perhaps a little before its British counterpart; and astrological periodicals of the kind of *Fate* and *Horoscope – Votre destin* – for instance, and *Sous le ciel* – came out during the middle 1930s.

One notable reference book has appeared more recently. During the war, the Vicomte Charles de Herbais de Thun, a Belgian astrologer, published a huge *Encyclopédie du mouvement astrologique de langue française*, containing short biographies, together with lists of their publications, of over 150 French astrologers from 1890 until the time of publication.

The most important French figure in astrology (although he himself would no doubt deny too close a connection) is undoubtedly M. Michel Gauquelin. He is at present researching at the Psychophysiological Laboratory at Strasbourg University. M. Gauquelin, who has a degree in psychology and statistics from the Sorbonne, is not an astrologer, but he has been engaged for over twenty years in the study of the relation between cosmic and biological phenomena. He had become interested in the work of Krafft and Choisnard, both of whom attempted statistical proof of certain astrological affirmations. But they had no real knowledge of statistics, and it was impossible for a statistician to accept their methods or findings. So Gauquelin set out his own research plan, and has examined Birth Charts in considerable numbers (they must by now total almost 100,000). The results of his investigations have been published in a series of books – *L'influence des astres, L'homme et les astres, L'hérédité planétaire*, and others – and most recently in a speculative work published in the US, *The cosmic clocks*.

In Germany interest in astrology revived in the 1880s. The influence of Madame Blavatsky was strong, through her admirer and neophyte Dr Wilhelm Hübbe-Schleiden. It was he who, with a rich businessman, Gutav Gebhard, founded the German theosophist movement. Interest in the subject steadily built up before the First World War, and continued to progress after 1918 – although it was officially discouraged, and at one time it was even illegal to provide predictions for money.

Naturally, when the Nazi party became prominent, professional and amateur astrologers busily drew up charts for its leaders. As early as 1931, Hitler's chart was reproduced and discussed in the astrological magazine *Zenit* (whose editor subsequently perished in a concentration camp). During the same year, Dr K.-G. Heimsoth discussed the charts of Goebbels, Goering, Strasser and Roehm. (Dr Heimsoth was murdered during the 1934 S.S. *Putsch*.) In the early 1930s there seems to have been a plethora of astrologers in Germany, but during the second half of the decade they disappeared underground because the Nazi party had become unsympathetic. In 1938, the last of a long line of German astrological congresses was held, and the Gestapo only permitted that on condition that the proceedings were not published.

It was during the 1930s that incidents began to build up which contributed to the extraordinary legends about Hitler's private astrologer; about Hess being 'crazed with astrology'; about the British government's secret astrologer, who taught Churchill the rudiments of the craft. (Four astrologers are currently distributing stories that they personally taught Mr Churchill at 10 Downing Street.)

The true story of the Nazis and the astrologers is to some extent more fascinating than the fiction. Ellic Howe tells it in *Urania's children*,[1] and it is unlikely that any future research will uncover much that is new. The story of Mr Howe's search for his material is a saga of perseverance and concentration.

The man accused of being Hitler's astrologer was Karl Ernst Krafft. It seems that a neutral diplomat brought his name to the attention of the British authorities during the early months of the war, via an extraordinary Germano-British astrologer, Louis de Wohl.

The story really started in 1939. Frau Goebbels was reading *Mysterien von Sonne und Seele* by Dr H. H. Kritzinger, which referred to an earlier book by a German postal official, Herr Loog, who had become interested in the prophecies of Nostradamus. These are not specifically astrological, although Nostradamus's contemporaries thought of him as an astrologer. He wrote so ambiguously, misspelled so persistently, used so many anagrams, so many abbreviations, that his work is a delight to anyone who

[1] op. cit.

wishes to predict anything.

Herr Loog interpreted and translated several of Nostradamus's 1,555 quatrains and Frau Goebbels fell on one which apparently foresaw a crisis centred on Poland, which would provoke the final downfall of Britain. Frau Goebbels, obviously extremely excited, nudged her husband, who in his turn summoned Kritzinger and instructed him to examine the other 1,554 quatrains and come up with something good for the propaganda machine. Kritzinger was unenthusiastic; so was Loog, to whom he passed on the message. So Kritzinger suggested Krafft as a Nostradamus expert who would undoubtedly be delighted to do the job. As indeed he was.

A Swiss citizen who had left Switzerland after some business difficulties, Krafft was in sympathy with the Nazis, and had managed to get himself a small regular income from the Reich-ssicherheitschauptamp (RSHA), Himmler's secret intelligence service, for whom he seems to have written an occasional memorandum on economic matters. Ellic Howe suggests plausibly that the RSHA was probably much more interested in Krafft's Swiss passport and the use that could be made of it, than in his somewhat questionable talents.

It so happened that the RSHA man who engaged Krafft was also interested in astrology; and in October 1939, Krafft wrote to this benefactor, Dr Heinrich Fesel, warning him that Hitler's life would be in danger during the first ten days of November. On November 8 there was an unsuccessful attempt to assassinate the Führer at the Burgerbräu beer-hall in Munich. Seven people were killed; but Hitler had left the building. Hearing the news, Krafft understandably but unwisely sent a telegram to Berlin, pointing out that he had told them so. The Gestapo arrested him early next morning. Interrogated in Berlin, he was able to talk himself out of what must have been a fairly tight corner, and was released. Late in 1939, Kritzinger called him to Berlin to work on Nostradamus.

During the early months of the war, Krafft was corresponding with an acquaintance in London on astrological matters. A German-born English astrologer, Louis de Wohl, heard that Krafft was working (apparently semi-officially) in Berlin, and became convinced – or pretended to be convinced – that Hitler believed in astrology, and that what Krafft was doing in the German capital was advising the Führer on the conduct of the war. In his book *The stars of war and peace*,[1] a book which is romantic enough to suggest considerable embroidery of the facts, de Wohl claimed that he discussed the matter with a Deputy Under-secretary of State at the Foreign Office, and later with Lord Halifax himself, and 'the heads of the various Service Departments'.

No one, it seemed, was over-anxious to employ de Wohl:

The very idea that one fine day a member of the House of Commons might get up and ask whether it was true that His Majesty's Government was employing an astrologer, made many of my new friends shudder [he wrote]. But at long last the niche was found. The fact that I had been living in Germany for over thirty years and thus knew a good deal about German psychology led to an excellent solution. It was called the Psychological Research Bureau, and it opened its offices at Grosvenor House, Park Lane, one of London's most fashionable hotels. . . . Considerably more than eight hours a day I spent on the unofficial side of my work; to check up on what Hitler was likely to be told by his astrological adviser.

Krafft was not as close to the Führer as may have been thought in London; in fact, he was never very close at all. Early in 1941 he had been warned off astrology, and even made to sign an agreement that he would not discuss astrology or Nostradamus in public (an injunction he promptly ignored). Perhaps by this time the German government had tumbled to the fact that the British were not themselves above using astrology as a weapon. Sefton Delmer, one of the most able workers in the Political Warfare Executive, had engaged de Wohl to write and prepare accurate forgeries of the German astrological magazine *Zenit* for distribution through the underground into Germany.

But it was Hess's defection to England that really finished German astrology for the duration of the war. It is supposed that Martin Borman was the first to seize on the fact that a minor member of Hess's staff was an amateur astrologer, as an excuse for

[1] Louis de Wohl, *The stars of war and peace* (Rider & Co., 1952).

the Deputy-Führer's action. Only four days after the flight, the
Völkischer Beobachter wrote:

As was well known in Party circles, Rudolf Hess was in poor
health for many years and latterly increasingly had recourse to
hypnotists, astrologers, and so on. The extent to which these
people were responsible for the mental confusion that led him to
his present step has still to be clarified.

And shortly afterwards came the *Aktion Hess*, with massive
arrests of a great number of people interested in the occult.
Borman signed a decree blanketing together 'astrologers, fortune-
tellers and other swindlers'. On June 12, 1941 Krafft was arrested.
Ironically, only three days after his arrest he was set to work with a
colleague, F. G. Goerner, at the Propaganda Ministry, on the
Charts of Timoshenko, Montgomery, Auchinleck, Roosevelt. He
took the work seriously, apparently believing that he was con-
tributing to the war effort. When he realised that he was simply
expected to turn out propaganda rubbish, he had a nervous break-
down (one of the results of which was that he sent a strong memo
to a senior propaganda minister predicting a large clutch of British
bombs for the latter's office). Early in 1943, Krafft was removed
from his tiny office at the Kommandentenstrasse, and put into a
small cell with thirty other prisoners in Lehrerstrasse Prison. He
caught typhus, and died in a train on the way to Buchenwald on
January 8, 1945.

It is an ironical, tragi-comical story; and there is much more to
it than in this brief summary – Mr Howe's book[1] examines the
whole relationship of astrology to the Nazi Government, factual
and fictional. Apart from the brief reference in his interminably
boring table-talk, Hitler's only contact with astrology seems to
have taken place during the Götterdämmerung of April 1945,
when in the bunker in Berlin, the US Ninth Army sixty miles
away in one direction, and the Russians about to cross the Oder in
the other, Goebbels was reading to his master from Carlyle's *History of Frederick the Great*. Prompted by the historian's description of how Frederick faced the darkest moments of the Seven
Years War, and of the miracle of the House of Brandenburg and

[1] *Urania's children,* op. cit.

Frederick's ultimate survival, Goebbels sent out to Himmler's headquarters for two horoscopes which were apparently filed there.

They were the charts of Hitler himself (drawn up for the moment when he became Chancellor) and of the Weimar Republic. Count Schwerin von Krosigk (who had been Minister of Finance from 1932 until the last day of the Third Reich) wrote in his diary:

An amazing fact has become evident, both horoscopes predicting the outbreak of the war in 1939, the victories until 1941, and the subsequent series of reversals, with the hardest blows during the first months of 1945, particularly during the first half of April. In the second half of April we were to experience a temporary success. Then there would be stagnation until August and peace that same month. For the following three years Germany would have a hard time, but starting in 1948 she would rise again.

Goebbels was so impressed that in a speech on April 6 he announced publicly that the Führer had been vouchsafed the news of the very hour of a change in Germany's fortunes:

The Führer has declared that even in this very year a change of fortune shall come. ... The true quality of genius is its consciousness and its sure knowledge of coming change. The Führer knows the exact hour of its arrival. Destiny has sent us this man so that we, in this time of great external and internal stress, shall testify to a miracle.

A week later, as the Chancellery burned after a violent air raid, Goebbels telephoned Hitler immediately: 'My Führer,' he said, 'I congratulate you! Roosevelt is dead! It is written in the stars that the second half of April will be the turning-point for us. This is Friday, April 13. It is the turning point.'

His secretary, Inge Haberzettel, noticed with great surprise that Goebbels was in ecstasy all day. Von Krosigk wrote: 'This was the Angel of History! We felt its wings flutter through the room! Was not that the fortune we awaited so anxiously?' It was not. The whole incident was one of the strangest and most macabre of all those during the last days of Hitler.

After the war it was not long before astrology broke into the German newspapers. Mass-Observation had noticed how the astrological columns appeared to have an encouraging effect upon the British during the darkest days of their war. Now astrologers in the German press spared no efforts to encourage their gloomy readers to rebuild their lives and the life of the country.

In Germany today, astrology is treated by leading astrologers with great and perhaps typically Germanic seriousness, as an empirical study. Reinhold Ebertin, the son of a prominent pre-war German astrologer, Elspeth Ebertin, can count on selling 2,000 copies at least of even the most technical of his textbooks.

Ebertin, the founder in 1928 of *Kosmobiologie*, the most reputable German astrological magazine, has worked out his own system of interpretation of a Birth Chart, which is in some ways anti-astrological – or at all events hostile to many traditional astrological concepts. He ignores house divisions, for instance, and pays scant regard to the signs of the Zodiac themselves. He was born in Silesia in 1901. He is a publisher, and a professional astrologer only in the sense that he is concerned in research and experimental work, and in forming his own theories; he has never done much consultant work. Originally a schoolmaster, in his late twenties he turned wholeheartedly to astrological studies, founding his specialist publishing firm. Beginning by publishing the most popular kind of astrological books, gradually his own interests outstripped this moderate course, and he began to work out his own astrological theories. In 1932 he organised a Congress of 'astrological pioneers' which was attended by representatives of various factions in the country. He was among the astrologers arrested after Hess's flight, and is said to have smuggled an ephemeris into prison in his sock, and, consulting it, to have decided that there was a good chance of his being released at a particular time. He was.

After the war, he rescued a single duplicating machine which he had managed to protect from damage, and started his publishing firm again in Aalen, where he restarted *Kosmobiologie* and in 1948 organised the first post-war astrological conference. This became an annual event, and resulted in the formation of the Kosmobiologische Akademie Aalen.

Ebertin's astrological textbooks, which are rather more specu-
lative than educative, are read with enormous interest not only in
Germany but by astrologers of a similar cast of mind everywhere.
Perhaps the most important is *Komination der Gestirneinflüsse*
(*The combination of stellar influences*), which was published in
1940 and revised ten years later.

With his son Dr Baldur Ebertin, a psychologist, he now works in
neurological clinics with a group of doctors, neurologists, psychologists, physicists, theoretical physicists, mathematicians and
chemists, on brain patterns, comparison of the indications of
specific diseases, analyses of various charts of psychologically disturbed people on a carefully controlled basis, and aims particularly
to concentrate the known facts of astrological analysis, with a view
to building a recognised methodology.

The President of the Kosmobiologische Akademie had been,
until his death, Dr Rudolph Tomaschek. One of the world's most
distinguished geophysicists, he had himself published some
interesting speculations on the nature of astrological influence. In
Tradition und Fortschritt der Klassischen Astrologie he places
emphasis on the 'correlation of astronomical facts with terrestrial
events', stressing that 'the truth of such correlations can be demonstrated by statistical methods; that is, the correlations between the
positions and aspects of the planets and angles with terrestrial
events. Their factual character is beyond doubt.'

He offers four theories in an attempt to explain why such correlations may appear. He dismisses as over-simple the possibility
that the planets actually *operate upon* events on earth, or that
they might trigger off earthly events which are anyway due to
happen. There might indeed be vibrations of some sort which
might act upon earth; but these are obviously at the moment
incapable of definition. He finds the theory of synchronicity
interesting – that all events within our reach are *total*, each a part
of the other. But as he points out, this is extremely difficult to
check, since it presupposes a *quality* of time. No moment can be
repeated, each moment is unique, and no experiment could take
place again and again under controlled conditions.

The theory with which Tomaschek is evidently most in sympathy is that the planets *symbolise* organic and cosmic forces

which are qualitative functions of time and space. This pre-supposes, he says, 'an animated universe, a spiritual coherence of the whole cosmos'. He quotes Heisenberg's Principle of Uncertainty, that it is not possible to determine the behaviour of an elementary particle in a strictly causal fashion. It is not possible to make an unambiguous forecast about it. Even the simplest particle is seen to possess a certain 'freedom'.

The states of consciousness which are within our comprehension (and this does not include, for instance, the state of consciousness which might be possessed by the planets or stars – Tomaschek cites Fred Hoyle's fantasy *The black cloud* in this connection)

> belong to . . . the microcosmic complexity which has developed via the protein molecules to organic life and eventually, by way of the organisation of the brain, to the thinking faculty and ego-consciousness. Although man, in respect of magnitude, stands between the atom and a heavenly body, he is not in the same line of evolution. Rather is the heavenly body the precondition of his existence.

Tomaschek wants to work towards 'a scientific understanding of the symbolism in astrology'. It is perhaps a typical Germanic approach to the question.[1]

---

[1] It is difficult to check on astrological activity behind the Iron Curtain. The Communist governments are not sympathetic to 'astrology', although 'cosmobiology' is not only tolerated but sometimes actively encouraged. (It is interesting to note the same language difference here as in *astro*naut and *cosmo*naut.)

There is the Czech government's Astrobiological Society at the Slovak Academy of the Czech Academy of Sciences, with Dr Eugen Jonáš at its head (see Chapter XI) and there are strong rumours of a Cosmobiological Institute at Kiev, headed by a Dr Emilyevich Kirsanov, where work is said to be going on in the correlation of planetary positions and certain symptoms of nervous diseases. But this has proved impossible to confirm.

XV

The Benefit of the Doubt

Most of us are so bound by the physical aspect of our lives, by what we can see and touch, that it is difficult for us to apprehend the untouchable. It is very easy to understand the scientist who remarked that for Marconi to send a message across the Atlantic was as impossible as for man to fly to the moon. Yet it would be a brave man who, living in the second half of the twentieth century (when wireless and the conquest of space are as familiar as television and the hydrogen bomb) would deny that the untouchable – almost the unthinkable – does often exist. It has become clearer than ever that there are universal laws which remain outside our comprehension. Lichtenberg remarked that 'if an angel were to tell us something of his philosophy, some of his propositions would sound like $2 \times 2 = 13$'. Similarly, some recent discoveries in science have made the proposition that $2 \times 2 = 4$ look fairly elementary. A speculative mind must be open to the ridiculous if it is not to risk being made to look ridiculous at last.

When I was first told the story of the Ascension, I felt that it was unlikely, for reasons of taste as well as mechanics. But religion, or the structure of the universe, have nothing to do with good or bad taste, and if they have anything to do with mechanics, those mechanics may obey rules quite unknown to us. So that one cannot properly call the astrological theory *unlikely*; it is not a word that has much meaning.

I now believe that astrologers can discover certain characteristics of one's personality by examining the position of the planets at the time of one's birth; and there seems a strong probability that some kind of prediction is possible, although there are obvious doubts about the extent to which exact predictions of any kind can at present be made.

This declaration is one which I would not have made two or three years ago; and even now it somewhat shocks me to find myself making it. Yet I believe that any reasonable man would have to make a similar declaration, after examining the evidence. What is that evidence? It is by no means wholly to be found in these pages. None of the facts and speculations I have presented would alone have been sufficient to persuade me. They are interesting, but far from conclusive; and as Dr Stevens underlines in his Appendix,[1] they were not obtained under proper test conditions. I do not believe that any of them have been faked, but it is certainly possible that some of them could be unreliable.

My conviction springs from various sources: from my own observations in my contacts with astrologers; from my observation of the reactions of their clients; from my examination of reports of medical, business, meteorological astrology. Each of these factors taken singly may be capable of dismissal; but taken altogether, I find them impressive. It may be argued that this is a slim basis for conviction, and indeed in the end acceptance of the astrological theory – a belief that certain observations about the nature of life on earth can be made after examination of the movements of the planets – may necessitate an act of faith.

But however this may be, in my view Mr Charles Harvey, Miss Ingrid Lind and Mr John Naylor could not have written their analyses of my character without some clues; and those clues were certainly not provided by me. Mr Harvey's statement of the relationship between me and my parents, and Mr Naylor's suggestion of my wife's birth-date did not, in Miss Lind's phrase, get into their analyses by knitting. Nor in general were their reports so vague that they could apply to anyone else. Other astrological reports I have seen from serious astrologers often include the same sort of detail, and seem to apply equally specifically to their subjects.

[1] See Appendix I.

Of course many of the statements made by astrologers are general and can be applied generally rather than specifically. I have attempted to make allowances for this, keeping in mind one's infinite capacity for self-deception. The area in which astrological reports seem weakest and most general is the area of prediction; and astrologers will admit this. Generalisation in prediction is, they say, unavoidable. They predict 'trends', and not events. This may be seen as an excuse; but is it not also honest? While the predictions made for me by the three astrologers I consulted (and, privately, by my wife) have often not appeared to be accurate, sometimes when I have checked them retrospectively they have proved to be so; and I have found that predictions of days of frustration in business, of extreme activity, of indolence, bad temper, feelings of well-being or depression, have sometimes been forecast some months in advance. But it seems clear that astrologers are at present only moving around the edge of a predictive field, supposing one to exist.

What sort of proof of the astrological theory would be universally accepted? Only, it may be, the kind of proof which is unlikely (as far as one can see) to emerge. But at least it is true that negative proof is as hard to come by, as positive. Various researchers have produced statistical evidence that astrology does not work; but their conclusions are almost always as suspect as conclusions on the other side of the argument. Michel Gauquelin, for instance, quotes approvingly in his book *The cosmic clocks* an experiment mounted by a scientist who 'had the patience to study the birth-dates of more than 2,000 famous painters and musicians: Libra has not ruled over the birth of these people more than the other signs . . .'. He also draws attention to the conclusions of an astronomer, J. Allen Hynk, who studied the birthdays of scientists, and found that they fall on random dates. But M. Gauquelin knows that in astrological terms the influence of Libra on painters and musicians, and of Aquarius on scientists, would make itself felt through the M.C., the Ascendant, the position of the Moon – by no means *solely* through the Sun-sign. The 'experiments' he quotes have no real astrological significance.

Statistical proof offered by astrologers has been, up to now, similarly suspect (although one or two large-scale astrological experiments, some of them already under way, others in a planning stage, may have been better designed, and may provide interesting evidence). The difficulty is that the astrological theory is so complex that statistical evidence can be interpreted in many different ways. It can also be, in itself, extremely complicated and difficult to analyse. Even supposing that one were able, for instance, to obtain the correct birth time and place of every passenger in an aircraft involved in a major air disaster, one could not expect their charts to show precisely the same indications. In fact a French astrologer, Volguine, published, in *Les cahiers astrologiques* for March 1966, a statistical analysis of the planetary positions at the time of 202 air crashes. Commenting on these, John Addey pointed out[1] that the methods used were unlikely to produce any *real* evidence. 'It is only when the circle of zodiacal, mundane and aspectual relationships are explored *in their fullness* (and not in terms of limited conventional divisions only) that the full dynamic of astrology is seen and rendered statistically accessible'.

If the circumstances of the air crashes were to be properly examined, astrologically, then one would presumably need not only the birth-times and places of everyone concerned in them (including those who serviced the planes, those who guided them from the ground, those who plotted the timetables and routes, etc.), but also the data of the builders of the planes, as well as the details of their first flights, the moments of take-off on the fatal flights, and perhaps additional data. The size of the problem becomes formidable; and until it is thought worthwhile to devote very considerable computer time to the examination of this kind of data on a broad scale, real statistical evidence will simply not be available. As Mr Addey put it:

> The best experience which it seems the patient, persistent and careful investigator can hope for, as long as he sticks to conventional astrological concepts of signs, houses and aspects, is to receive a fair but tantalisingly small – just too small – confirmation of the general principles and concepts of traditional astrology. But the margin of success is nearly always too slender to be convincing to others.[2]

[1] *Astrological Journal*, vol. VIII, No. 3 (Summer 1966).
[2] *ibid*.

The slowly changing climate of opinion about astrology has been affected not so much by astrological experiments, as by a slow leakage of convincing borderline information, some of it appearing in the press as general news. An American researcher is reported to have studied many thousands of birth dates before concluding that the people born in New England in March tend to live on an average four years longer than people born in July; a British demographer studies the physical data of 21,000 troops and finds an obvious relation between their weight and height and the season of their birth; a New York researcher finds that the IQ of schoolchildren there is higher for those born in May, June, September and October than at other seasons, and is at its lowest for those born in January and February.

Sometimes it is possible to explain these figures non-astrologically. When one hears that there have always been more births in the northern hemisphere in May and June than in November and December, one might argue that the warmth of the weather in August is more conducive to procreation than the cold of February (even if there has been no change in the statistics since the advent of cheaper and easier means of heating the home). But more often than not, 'astrological' statistics are received in a mordant silence.

But, if conclusive proof of the viability of the astrological theory were to appear tomorrow morning, we would be no nearer to discovering why or how it worked (although the resulting concentration of scientific attention might reveal some acceptable solution). M. Gauquelin believes that a child at birth inherits from his parents a sensitivity to the 'planetary clocks' which, he argues, influence the reproductive cycles of certain sea animals, the behaviour of oysters, the breathing of embryos in fertilised hens' eggs (aware of the rising and setting of the sun despite being kept at a uniform temperature and in a constant light). But is this theory any more likely than the conventional astrological one? Assuming that there is an unearthly (I do not mean an occult) force which reaches the embryo in the hen's egg through the protective envelopes of space, atmosphere, sea, eggshell, laboratory, or whatever, could it not also reach the human embryo in the womb and have its effect upon the infinitely delicate process of cell formation? If there is any truth in the fact that a physical influence from the planets acts on human beings at all (and I cannot personally accept a force which is *not* physical in its effects) then it must surely act at its strongest during the very early stages of development in the womb.

Why then, the apparently infinitely important 'moment of birth' calculated to the minute? What about the place of birth? What if a mother travels ten thousand miles in the weeks after the child's conception? My credulity of an astrological theory stops a long way short of the notion that at the moment of birth, and only at that precise moment, some extraordinary terrestrial force implants its seal upon the newborn child. Yet I cannot deny that astrologers, working from the moment of *my* birth, appear to have produced certain accurate facts about my life and character. Was I, then, at some point subject to the action of 'rays from outer space' – for such a phrase, straight out of science fiction, seems the only applicable one?

Again, suppose that this is true: then how *broad* is the astrological system? If it works for humans, then does it work also for animals, birds, insects? As far as I know, there has been no serious attempt to discover this. The two dogs with whose characters I am most familiar conform roughly to their astrological types. But would one expect to find an astrological influence in the life of a fly, or an elephant, or a cabbage? Surely the astrological influence would not be in proportion to a living organism's size or longevity, but to its intelligence. One would expect a more decided influence on a human than a horse. But the only reason why the astrological theory should not work for animals as for man is presumably theological!

If one links the astrological influence with intelligence, with an effect on the *mind* (either at birth or subsequently), where does this leave the political astrologer? How does one explain such phenomenon as the forecasting of the sinking of the *Titanic*, deduced from a chart drawn up for the moment of her launching? These are not questions an astrologer is able to answer. If they are ever answered, it will surely be by scientists. And the scientists apparently are not interested. For the first time in the five or six thousand years during which man has been examining the astrological theory, it may at last be possible to prove conclusively whether or not it works. It is difficult to understand why not one scientist has given the matter his serious attention.

The advantages of a properly supported astrological theory are obvious. But even without them, what a fascinating contribution would be made to our conception of the universe if the theory were supported by scientific evidence. Can no one be persuaded that a serious examination is worthwhile?

Just as I find the scientific mind closed to the idea, so a great number of intelligent laymen and women similarly close their minds. Without having examined the propositions of astrology seriously, without having looked at the inexplicable accuracy of many astrological analyses, they automatically dismiss the possibility that the theory may be capable of proof. Of the sceptics who have been willing to listen, and to whom I have put some of the questions in my own mind, none has had any alternative explanation to offer for, for instance, the accuracy of astrological analysis of character. The one thing they seem clear about is that whatever is responsible for that acuracy, it can have nothing to do with astrology. One is tempted to recall Sir Isaac Newton's reputed comment when Edmund Halley criticised him for accepting astrology: 'Sir, I have studied the subject; you have not.'

When one considers the great number of astrologers working all over the world, at the beginning of the 1970s – as consultants, in medicine, weather forecasting, business, psychiatry; when one considers that they are often very highly paid for their services by people who are unlikely to pour good money after bad; when one considers the number of accurate forecasts made often within narrowly circumscribed limits; when one looks at the slowly but steadily growing evidence of a planetary influence on terrestrial life, is it reasonable still to postpone a proper, scientific examination of the whole field of astrology?

I believe that it is not.

Appendices

Appendixes

Appendix I

A PSYCHIATRIST'S VIEW
Anthony Stevens, M.A., B.M., B.Ch., D.P.M.

What am I, a man of science, doing writing an appendix to a book on astrology? It is an interesting sign of the times that I am prepared to consider it, for, but a short while ago, to appear between such covers as these, even in the company of Mr Parker, would have been to commit professional suicide. Enough eyebrows will be raised as it is; and so I had better explain at once that it is not astrology as an art which compels my attention but the extraordinary come-back which this primordial craft has made on the contemporary scene. How is one to explain this strange phenomenon? What can it signify?

I cannot pretend to give definite answers to these questions, although I realise that the reader may expect me to try. That I have been trained in the disciplines of normal and abnormal psychology does not, in my view, confer on me any special authority to write on the questions raised by Mr Parker's book. The reflections which I offer are no more than the free associations of a psychiatrist relaxing on his couch; my words have no greater value than what the reader feels they are worth.

I sound this note of warning because it seems to me that Mr Parker's kind invitation shows that he shares the common illusion that psychiatrists are scientists who know all that is worth knowing about 'what makes people tick'; why else should he choose me to assess the accuracy of three astrological analyses of his character, and evaluate his own objectivity in reviewing them?

It is not perhaps widely appreciated that psychology, psychiatry and psycho-analysis represent three quite distinct disciplines and that only the first of them has any claim to be scientific. Psychology moved away from its parent, philosophy, over a hundred years ago to embark on an ambitious attempt to establish itself as an empirical science of mind whose status would bear comparison with that of Newtonian physics. Galling though it is to admit in a book on astrology, the attempt has proved something of a flop, for after more than a century of continuous endeavour, all that academic psychology has to show for itself is a collection of facts, a number of generalisations, a handful of 'laws' and no firmly established corpus of scientific theory. Psychiatry and psycho-analysis on the other hand are not concerned with the investigation of normal mental processes but with the comprehension and treatment of abnormal mental and emotional states. Psychiatrists are doctors first and foremost: few have more than a superficial training in academic psychology (in this respect I can count myself a privileged exception). Psycho-analysts may also be doctors but they confine their activities to the use of one therapeutic method, namely the analytic technique advocated by Sigmund Freud.

Analysts of the school founded by C. G. Jung are called 'analytical psychologists', but they have little in common with experimental psychologists, by whom they are completely disowned. Adlerians call themselves 'individual psychologists'. But these semantic distinctions between analysts of the various schools have never caught on, and to the lay public they are all 'psycho-analysts'. It is in this lay sense that I use the term here. In this country the majority of psychiatrists are not analysts and, contrary to common belief, do not adhere to any analytic school. Like analysts, however, many psychiatrists are psychotherapists in the sense that they endeavour to treat their patients' minds by using their own.

No psychiatrist or psycho-analyst can hope to be scientific in his practice: he hasn't time. If he waited for the experimental psychologists to test in their laboratories all the hypotheses on which his work is based, he and his patients would be dead before the results were ready for publication. That psychotherapists are unscientific in their procedures however causes a number of experimental psychologists to look down their noses at them – much as I imagine scientists of all disciplines must look down their noses at astrologers. I find this comparison instructive.

In the course of reading Mr Parker's book I have been struck repeatedly by the similarities which exist between astrology and psycho-analysis. They both represent systems in which every observation made by the astrologer or the analyst is referred to existing hypotheses without ever questioning the hypotheses themselves. They both provide a frame of reference, a vocabulary, a syntax in terms of which two people may formulate a common understanding, so that what was previously unknown or experienced in isolation may be comprehended and shared. From what Miss Lind says it is apparent that *transference* plays an important part in her relationship with her clients, which goes far to explain why they seem to accept her occult notions as uncritically as a reclining patient drinking in the Freudian interpretations of his analyst. The quotation on pages 88–9 from an article in *Time* magazine could be applied just as well to psychotherapy, whether 'analytically orientated' or not. Only a few words need changing.

> Sensitivity, intuition and maybe even clairvoyance makes the difference between . . . tomfoolery and 'good' astrology [psychotherapy]. The good astrologer [therapist] senses the mood of his client [patient], perceives his problems and finds the most positive way of fitting them into the context of the horoscope [analytic theory]. Then he goes ahead, shaping predictions so that they amount to constructive counsel. . . . There are many troubled people who refuse to accept personal responsibility for their lives, insisting that some outer force is in control. For these, a first-class astrologer [psychiatrist] can seem a necessity – and perhaps he is. [I'm *sure* he is!]

If, then, the astrologer and the psychotherapist have so much in common, why is it that a number of people choose to become clients of the former rather than patients of the latter? The psychiatrist, it has often been suggested, is taking over the rôle once played in our society by the priest; but evidently a growing

number of men and women consider this rôle to be more adequately filled by the astrologer. Why?

Historically, one may regard astrology, like alchemy, as a stage
in man's intellectual progress from magic to natural science: it
arose directly from the human obsession with seeking explanations. Before modern technology made him overweening,
man saw himself at the centre of a mysterious universe whose
behaviour he experienced as both arbitrary and capricious. Any
system, however absurd, attracted him if it could impose order on
this fearful chaos, particularly if it gave him the power to predict
disasters before they overwhelmed him. And so he relied on quaint
magical-symbolical formulations until, in the seventeenth century,
the conviction grew on him that the universe itself might be
governed by natural laws which could with certainty be established by systematic observation and experiment.

> *Nature and Nature's laws lay hid in night;*
> *God said: 'Let Newton be,' and all was light.*

But the light which Newton lit was to prove a mixed blessing for
mankind. The primordial longings which gave birth to astrology and alchemy were not to be gratified by the new sciences,
astronomy and chemistry, which superseded them. The old astrologers had not been interested in the real nature of the stars any
more than the alchemists in the real nature of matter; for both,
heavens and matter constituted an enormous screen on which they
might gape transfixed at their own unconscious projections. But
when Newton's light came on, ending this magic peep-show, what
could the astronomer, who walked so boldly on to the stage, tell a
man in the audience who wanted to know about his personal
destiny, and how could a chemist help him in his quest for personal
transmutation? In order to become scientifically sophisticated we
had to pay a heavy price; we were bereft of our sense of intimate
participation in the universe we inhabit. By becoming objective
about the stars and aloof to matter man not only made natural
science possible but precipitated his final ejection from the Garden
of Eden; he bit deep into the apple which fell on Newton's
head.

We are, however, of the same species as those men who only

yesterday, in biological time, inhabited the pre-Newtonian twi-
light; their symbolical needs, which the new sciences ignored,
linger on in us. Depth psychologists of all schools are agreed that
repressed components lose neither their identity nor their li-
bidinous charge in the unconscious and may once again achieve
direct expression should the repression be removed; it is also held
by Jungians that any one-sided attitude, if persisted in, either on
the cultural or the personal level, eventually goes over into its
opposite. Thus, it would not seem far-fetched to argue that the
contemporary resurrection of astrology is symptomatic of a quick-
ening of dormant elements banished too long from individual consciousness and cultural acceptance.

'The unconscious primordial mind,' wrote Baynes, 'in which
are to be found all those living contents of the soul which have not
been lived out, is liable to erupt like a volcano as soon as the
repressive civilised crust wears thin.'[1] In the present century the
repressive processes on which European culture has rested are
being steadily eroded with the consequent eruption, at the collective level and on an unprecedented scale, of previously in-
hibited erotic and aggressive impulses. This phenomenon is in no
small measure due to the impact of 'psychoanalytic permissiveness'
on our culture. It is the irony of Freud's work that his insights at
one and the same time warned us of the social consequences of
undoing repression and made these consequences inevitable.

Permissiveness has not, however, resulted solely in the
uninhibited expression of sexual and aggressive behaviour, but
also in the 'hippy' phenomenon characteristic of what astrologers
have started to call the Aquarian generation. When Jung broke
with Freud it was because of his conviction that the Freudian view
of man was unduly limited: Jung conceived the unconscious as
inhering components far more extensive, far richer in creative
potential, than the repressed infantile wishes of Freudian psychology; Jung also maintained that *libido* could not be identified
with a purely biological sex drive, but carried much wider
implications of a spiritual as well as an erotic or aggressive
nature. Contemporary events would tend to vindicate him. The

[1] H. G. Baynes, *Analytical psychology and the English mind* (Methuen,
1950).

'Aquarian generation' is not just preoccupied with sexual activity; it is equally concerned with spiritual experience. The remarkable affinity shown by these young people for contemplative disciplines, psychedelic adventures and various esoteric cults bears witness to their sense of alienation from a culture dominated by scientific materialism which, through its detachment from subjective considerations, has abdicated responsibility for the effects it has on human life. Their free use of zodiacal symbolism and interest in astrological enquiry are, it seems to me, specific examples of a general contemporary quest for new formulations: they wish to make a new order out of chaos which they may call their own. That they should regress temporarily to a pre-scientific stage of cultural development may be understood as a *réculer pour mieux sauter,* a mobilisation of dynamic modes of collective experience which have lain hidden beneath the 'repressive civilised crust' for three centuries and whose energy is required if a new *Weltanschauung* is to arise. Truly the Christian era is ending and a new order must be found if mankind is not to be swallowed by a new Dark Age, presumably synonymous with extinction.

The new science of psychology has been unable to assist in this quest because, like the physical sciences, it has concerned itself too exclusively with the inessential goals of human interest while ignoring the essential ones. Its preoccupation with the technology of human sensory perception, linguistics, information storage and so on, has ensured that the one thing which has been rigorously excluded from the psychological laboratories is the human mind: indeed, 'mind' is a four-letter word which scientific puritanism, the only form of puritanism left to us, has forbidden us to use. The same taboo which has kept the 'mind' out of the laboratories has served to exorcise the 'psyche' from psychiatric consulting rooms, though to a lesser extent in the United States than in the United Kingdom. However, whether psychiatrists choose to recognise the fact or not, the patients who enter their consulting-rooms continue to bring their psyches with them; and since the National Health Service was inaugurated, a multitude of unhappy men and women have waited in out-patient departments in search of wise counsel, only to receive, when their turn came, a bottle of pills.

Does astrology, then, provide us with a satisfactory alternative?

I can only speak for myself when I say that it does not. Astrology, to me, seems to represent not so much a useful science as a delusional system, and in this sense it is comparable, in my view, to organised religion. A working psychiatric definition of a delusion is a false belief which cannot be corrected by an appeal to reason, and which is out of keeping with the cultural and educational background of the individual entertaining it. A feature of delusions is the emotional intensity with which they are held, and it is perhaps this characteristic which is even more striking than their falsity: hence the apparently unshakable conviction with which astrologers as disparate as Mr Harvey and Miss Lind express their beliefs.

In their most bizarre form, delusional systems are encountered in patients suffering from paranoid schizophrenia; they afford a further example of man's need for explanations. To suffer from schizophrenia is to undergo an experience of progressive personality disintegration of a most disagreeable kind, interrupted from time to time by crises of personal identity during which the individual may feel that his sexual and aggressive impulses do not belong to him but are in fact alien intruders forced into his mind by the agents of a sinister conspiracy whose sole intention is to produce the unbearable state from which he is suffering. Many paranoid delusional systems possess remarkable internal consistency, making perfectly good sense if one is prepared to accept, for the sake of argument, the fundamental assumptions on which the system is based. While schizophrenic delusions represent an attempt on the part of the patient to render his circumstances explicable and to create some kind of order out of his own private chaos, astrology, I submit, represents a similar attempt operating at a collective level.

I personally do not believe that the best means of combating materialism is to go back on the scientific revolution and regress to a cosmology founded on magical modes of thought. As a psychiatrist I spend my life helping to free people from their delusional systems, and I cannot bring myself to feel that what is right for my patients is wrong for our culture. My first duty as a psychotherapist is to encourage my patient to assume responsibility for his inner experiences, not to disown them and project them outside: for it is only by finding the courage to overthrow his paranoia that the individual becomes capable of psychological growth. Jung's major contribution to psychotherapy lay in his insistence on the inner life as being an autonomous fact of nature which must be taken seriously in its own right if it is not to be devalued by the insidious encroachment of the materialist view. In seeking to explain our moods and feelings by attributing them to some external influence, such as astrological or other metaphysical powers, we are in a paranoid manner of speaking, playing into the enemy's hands. If you then ask me, once the projection has been taken back and responsibility for its components assumed, how we are to proceed, on the individual and cultural level, towards a full realisation of the dignity and meaning of our lives, then I would say that it can only be through the mutualities of relationship, catalysed by love. 'If you consider the individual by himself,' wrote Martin Buber, 'then you see of man just as much as you see of the moon; only man with man provides a full image.' Fulfilment of the potential of our inner lives requires intimate connection with others: we cannot go it alone. A paradigm for any psychologically creative relationship is the analytic *transference* relationship which James Hillman has aptly described as a 'league of the two through thick and thin'. By revealing himself wholly to his analyst, holding nothing back, the analysand becomes freed from paranoid concealment while the analyst, by becoming privy to his innermost secrets, assumes a unique responsibility for his ultimate fate. It is ironical that people who turn to astrologers at a time of crisis are probably searching for such a relationship. While I have no doubt that what Mr Parker calls 'good astrologers' go some way towards meeting this need, my quarrel with them is that instead of freeing their client from his paranoia, they reinforce it by dragging him into a shared paranoia, a *folie à deux*, in which both astrologer and client subscribe to the same delusional system. This is not to argue that their association is necessarily harmful or productive of mental illness, for I use the term paranoia in its widest sense: an attitude of mind which sees events as being influenced from behind the scenes or from 'out there'. Astrology, in my view, is not so much anti-therapeutic as a-therapeutic, producing a psychologically sterile liaison between client and astrologer which stultifies creativity instead of making it possible: not 'know thyself' but 'know thy stars'. At this crucial point, the similarity between astrology and psycho-analysis ends: if my own fate should bring me to the cross-roads, I know to which discipline I should turn for help.

Astrology and synchronicity

When one examines in detail with a schizophrenic patient the development of his delusional system, one discovers that it is invariably founded upon a series of 'meaningful coincidences', coincidences that is to say which are meaningful to *him*. Taken individually, these events are unimpressive, but collectively they represent for the patient overwhelming evidence that his beliefs are not delusions but facts, and for the psychiatrist an obstacle which his therapeutic endeavours are often powerless to overcome. Such experiences are not peculiar to schizophrenics, however; we all have them from time to time, and their significance for scientific theory is not inconsiderable.

Newton's light must have given a noticeable flicker earlier this century when physicists were disconcerted to find that they could not observe small, fast-moving particles without altering their behaviour, and were forced to confess that, when it came to considering the position and velocity of such particles, they were unable to make precise predictions. 'The scientific world view,' wrote Heisenberg in *The physicist's concept of nature*,[1] 'has ceased to be a scientific view in the true sense of the word.' Thus the absolute validity of natural law was debased and made relative. Natural laws were, after all, only statistical truths applicable to macrophysical quantities, prediction only being possible where the quantities were large enough to be statistically meaningful. It follows that the experimental method of enquiry is capable of establishing only the occurrence of those events which are regular and capable of reproduction; it cannot be used to investigate events which are either rare or unique.

The relevance of this conclusion for the study of phenomena such as those of extra-sensory perception, astrological prediction,

[1] Hutchinson, 1958.

and the 'synchronistic' happenings of everyday life, was pointed out by Jung, as Mr Parker has described in Chapter V. To ascribe events not susceptible to a causal explanation to 'coincidence' or 'chance' is not to offer an explanation of why they should occur: 'chance' is the blanket term we use to cover up those happenings whose causality we are unable to divine. However, brain-washed as we are by the 'scientific world view', we find it impossible to conceive of events which are connected non-causally or which may be capable of a non-causal explanation. Nevertheless, we are clearly not justified in inferring that such events do not occur. Their occurrence, or at least the possibility of their occurrence, follows as Jung has argued from the premise of statistical truth. It could be, therefore, that parapsychology and astrological charac- ter analysis are realms in which acausal events not only are pos- sible but actually occur.

Unlike astrology, parapsychology has succeeded in achieving some degree of academic respectability, especially in Duke Uni- versity, USA. In the decades since Professor J. B. Rhine set up his laboratory there a vast mass of data has been accumulated, under strictly controlled conditions, capable of convincing any but the most hardened sceptics that there are occasions on which certain apparently gifted individuals are capable of communicating with each other by extra-sensory means. So far, however, little infor- mation has emerged which could help to explain the *modus oper- andi* of such extraordinary phenomena, and it is this theoretical failure which has caused sceptics to reject all parapsychological phenomena, however convincing the evidence for them may be. The sceptics insist that since psi-phenomena are incompatible with a causal view of the universe, then those who have observed them must be the victims of illusion: the observations, not the model, must be wrong. If, on the other hand, any psi-phenomena occur at all, then it must follow that the prevailing scientific concepts of the nature of man and the universe are urgently in need of revision. We must ask ourselves whether the scientific attitudes which have increasingly dominated our culture since the time of the Re- naissance have after all seriously limited our field of vision, pre- venting our contemplation of other possibilities.

When we turn from parapsychology to astrology we may draw

certain parallels. Most educated men and women would probably justify their rejection of astrology by saying that they cannot see how there could be any causal connection between the everyday occurrences of their lives and the positions of the planets at the time of their birth. I know that it is on this statement that my own scepticism rests. However, if we are entirely objective about it, should we not admit that we may be committing the same error of blindness as the eminent academics who flatly deny the findings of parapsychology because they conflict with their traditional beliefs? Why should we reject the inexplicable assertions of astrologers while accepting the no less inexplicable endings of the parapsychologists? Without doubt, most of us would reply that ESP findings have been gathered by the use of experimental method, under conditions which are both controlled and reproducible, whereas astrological data have not been subjected to the same rigorous scrutiny and cannot therefore be regarded as established facts capable of replication and statistical verification.[1] Clearly, if astrology wishes to rival parapsychology in academic respectability it must make itself accessible to scientific investigation – which brings me to Mr Parker's astrological experiment.

Before discussing the results of this experiment I feel it only honest to confess that my status as 'psychologist' and 'psychiatrist' does not, in my opinion, qualify me to make authoritative pronouncements concerning Mr Parker's character, any more than it permits me to assume a cloak of infallibility should I attempt to determine the relative merits of the three astrological reports discussed in Chapter IV. Indeed, there is no sphere in which psychology has proved more disappointing than in the study of human personality, a fact which is as true now as it was when Jung planned his own astrological experiment twenty years ago. Jung chose to take the objectively verifiable fact of marriage as the focus of his study rather than the more elusive variable of personality precisely because of the uncertain status of personality assessment as an applied branch of psychology.

It is difficult to refute the assertion that knowledge of character

[1] The astrological enquiries of M. Gauquelin, described in Chapter XV, were certainly made under strict control. – Author.

is a highly subjective affair [he wrote], because in charac-
terology there are no infallible or even reliable signs that can be
in any way measured or calculated. . . . The absence of reliable
criteria for determining traits of character, makes the meaningful coincidence of horoscope structure and individual
character seem inapplicable.

Mr Parker, however, apparently untroubled by such scruples, has
rushed in where Carl Jung feared to tread. One cannot but commend his pluck, if being somewhat dumbfounded by his aud-
acity![1]

Notwithstanding the difficulties involved in analysing the
results, an experiment such as the one Mr Parker envisaged is not
without interesting possibilities. Any positive findings it might
yield, however, would depend for their persuasiveness on the
rigour of the experimental design, and one might consider using,
for example, a strategy such as the following:

(1) Character analyses would be commissioned from a number
of astrologers who should not be acquainted with the subject nor
with anyone who knew him.

(2) Each astrologer should be sent the birth date under an alias
so that there could be no question of his discovering the subject's
identity.

(3) The subject should observe complete secrecy about the experiment, telling no one that he had requested 'astroanalyses', nor
revealing the identity of the astrologers concerned.

(4) The astrologers selected for the experiment should be known
to work independently of one another, so as to eliminate the possibility of collusion between them.

(5) The subject should be investigated by a small team of
psychologists to permit them to collect crucial biographical details
and prepare as detailed a personality profile as their primitive
science would allow.

(6) The astrologers' and psychologists' reports should be sub-

---

[1] Dr Stevens fails to recognise that I never proposed an 'experiment'; my
purpose was partly to show the kind of work astrologers are doing, and
partly to satisfy an amateur curiosity. But I take his point. – Author.

mitted to an independent panel of judges, none of whom should
be acquainted with the subject. The judges would examine the
astrologers' reports to assess their degree of consistency with each
other and with the data independently collected by the team of
psychologists.

(7) Finally, when the judges had completed their assessment,
the subject might be permitted to reveal himself and express his
personal view of what the astrologers and, for that matter, the
psychologists, had said about him.

Although such an experimental design leaves much to be desired, it would nevertheless go some way towards shielding Mr
Parker from the following criticisms which no sceptic could fail to
level at him:

(1) Mrs Parker, herself a well known astrologer, not only knew
that the experiment was in progress but was also personally acquainted with two of the astrologers selected. Mrs Parker assures
me that at no time did she speak to the lady and gentleman in
question (Miss Lind and Mr Harvey), either about the experiment
or her husband's personality characteristics. While I have no hesi-
tation in accepting her word, some may feel less inclined to be so
charitable.

(2) Mr Parker had made the acquaintance of Mr Harvey
before asking him to work on his horoscope. He tells me that his
meeting was casual, and brief, and that Mr Harvey had no cause
at the time to regard him as a prospective client. However, he
would have known him to be a journalist and broadcaster (so
would Miss Lind); to say nothing of being the husband of his wife;
and it is not unlikely that Mr Harvey would have registered
definite impressions which would have been of considerable assistance to him when writing his report. Furthermore, knowing
Mr Parker's identity and profession, it would not have proved
difficult for either astrologer to discover far more about him had
they wanted to. I don't suppose for one moment that they did; but
that is hardly the point.

(3) When Mr Parker approached Mr Harvey and Miss Lind he
did not make a secret of his experiment or his intention to publish
the results. Moreover, he cannot positively assure me that he did

not inform each of them that he was going to commission a horoscope from the other. So the possibility of collusion between them
cannot be ruled out (though it seems unlikely, in view of the fact
that Mr Harvey has been outspoken in his criticism of 'occult'
astrology). However, whether they felt tempted to collaborate in
Mr Parker's horoscope or not, knowing that he intended to publish their reports cannot have weakened their resolve to make a
good job of him or discouraged them from making the most of
those things about him which they already knew.

(4) A sceptic would be quite justified in objecting that Mr
Parker is not the best person to assess his own character or to judge
the extent to which the three astrologers have caught his likeness.
One does not have to be a psychology graduate to know how
difficult it is to be entirely objective about ourselves. Few of us
possess the genius for introversion of a Proust or Jung, and most of
us pass through life unconscious of the psychic determinants of our
conscious personalities. How many men ever truly come to know
themselves? Certainly, those of us who have gone through the
expensive and laborious processes of an analysis achieve some
degree of self-awareness, but we can never be entirely sure how
genuine such awareness is, or how far we have allowed ourselves to
be stretched on the Procrustean couch of our analyst's theoretical
assumptions.

It is perhaps this very uncertainty that makes us thirsty for self-
knowledge and gives credence to those who claim they can supply
us with what we want to know. There can be no doubt most of us
find our psyches a source of endless fascination, and few utterances
of other people are more important to us than those which concern
ourselves, especially if the persons who make them are 'experts' of
one kind or another. In this respect, we are all, to a greater or less
extent, gullible and asking to be conned. Man's success as a social
animal is in no small measure due to his suggestibility; but since
time immemorial it is this suggestibility which has kept quacks of
all professions, including my own, in business. There is no end to
what you can make people believe, provided you are skilled in the
art of persuasive presentation.

I do not wish to imply that Mr Parker is any more suggestible
than the next man; but he is human, after all, and must as a

consequence share his measure of suggestibility with the rest of us. Thus it is that by electing himself the final adjudicator of the three astrological reports he lays himself open to the objections of bias and subjectivity.

(5) By inviting a psychiatrist who is a friend to assess the objectivity of his personal assessment, Mr Parker does not defend himself adequately from objection (4). The mere fact of our friendship makes it as difficult for me to be objective about him as it is for him to be objective about himself. It is an occupational hazard run by all psychiatrists to be asked at parties whether they are not forever analysing their friends. Far from it: when we knock off at the end of the day, we put away the tools of our trade with the same feeling of relief as a dentist or a plumber's mate. One of the major consolations of friends for a psychiatrist is that they are people whom he doesn't have to treat. Consequently I do not consider that my opinion of Mr Parker's precision in Chapter IV possesses any greater value than that which any other friend may have offered. For what it is worth, however, I will say that I think he has been admirably frank in reviewing the three astrological reports on his character, and that as far as I am aware his evaluation of their accuracy is as honest and objective as it is possible for a man to be.

Even allowing for the serious limitations of Mr Parker's experimental design, it is clear that the astrologers scored some bull's-eyes which it is difficult to dismiss as smart guesswork. This is particularly true of Mr Naylor, the only one of the three not to know Mr Parker, to receive his birth-data under an alias, and not to be aware that he was participating in an experiment the results of which were to be published: his remarks about Mr Parker's 'restless temperament', his 'quick and assimilative mentality', and his obvious possession of 'powers of expression in speech and writing' are particularly impressive to anyone who knows him as well as I do; to say nothing of the bald statement that anybody 'born within a few days of January 25 or July 27 . . . would be likely to affect [his] life and affairs considerably for good or ill. There would be a kind of link of destiny between [them], as it were.' No one can deny Mrs Parker (whose birthday is on July 27) a 'link of destiny' with her husband, or the considerable effect she has had on his life and affairs.

Thus, although Mr Parker's 'experiment' will convince nobody who has an elementary grounding in scientific method, it at least calls attention to the challenging possibility, however unlikely it may seem, that astrology can tell us more about ourselves than we can 'explain' by 'chance'. I join with Mr Parker in hoping that he may have provoked some Quixotic scientist to brave the contumely of his peers and conduct a well-designed investigation into the validity of what astrologers claim they can do. For it seems possible that if we could only comprehend the mystery which shrouds these and other synchronistic phenomena we might find ourselves at last freed from our thraldom to delusional systems and on the threshold of an era, predicted by St John the Divine, when man would be so completely in possession of his fate as to require no temples and, one might add, no horoscopes.

Appendix II

I reprint the whole of an astrological analysis prepared for a thirty-seven year old client who approached my wife in 1969. She had not met him before preparing the work, nor has she met him since. I am grateful to him for allowing me to reproduce this report, which – except for a fictionalised name – is set out here precisely as he received it.

ASTROANALYSIS FOR JOHN JONES
Julia L. Parker
August 1969

Astrology is not an art by which the future can be foretold in detail. Astrologers are not fortune-tellers.

Over the centuries it has been discovered that by measuring the movements of the planets within our solar system, deductions can be accurately made about the lives of human beings. We do not know why astrology works. We only know that the study of our subject in depth over a period of years has proved that it does. The study has been going on for centuries, and we are still learning and extending our knowledge yearly. While we have great respect for tradition, we now work on modern psychological lines, and our results often coincide with the teachings of Jung.

Only astrological deductions have been used in this analysis, and no clairvoyance whatsoever has been employed.

The signs of the Zodiac are of varying importance in different Natal Charts. Newspaper and magazine astrology has emphasised the one that contains the Sun, since everyone knows their Sun-sign simply by knowing their birthday. Natal astrology is as individual as people themselves, and the sign ascending over the Eastern horizon at the time of birth is of equal or even greater importance than the position of the Sun. The actual degree rising in this sign can only be calculated when the time of birth is accurately known, and is therefore individual to the person for whom the Chart is calculated.

Your Chart shows that when you were born the sign ascending was Cancer, and the sign containing the Sun was Virgo.

Basically, you have very much a combination of the known characteristics of these two signs, but there are many other important factors – including the position of the Moon, relationships between the planets, and so on – which have to be carefully considered. I have not used astrological terminology in this analysis; I have, however, a record of the source of all deductions drawn from your Chart in my files for future reference.

It is possible that you may not have seen a Birth Chart set out like this one [Fig. 2] before. The large circle on the printed form shows the twelve signs of the Zodiac as they were positioned when you were born. The twelve divisions of the large innermost part of the circle are called Houses, and relate to yourself, your finances, your career, and so on. Within these, and the Signs, are placed the planets – represented by their traditional symbols *glyphs*. The red, black and dotted lines are called *aspects,* and represent the relationships between the planets. Planets are 'in aspect' when there are certain specific angular distances between them.

On the left of the form are other traditional indications that I have had to take into consideration when interpreting your Chart. The details in the squares at the bottom of the form set out the aspects in another way, and the various time-adjustments that have had to be made to convert your birth-time into astrological data are also shown.

JOHN JONES ESQ., BORN WITH CANCER RISING, THE SUN IN VIRGO, AND UNDER THE MID-HEAVEN OF AQUARIUS.

Asc ♋, ☉ ♍, Mc ♒.

In the letter you wrote a few weeks ago, you asked me many

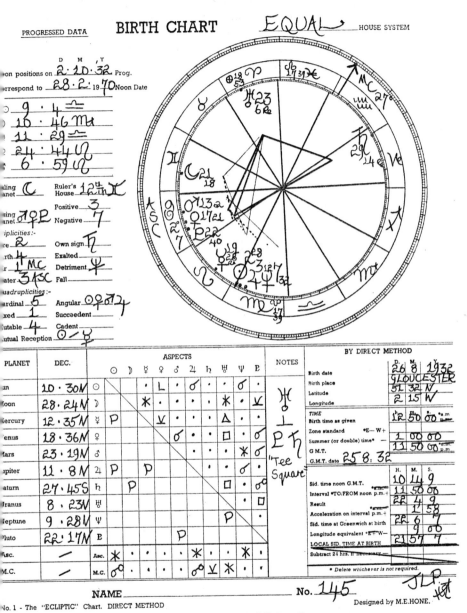

Fig. 2. Birth Chart of John Jones

questions, and I will endeavour to answer as many of them as possible, either in this section of the Report or the second. But it would, I am afraid, be unethical for me to answer one or two of your queries. For instance, astrologers do not predict death – there are so many astrological factors involved at such times that it is well-nigh impossible to do so. Neither do we predict events as such: as far as the progressed section of a Report is concerned, we deal with *trends* and with *tendencies*; we would never say, for instance, 'on such-and-such a day you will win £1,000'! Any astrologer who attempted such a statement would probably be a charlatan or a clairvoyant, and I am neither.

I am sure you will appreciate the situation, and bear with me. I hope you will be interested and perhaps helped by my comments.

A powerful tenacity and well-developed critical faculties are two important facets of your personality; and while you have the ability to see through to a satisfactory conclusion any project you may undertake, it is very likely that although you are well able to consider every aspect of problems in detail, you will retain breadth of vision – thus being able to keep a sense of perspective, and not getting too bogged down with detail in the process.

You are probably motivated by an enormously powerful driving force which spurs you on towards greater achievement and success in life. A sense of achievement is important to you: it is also important to you to get a great deal out of life, and to be successful. However, I feel that in some respects it is the *achievement* of your aims and objectives that is more important to you than the objectives themselves. Once having achieved a particular objective, you probably feel that it is behind you, and you are at once ready to set off again on the next ambition, for the next experience life has in store for you. This is excellent, and does in a way I think sum up your attitude to life.

Continuing the theme a little futher, it may well be that an easy flow of this particular expression of yourself has not been simple for you. It may well be that you have had stumbling-blocks to overcome. This sounds like a generalisation – everyone has to live through difficult periods – but you will certainly have felt at times that you have been completely thwarted, that progress has ground to a halt maybe both in your career and in your personal life; and at such times you will indeed have had to swim against the tide.

I do not think that periods such as these are easy for you to live through. You are a sensitive person – probably far more so than your friends would realise. So when difficult periods occur for you, your natural reaction is more than likely to be to conceal your feelings behind a powerful defensive system, and retire into your shell nursing your wounds. But you probably feel all the time that you would like to hit back at whatever or whoever is blocking your progress.

At this point another facet of your personality comes into its own; if you do *not* 'hit back', it is because of your highly developed reasoning powers. You can cross-question yourself, and in the long run you probably feel that things are best left as they are; so you push your feelings into the back of your mind.

In many ways this trait seems to be directly linked with your built-in defensive system; and while your immediate response may be to go into battle, it is probably better for you in the long run to curb impulsiveness, and let your reasoning power dominate over any aggression which might have a tendency to throw you in at the deep end under difficult conditions.

In many ways there is a great deal of the individualist about you; there is very little in you that wants to be run-of-the-mill and ordinary. This is a splendid facet of your personality, and one which should keep you lively and vital. Try if possible to keep this spark alive in yourself, and do not for instance take on a dull job which you would find tied you to a nine-to-five round, or would be 'routine', just because it may promise financial security.

Although I am certain that you have the ability to live a well-ordered and well-disciplined life, and can probably cope with quite difficult conditions (your years in the army, for instance, although going against the grain in some respects, were by no means wasted, since they probably had an appeal of their own) I do not think a very ordered life is particularly positive for you. You are more likely to be at one with yourself when you have a sense of freedom to do what you want to do *in your own way*. In other words, while you can take discipline, and do run-of-the-mill work, you should constantly question yourself, since this may not be a positive way for you to live, even if it means material progress. Your reaction to orders may well be that of Lord Nelson on one celebrated occasion!

Before going into the question of your career potential in detail I think this is the point when I might put a few matters to you which could have a bearing on your future personal development, and on your general attitude to life. I think it may be a good thing for you to reassess yourself (there is an indication bearing on this, which I will deal with in the next section). I wonder if you are aiming high enough, with regard to some aspects of your life? It may be, I think, that in some respects you may be neglecting certain higher aspects of your life in tending to be over-involved with material things. Far be it from me to say that material progress is unimportant – it is of course extremely so; but progress in a material sense should be accompanied by the development of the less materialistic tendencies, of cultural and spiritual interests.

I hope I am not the sort of astrologer who preaches to her clients, and if I seem to be doing so, please forgive me; but it is my job to assess potentialities, and I am going to stick my neck out! You have a strong humanitarian streak, and an inner need to use this gift on a high level. If, for instance, you had decided to become a doctor, this particular facet of your personality would have been positively externalised. However, as you are following a very different profession, it may be that this potential is lacking externalisation. I think it would be an excellent thing for you to have some interest which is totally different from your career, and which exploits another aspect of your psyche. I am quite certain that you have an inner need to express a great fund of natural affection, and a quality which is enormously protective, kind and gentle; and while I have no intention of telling you to go off to some far-flung corner of the earth and tend the sick, I am certain that involvement perhaps with some charity or fund-raising *for* charity would be satisfying for you. If something of the sort does not appeal to you, perhaps there is an aspect of life which moves you deeply: some cause, the prevention of accidents or something of the sort, that you feel strongly about. My advice to you would be to do something about it. Both you and the cause would benefit immeasurably if you do. There are several reasons for my saying this; some of course I have already mentioned, and the first and foremost is that your potentiality for humanitarian action is very strong in your psychological make-up. Secondly, I am inclined to think that you may not have developed this aspect of your personality – you may have pushed it aside, simply because of your involvement with your career; and finally, you are heading for a period of reassessment which could help you to see yourself from the outside.

A somewhat negative indication which you should guard against at all times, is a tendency towards over-concentration on yourself. You have more than likely over the years realised that this could be so, and by now have come to terms with the tendency, being able to bring other facets of your personality into play to overcome it. Again, I feel that involvement with some interest that is anything but worldly, and could be of help to society in general, would counter-balance this possibly negative trait.

The first of your queries I would like to deal with is the one about your career. I think your position as an advertising manager is an excellent one for you. However, it would be possible for you to develop this, expanding your field of operations. You probably have quite a flair for appealing to a mass audience. Could the emphasis change from a business publication to greater involvement with pure advertising? I think that if you worked for, or had your own advertising agency, it would suit you very well indeed. You have the ability to get a message over to the public – to *sell*, and especially to sell *ideas* – and you have originality in plenty; it is probably not difficult for you to come up with something 'different' or new. I do not know a great deal about the world of advertising, but perhaps you will be able to make some sort of coherent sense out of these rather general comments. If you are baffled by them, do put me in the picture from your point of view, and I will reassess the situation and review my remarks.

As far as having your own business is concerned, yes – I think this would be excellent for you. I am certain that it would be preferable to going into partnership. You need to be very much on the defensive as far as business partners are concerned; and unless the person you are to work with is very much older than yourself, my advice would be to go it alone. You have an independent streak which makes it much more likely for you to be successful when working alone in your own way, without hindrance from anyone else. Perhaps ideally you could find someone who would provide some capital, and then take a cut from the profits; that would be a solution. But do *not* have a business partner of approximately your own age under your feet all day. I do not think it would work out well for you, and you should be very careful in this respect. An older person could be an asset; a contemporary or near-contemporary, a disaster.

As far as the financial question is concerned, you are well-endowed: you are naturally very shrewd and clever in this respect. Possibly you have a tendency to over-invest, and you should watch this with care, since you might tend to be swept off your feet at times, when your natural caution and shrewdness could go by the board. The current trends in your financial life will be dealt with later. There are certain fields which should be excellent for you (you may care to comment on whether they have been so in the past): agriculture (including dairy produce), radio and TV shares (the producing companies rather than TV or radio manufacture), air lines, scientific instrument manufacturers – all these could be fields for successful investment. I am tempted to add the fishing industry and possibly shipping; but I would like your reaction to this. Have you had success or failure with these particular industries in the past?

As far as personal relationships are concerned, you are an emotional person and have a very great deal to give to the other person. You have a deep-rooted psychological urge to protect a partner, and to take care of her in a delightfully cherishing way, and as this is true in emotional relationships now, so of course it could be if, later, you marry and become a father: you will make an excellent father, although you may have to be a little careful that you are not over-strict or over-critical at times towards your children.

I would of course be predicting an event (or a non-event!) if I said that you would or would not marry: and in any event this kind of indication will be covered later. But looking at your Birth Chart as far as marriage is concerned, I can say that there is a *possibility* that if you do marry your wife may be rather older than yourself.

It is obvious that you should be on the defensive before committing yourself to marriage. Everyone must be, of course; but it is particularly the case with you. In some respects partnership in marriage (as in business) could be rather tricky with you, and unless you give yourself rather longer than you perhaps feel you really need to make up your mind about a person, a certain disillusionment and disappointment could be the result, perhaps spoiling the relationship for you. So, obviously, you should be on your guard should you find someone you feel you would like to marry. Even if you are certain that she is right for you, consciously give yourself plenty of time really to get to know her before committing yourself to a legal marriage. I will go into your relationship with Peter in the next section.

As far as your question about the second half of your life is concerned, and the possibility of it being more comfortable than the first – again, this tends to border on the sort of question astrologers do not like to make dogmatic or sweeping statements about; but I think anyway that you may be in a position to answer the question yourself. Astrologically speaking, there was an important indication of a change round about 1967–8, and perhaps this had a bearing on the better-than-average investments of which you spoke. If from then on, your life has assumed a new and possibly more comfortable aspect, then it could well be that you are up to a point set reasonably fair for a very long time. However, you must understand that it is quite impossible to be cut and dried about this; there will be difficult years and pleasant times; it is too difficult a question, and basically impossible to answer.

Again, to assess retirement would keep me busy working on your Chart for about two months, and doing nothing else! Similarly, it would take even longer for me to assess the possibilities as to which of your parents may die first – apart from the timefactor, one would need both parents' birth data; and in any event such an examination would be totally unorthodox, and I could not consent to do it.

If a period of stress is indicated in the next year or two, I can of course say that it may have a bearing on family relationships, should this indeed appear to be so; or if there seems to be a possibility of an inheritance I can of course tell you. But to say that a parent will die on such-and-such a date and leave you such-and-such a sum would need a crystal ball and a fortune-teller; it is not my job.

As far as your health is concerned, there is a possibility that you may tend to worry about it rather a lot. In point of fact, proneness to worry in general is something you may well have to live with. It could in itself of course affect your health, and sheer worry could lower your vitality, perhaps leading eventually to stomach upsets or strain on your nervous system and digestion. It is impossible for me to say that you should not worry; one is either the type to worry, or not. The only advice I can give is that you should be thoroughly aware of the tendency for worry or tension to bother you, and try if possible to see the early symptoms, avoiding a build-up of negative conditions. For instance, you could when worried tend to get a certain amount of indigestion, or stomach pains. It sometimes helps if you can talk over your worries with another person; you may have a tendency to keep your worries to yourself, and this does not help. Try to externalise them as much as possible.

I wonder if your interest in your health is extended to an interest in diet? You could be interested in vegetarianism, for instance.

You may be interested to know that there is an astrological tradition that links places with the signs of the Zodiac. In your case there is an affinity between your Chart and the Chart of the USA itself; and it is not surprising that you are so strongly tied to that country.

POSSIBLE DEVELOPMENT OF POTENTIALITIES OF
THE BIRTH-CHART KNOWN ASTROLOGICALLY AS
'PROGRESSIONS' FOR JOHN JONES

I have calculated dates as accurately as possible in this section, but they mark the times at which trends are working in your life, as opposed to definite dates.

On the left-hand side of the second printed form [Fig. 3] you will see a series of circles one within the other. You will notice that the centre two circles are identical to those on your Birth Chart. On the next band, the glyphs, Ascendant and Mid-Heaven are repeated, but are in different positions. As your Birth Chart represents the positions of the planets at the time and place when you were born, so this band shows them in their relationship to you at the present time. They are, in fact, in their positions for October 2, 1932 – thirty-eight days after you were born. One day's planetary motion represents one year in your life.

You will see another strange date on this form: this is your Noon Date, and is the day in the year (calculated from your Birth Time) around which the conditions indicated by these positions begin to have their effect on you.

In the outside circle you will see some glyphs followed by the letter *T*. These are the heavy, slower-moving planets as they are on your Noon Date, but in the year 1970. Their positions are interpreted.

On the right-hand side of the form, the top section sets out what aspects are going to be exact for you during the coming twelve months or so. The large section below shows where the Moon is, and its relationship to the other planets, and the relationship between the heavy planets and your natal planets for the twelve month period under consideration.

JOHN JONES, PROGRESSED ASCENDANT LEO, PROGRESSED
SUN IN LIBRA, PROGRESSED MID-HEAVEN ARIES

At the present time, your progressed Birth Chart is not greatly active. However, there are a few indications for me to interpret, and at the same time I shall be able to comment on the various points in your letter which I have not yet covered.

Perhaps the most fascinating query is about your relationship with Peter. I have worked briefly on his Chart, and I cannot say how splendidly it fits in with yours. There is much which is

CHART FOR PROGRESSIONS AND TRANSITS

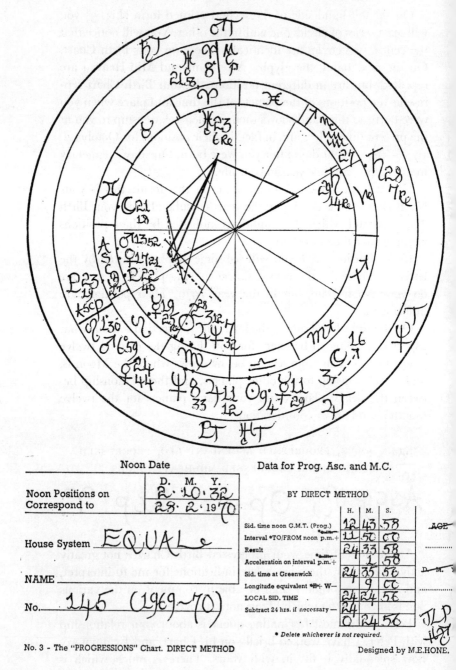

Fig. 3. Progressions and transits for John Jones

TAL ANETS MERICAL DER	SOLAR	MUTUAL		
				"O.D."
♎ 7 ♋				
2·28♍	☉ p ⊻ ♆ p 1968~69	☿ p ⊻ ♃ p 1970		☿ △ ♄ 1969
3·12♍				☾ ☍ ♄ 1968~69
7·32♍				
13 52♋		♀ p △ ♅ R 1968~69		
17·21♋				
9·25♌				
21·18♊		♀ p ⊻ ♇ R + p 1968 69		
22·18♋				
23·6♀				
27·00♅				
29·14♆R				

Date Month	Moons Long.	To Natal	To Prog.	♇	♆	♅	♄	♃	♂	NOTES: NEW MOONS
SEPT '69	3·16	✶♃				N	△♆24	□♂24	☌☾6 ☌Asc24	✶♀ ⊻♆ (♍) 11th
OCT	4·31				□MC 11	O	8	□♀13-16 ✶♆22-25	☌♂11 ☌♀17 ☌♃24	□♀ ✶♆ (♎) 11th
NOV	5·46			⊼MC 23	8	T	△♃17 30	✶☾1-4 □♇5-9 ☌♅10-13	☌♄3	△♀(♏) 9th
DEC	7·1	✶♀	□♂		✶♄10	R	△☉2	△MC9 □♄11-16	☌♀1 ☌MC12 ☌☉19	⊼♀(♐) 9th
JAN '70	8·16		✶♆ ⊼MC		4	A		△Asc4-7 ✶☉6 ✶♃7-14	☌♃25	☌♀(♑) 8th
FEB	9·31		⊻☉	7		N	4 △♃5-19		☌♅26	⊼♀(♒) 6th
MAR	10·46		⊻☿ ✶♃			S	△♆23 30	✶♃29		△♀(♓) 7th
APL	12·00					I		△Asc5-7 ✶☉1-4		□♀(♈) 6th
MAY	13·15	△♂			✶♄4	T	✶♂10 17	□♄1-8 △MC16-30	☌☾20	✶♀(♉) 8th
JUN	14·29				10	S	✶♀12 20		☌Asc5 ☌♂23 ☌☿29	⊻♀♂(♊) 5th
JLY	15·44						□☿1 10	△MC 20-30	☌♇7	☌♂(♋) 4th
AUG	16·58	△♀ ↓					✶♇9 ↓ 1st Oct	□♄8 15	☌☿14	⊻♆(♌) 2nd

enormously positive between the two Charts from an astrological point of view, which means that your relationship is excellent for both of you. Much of what joins you is permanent, and I do not think there is much likelihood of your splitting up. It would, I think, be a very great pity if you did. Although you are of course very different people, recognition of your respective personality-traits and identification with each other's objectives in life is very apparent indeed. I am certain that you contribute a very great deal to each other's general happiness and psychological well-being; you are both enormously 'in tune' with the other. It may even be that you are almost too much so in some respects, and that probably if one of you is thinking out a line of action, the other has already got there before he has had a chance to complete his plan!

As far as I can see, I do not think there is (as I say) much of a possibility of your splitting up. If you did, I think it is unlikely that you would sever your relationship completely, or lose touch permanently. You would both lose a great deal if you did, and would both no doubt realise this and come to your senses after a time.

As far as new relationships are concerned, and 'what they would be like' – this is impossible to say. Astrologers can of course assess times when new friends are likely to be made, or when there is a particular emphasis on emotional relationships – possible marriage, for instance. But one needs the Chart of the other person concerned to help a client judge the possibility of the development of a friendship, whether it is going to be a 'passing fancy', or whatever.

As far as your health is concerned, for the coming year or so I do not think you have any cause to worry. It may be that you are coming to the end of some slightly lowering conditions as far as your vitality is concerned. Possibly over the past year or so you could have been below par rather more often than usual, and this might have given you a certain amount of cause for concern. However, the indication which caused this is easing, and for the next year or so (generally speaking) you have no cause to worry about your health. There may be times when minor upsets could bother you; I will deal with these later. But there is no indication of any serious difficulty.

As far as travel is concerned, you could find that you will travel more than usual from about the present time and for the next eighteen months. A minor indication working in your Chart is in favour of this. It would be for instance an excellent time for you to plan a long trip, if it could be arranged. Have you ever been to Morocco? You might well find this a particularly interesting country, during the next year or so! I will indicate particularly pleasant periods for travel in the summaries later on.

This is also an excellent time for study. Are you interested in languages? If so, you would find it particularly stimulating to develop this interest for the next year or so. Other spare time activities you might like to think about could be archaeology or history.

You ask me about your relationship with your parents. It may well be that the relationship with your Mother has been rather more satisfactory than that with your Father; there is an indication of friendship between you and your Father, but the relationship may tend to be somewhat shallow, whereas your Mother has more than likely been the one to spur you on and to stimulate you intellectually. Again, I do not think you will have any difficulty as far as your parents are concerned during the next year or so. Here again, any short-term indications will be covered in the monthly summaries.

MONTHLY SUMMARIES

What I have written so far in this section is an interpretation of the long-term indications working in your Chart at the present time and for the coming year or so. What follows is an interpretation of the short-term indications: these last for varying periods of time, anything from a day or so to about two months.

1969

September
A progressive month: conditions are good for investment over the period as a whole, but it might be advisable for you to hold back between the 6th and 7th, and after the 24th. At these times you

could tend to take risks and therefore may be somewhat rash.
Towards the end of the month be particularly on the defensive if
you are driving, as your risk-taking could affect you in this way.
You may find it all too easy to overtake when you shouldn't. If you
cook or are handling sharp tools, again be a little more careful
than usual. These conditions ease after October 2, but return for a
day or so around October 11.

October

A pleasant month as far as your social life is concerned; but financially, I must warn you of possible over-extravagance – perhaps
incurred through entertaining. These conditions are most likely to
be to the fore around the 13th to the 15th. You may be particularly busy around the 11th, and again later on – about the
24th/26th, when all hell could break loose! If you have to travel
the last week of the month is perhaps the best time for you to do so.
You may find it a little difficult to concentrate on the job in hand
for much of the month; if this is so, my only advice is consciously
to *let* yourself have a little 'drift' – it will do you good, providing
of course that you can consciously pull yourself back to earth
again afterwards!

November

Most of the indications for this month are working for you during
the first two weeks or so. Financially speaking, between the 1st and
the 4th conditions are excellent: a time to invest if you feel you
would like to. However, at the same time you could have a certain
amount of tension, and this may be due to frustrating delays. Try
not to get worried or tense; if anything bothers you, difficulties
should be behind you after the 15th. From the 17th, constructive
progress should be made; it is for instance an excellent time for
you to catch up on any backlog of routine work – it could seem
rather less dull if you get down to it around then!

December

Conditions are excellent during the first week of this month: if you
have plans to put into action, or ideas to put to those in authority,
this is an excellent time to exert yourself. It is likely to be a busy

and progressive period. After the 16th, conditions tend to deteriorate, and although you are likely to be busy, you could come up against a few brick walls. If you are thinking of visiting your family at this time I think it may be better to plan to spend New Year with them rather than Christmas; the indications show that you would be happier with them at that time.

1970

January

The indications for the first two weeks of the New Year are excellent. When a client has such a progressive group of transits, it is sometimes difficult for me to tell him exactly how to get the best out of them! If you are in the mood to concentrate on career or financial matters, these should make splendid progress. On the other hand, if you come home for a while (or take a holiday abroad) you will undoubtedly enjoy yourself in that way as well: it is up to you to make the decision!

February

If you have any plans for minor domestic changes, this could be an excellent time for you to make the necessary arrangements. The 2nd and 27th are two days on which to enjoy yourself, and negative dates are the 7th and the 15th. The 26th possibly will be the busiest day of the month. Progress is likely to be constructive but perhaps rather slow as a whole during February.

March

If you have the opportunity to travel during March it would be an excellent time for you to do so if it was not possible for you to come home earlier, then conditions working for you in March are excellent. Between the 23rd and the end of the month your inspiration is highlighted: any scheme that you may have in mind, even if it is 'way out', should go ahead very well.

April

More positive financial indications are with you between the 7th and 14th of the month; you should do very well at this time, but keep both feet on the ground and do not let yourself be carried away. The 3rd is lively: the unexpected may happen!

May

Of the months I am considering, this could well be the most hectic. You are likely to be very busy, and because of this you could feel a certain amount of strain on your health. If you find that you are having to rush around hither and yon, consciously make yourself slow up and take a deep breath! The best period is between the 16th and the 30th of the month; but I must stress that the pace of life could well be frantic – even at times annoyingly so – so hold on and don't strain yourself.

June

The hectic time is with you at times during June: these are likely to be for the first week and again around the 25th of the month. There is accent on your love life between the 12th and the 20th. You should proceed with considerable care at this time, since you could run into minor difficulties. You should, however, have any complications behind you by the 29th of the month – the 26th being a possible date to patch up any difficulties.

July

There is a possibility that you may be feeling rather depressed during the first ten days of July. If negative feelings bother you, try not to let them turn to worry since, as we have already said, this could upset your health. Conditions are quite different for you after the 20th, when you really should be able to get a great deal out of life. During those ten days, financial interests are positively accentuated, and the month ends on a particularly lively note.

August

It might be advisable for you to take a short break between the 3rd and the 5th. Could you have a day or two in the country perhaps? Conditions are rather heavy going for you between the 8th and the 15th, so do not expect too much progress. Between the 17th and the 19th you should be feeling very much on form mentally: this is likely to make up for any dead-slow-and-stop times earlier in the month. From the 9th, and until the 1st October, I do

not think you should make investments: there is an indication
working at this time that could cause you quite a lot of difficulty in
this respect. I think I am going to stick my neck out as far as to say
lay off any financial risks altogether. If I had worked on your
progressed Chart regularly for some years I could be rather more
precise in my interpretation of this particular indication. As it
stands, I think my best advice to you is that it could hit you below
the belt as far as finances are concerned.

However, I must look at the indication in another way, and also
warn you to be somewhat on the defensive as far as personal
relationships or business partnerships are concerned.

I am sorry to end this summary on a rather negative note, but I
feel I must put you in the picture. If the going is difficult, at least
you will know that it eases at the end of September.

If you would care to make notes of the accuracy or inaccuracy
of my interpretation of these trends in the coming twelve months,
this would be enormously helpful later on, should you wish me to
write a further instalment!

A Select
Glossary of Astrological Terms

These short definitions are by nature over-simplified; their astrological significance can only be fully appreciated in a textbook context.

ASCENDANT or Ascending Sign. The sign of the Zodiac rising over the eastern horizon at the time of one's birth.

ASPECT. The angle made by the line drawn from one planet to the centre of the earth, and the line from another to the same point.

BIRTH CHART. A Chart showing the position of the Sun, Moon and planets as they would be seen at the moment of one's birth, and from the place of birth.

CUSP. The dividing points between planetary Houses and signs.

ECLIPTIC. The apparent path of the Sun around the Earth.

EPHEMERIS. A publication containing the positions of the Sun, Moon and planets at noon Greenwich Mean Time for every day of the year of publication.

GLYPH. The written symbol signifying the Sun, Moon, each of the planets, and each sign of the Zodiac.

HOROSCOPE. See *Birth Chart*. Laymen will refer to a Birth Chart, an astrological analysis, or a newspaper column as a 'horoscope'. On the whole, professional astrologers eschew the term.

HOUSES. Twelve traditional divisions of the astrological Birth Chart arrived at by calculation from the birth data. Each House traditionally affects a different area of the subject's life. There are various systems of House Division.

M.C. or Medium Coeli; Mid-Heaven. The degree at which the ecliptic reaches its highest point at the meridian of any place at a given time.

NODES. The points at which the Moon's and planets' apparent path around the earth intersects the ecliptic.

PROGRESSED CHART. A Birth Chart re-drawn so that it has relevance to its subject's future. The *progression* of a Chart involves its recalculation by the use of the Ephemeris for the year for which *progressions* (laymen would say 'forecasts') are required.

RECTIFICATION. The means employed by an astrologer to draw up an accurate Birth Chart when the precise time of birth is not known.

SIDEREAL TIME. The actual time the earth takes to revolve on its axis: i.e. the time between the successive meridional transits of a star – usually the first point in Aries; not twenty-four hours, but $23' 56'' 9°$.

SUN-SIGN. The sign of the Zodiac through which the Sun is passing at the moment of one's birth. Since this depends on the time of year when one is born, it is commonly the single astrological fact which everyone knows.

TRANSIT. The movement of a planet over another planet, or over some given point in the Birth Chart.

ZODIAC. Mythical figures outlined by drawings making use of certain constellations. These form the background against which the planets are seen to move. The Sun is said to be 'in' Gemini when, from earth, it is seen against the pattern of stars over which the ancients drew the figures of the heavenly twins. It is emphasised that astrologers do *not* now make use of the Zodiac except as a convenient method of naming fields of the ecliptic.

Index

Index